PRAISE FOR DOMINIQUE MORISSEAU AND THE DE...

"Dominique is a healer . . . There's a disease in African-American communities—it's a metaphor in a sense, but it's a reality that I face—and the disease is ignorance. We rarely get to see African-American people at the center of the world, the salt-of-the-earth, wonderful, angry, joyous, loving, beautiful people. Dominique takes the marginalized people and gives them a story, gives them a voice. So she heals that disease."

—Ruben Satiago-Husdon, director

"Like August Wilson, this playwright has heart, along with a sense of historical moments that define the lives of ordinary Americans."

—Variety

"Inspiring . . . *Skeleton Crew* is a fitting elegy to the hardest working people in America, who far too often get the short end of the stick."

—Theatermania

"*Detroit '67* is Morisseau's aching paean to her natal city . . . A deft playwright, Morisseau plays expertly with social mores and expectations . . . She reframes commonplace things so that we see them in new light."

—Star Tribune

"This is a writer who has a flawless ear . . . Dominique Morisseau has been cutting a wide and spectacular path through the writers' ranks . . . A writer not to be ignored."

—Deadline

"Equally invested in the politics of the everyday as she is in the humor that makes the everyday bearable, Morisseau's especially strong when it comes to tone; she knows how her characters sound, and how they sound in relation to what their interlocutor is and isn't saying."

—NEW YORKER

"*Paradise Blue* was perhaps the finest new play of the year . . . I was surprised by the ending. I was surprised by the structure. I was enthralled by the experience from top to bottom . . . Perfection."

—BERKSHIRE EDGE

"Morisseau's jazz-infused *Paradise Blue* upends expectations."

—NEW YORK TIMES

"Smart, heart-wrenching and engrossing . . . In *Detroit '67*, it's police violence against black men that comes in for Morisseau's trademark treatment, which is sensitive and unsparing at once . . . Its intelligence and sensitivity to the complexity of the issues at play in Detroit—and across the country—shines through at nearly every moment."

—THE BUFFALO NEWS

"The questions in *Detroit '67* are both big and small. Who started the riots? Was it about race? Will the people affected by the violence be able to pick up the pieces? Racial conflict is the primary culprit for the unrest. On the other hand, Morisseau wants us to dig deeper. She wants us to validate the lives of the revolutionaries who fought for civil rights and honor those who struggled to exist. Funny and informative, *Detroit '67* tackles the turbulence of the time while finding a way, through all of the dilapidation, to recognize a defining generation."

—BET.COM

THE DETROIT PROJECT

BOOKS BY DOMINIQUE MORISSEAU PUBLISHED BY TCG

The Detroit Project

INCLUDES:

DETROIT '67

PARADISE BLUE

SKELETON CREW

Pipeline
(forthcoming)

THE DETROIT PROJECT

DOMINIQUE MORISSEAU

THEATRE COMMUNICATIONS GROUP   NEW YORK   2018

The Detroit Project is copyright © 2018 by Dominique Morisseau

Paradise Blue, Detroit '67 and *Skeleton Crew* are copyright © 2018 by Dominique Morisseau

The Detroit Project is published by Theatre Communications Group, Inc., 520 Eighth Avenue, 24th Floor, New York, NY 10018-4156

All rights reserved. Except for brief passages quoted in newspaper, magazine, radio or television reviews, no part of this book may be reproduced in any form or by any means, electronic or mechanical, including photocopying or recording, or by an information storage and retrieval system, without permission in writing from the publisher.

Professionals and amateurs are hereby warned that this material, being fully protected under the Copyright Laws of the United States of America and all other countries of the Berne and Universal Copyright Conventions, is subject to a royalty. All rights, including but not limited to, professional, amateur, recording, motion picture, recitation, lecturing, public reading, radio and television broadcasting, and the rights of translation into foreign languages are expressly reserved. Particular emphasis is placed on the question of readings and all uses of this book by educational institutions, permission for which must be secured from the author's representative: Jonathan Mills, Paradigm Agency, 360 Park Avenue South, 16th floor, New York, NY 10010, (212) 897-6400.

Page 10-11 and 30: Georgia Douglas Johnson, "The Heart of a Woman" and "My Little Dreams," *The Heart of a Woman and Other Poems*, The Cornhill Company, Boston, 1918. Page 65-66: "Calling Dreams," *Bronze*, B.J. Brimmer Company, Boston, 1922. Public domain. Page 181-182: The Four Tops, "Reach Out, I'll Be There," written by Lamont Dozier, Brian Holland, and Edward Holland, Jr. Copyright © 1966 Jobete Music Co. All rights reserved.

The publication of *The Detroit Project* by Dominique Morisseau, through TCG's Book Program, is made possible in part by the New York State Council on the Arts with the support of Governor Andrew Cuomo and the New York State Legislature.

Special thanks to the Vilcek Foundation for its generous support of this publication.

TCG books are exclusively distributed to the book trade by Consortium Book Sales and Distribution.

Library of Congress Cataloging-in-Publication Data
Library of Congress Control Numbers:
2017023089 (print) / 2017026006 (ebook)
ISBN 978-1-55936-538-3 (softcover) / ISBN 978-1-55936-858-2 (ebook)
A catalog record for this book is available from the Library of Congress.

Book design and composition by Lisa Govan
Cover design by Joan Wong

First Edition, June 2018
Third Printing, February 2023

CONTENTS

Detroit is my family. My best friends. My husband.
My first love. My creative genesis. My heart.

This is for your imperfection. Your truth.
And your ongoing survival through the decades.

#lifelongdetroitgirl

PARADISE BLUE

For Pearl Cleage, because of her inspiration to me as a writer. Because of her love of black women in her work. Because of her love of Detroit. And because of her essay, "Mad at Miles"— which gave me the ammunition and bravery to deal with community accountability in and out of my art.

And for the elders who remember a very different Detroit.

peaceandlovedominique;)

Paradise Blue received its world premiere at the Williamstown Theatre Festival (Mandy Greenfield, Artistic Director) on July 22, 2015. It was directed by Ruben Santiago-Hudson. The set design was by Neil Patel, the costume design was by Clint Ramos, the lighting design was by Rui Rita, the sound design was by Darron L. West, the original music was by Kenny Rampton and Bill Sims, Jr.; the production stage manager was Lloyd Davis, Jr. The cast was:

PUMPKIN	Kristolyn Lloyd
BLUE	Blair Underwood
CORN	Keith Randolph Smith
P-SAM	André Holland
SILVER	de'Adre Aziza

Paradise Blue was produced at Signature Theatre (Paige Evans, Artistic Director; Harold Wolpert, Executive Director) on April 24, 2018. It was directed by Ruben Santiago-Hudson. The set design was by Neil Patel, the costume design was by Clint Ramos, the lighting design was by Rui Rita, the sound design was by Darron L. West, the original music was by Kenny Rampton; the production stage manager was Laura Wilson. The cast was:

PUMPKIN	Kristolyn Lloyd
BLUE	J. Alphonse Nicholson
CORN	Keith Randolph Smith
P-SAM	Francois Battiste
SILVER	Simone Missick

Paradise Blue is a recipient of the 2015 Edgerton Foundation New Play Award.

CHARACTERS

PUMPKIN, black woman, late twenties to early thirties. Pretty in a plain way. Simple, sweet. Waitress, cook and caretaker of Paradise Club. A loving thing with a soft touch. Adores poetry.

BLUE, black man, mid to late thirties or early forties. Proprietor of Paradise Club. Handsome, mysterious, sexy. Quietly dangerous. Aloof. A hard shell and a hard interior. Battling many demons. A gifted trumpeter.

CORN (AKA CORNELIUS), black man, late forties to early fifties. Slightly chubby. Easygoing and thoughtful, a real sweetheart with a weakness for love. The piano man.

P-SAM (AKA PERCUSSION SAM), black man, mid to late thirties. Busybody, sweet-talker, hustler. Always eager for his next gig. The percussionist.

SILVER, black woman, late thirties to early forties. Mysterious, sexy, charming. Spicy. Gritty and raw in a way that men find irresistible. Has a meeeeaaaannnn walk.

Detroit, Michigan, in a small black community known as Black Bottom, on the downtown strip known as Paradise Valley. Paradise Club. 1949.

A " / " indicates where the next line of dialogue begins.

ACT ONE

In darkness:

A trumpet wails a painful tune. It is long and sorrowful, almost a dirge.

At rise:

A soft light comes up on Blue. He is silhouetted with his trumpet in hand, the source behind the trumpet's wail. Beads of sweat dance down his face as his notes pierce the air.

The trumpet sings as the tune becomes increasingly beautiful.

Then suddenly, a white light washes over Blue. He plays a long note. It is the most beautiful note we've ever heard.

Finally, he stops, stands there . . . dripping with sweat. Crying.

The white light over him becomes even brighter.

He smiles, overcome with peace.

A gunshot.

Blackout.

SCENE ONE

Lights up on an empty nightclub. This is Paradise. A sign in the window that says so is unlit.

A cardboard sign in the window says, BASSIST WANTED—ASK FOR BLUE.

A second cardboard sign in the window says, ROOMS UPSTAIRS AVAILABLE FOR RENT—ASK FOR BLUE.

Chairs are mounted on tables. A bar is stage left. Stools are mounted atop. A heap of swept trash sits in the middle of the floor with an abandoned broom nearby.

Pumpkin, a young, pretty, simple woman, enters from the kitchen with a dustpan in one hand and a book of poetry in the other.

She reads with complete engagement, doing an odd job of trying to sweep up the trash without losing her page as she reads.

PUMPKIN *(Reciting aloud)*:
> The heart of a woman goes forth with the dawn,
> As a lone bird, soft winging, so restlessly on,
> Afar o'er life's turrets and vales does it roam
> In the wake of those echoes the heart calls home.

(She carries the dustpan over to the trash can, trying pitifully to balance it all. A trail of trash spills along the way.)

> The heart of a woman falls back with the night,
> And enters some alien cage—

(She notices the trash that she's spilled. She doubles back and sweeps it up, then proceeds to the can again, engulfed in the poetry.)

> And enters some alien cage in its plight,
> And tries to forget it has dreamed of the stars
> While it—

(More trash spills.)

Ah fudge!

(She scoops up the trash, dropping the book.)

(As swear words) Mother fudge and grits!!!

(She picks up the book. She carefully balances the trash and the book, heads closer to the trash can.)

> And tries to forget it has dreamed of the stars
> While it—breaks,
> breaks,
> breaks
> on the sheltering bars.

(Finally, she dumps the trash into the trash can. The book falls in as well.)

Fudge grits and jam!

(She digs into the trash can to retrieve the book. She wipes it free of food and other garbage nasties and flips through the pages.)

My greatest apologies Missus . . . *(Reads the name on the cover)* . . . Missus Georgia Douglas Johnson. I would never purposefully treat your beautiful words like Paradise Valley trash. No ma'am. Your words don't deserve none of yesterday's apple tart or steak and peas. And certainly it don't deserve none of Corn's peanut shells or Blue's broken whiskey bottles. Your words deserve to be memorized by every waking mind in Black Bottom. Yes, ma'am. Pumpkin's gonna recite your words to whoever needs some . . . elegance in their day.

(The door to the club opens and Cornelius [aka Corn] enters, followed by Percussion Sam [aka P-Sam]. P-Sam grabs the cardboard sign from the window.)

CORN: Hey there Pumpkin. Good morning to ya.

PUMPKIN: Hey there Corn. Hey P-Sam.

P-SAM: Where Blue?

PUMPKIN: Left out this mornin'. Had to go take care of some business downtown, he say. Ya'll hungry? Got some coffee and toast in the back.

CORN: That'd be all right with me.

(P-Sam holds out the sign.)

P-SAM: When he put this up?

(Pumpkin looks at the sign.)

PUMPKIN: Don't know. Musta done it just this morning. Wasn't there last night.

P-SAM: You see this, Corn? You know what this mean?

CORN: Mean "Good-bye, Joe."

P-SAM: I told you, Corn. Didn't I tell you? A little tiff. Little tiff my backside. You said it was just a little tiff and now we got to find a new bassist.

CORN: I thought it was little.

P-SAM: Ain't nothin' little when it come to Blue. Didn't I tell you? Soon as he get that bit of anger in him, somethin' little always turn into somethin' jumbo size. I told you.

PUMPKIN: He done fired Joe?

CORN: Blue and Joe got into a little tiff last night—

P-SAM: Little my tailbone.

CORN: Joe wanted more off the top. Wanted Blue to start paying up front, before we play 'steada after.

P-SAM: And what's wrong with that? Ain't nothin' wrong with wanting your money up front—

CORN: But everybody know Blue like it the way Blue like it. Blue been payin' *after* since we been playing together. You don't know cuz you ain't been playin' with him long as me. We been playin' together since he first got this place. I knew his daddy before he left it to him.

P-SAM: That don't mean a hill of beans. If Joe wanna get paid first, ain't nothin' wrong with that.

CORN: Joe don't understand 'bout the way Blue mind work. That's what I'm trying to tell you. Blue don't like nobody questioning his loyalty. Pumpkin know what I'm sayin', don't you, Pumpkin.

PUMPKIN: I know. Blue like things his way cuz that's the only way he understand. Stuff gotta make sense to him. *(Shift)* I'm gonna go get your coffee and toast.

(Pumpkin heads into the back.)

P-SAM: You know as well as I do that Joe was right. Sometimes Blue make you wait all night till he get the money square. By that time the woman you was leavin' with done already left with some other moe. He make you wait on his time all the time and it ain't right. Joe just speakin' his mind . . . and good for him, Corn. Good for Joe.

CORN: I'm just tellin' ya, Blue got a type of organization to his mind. Joe confusing a lot of that organization. Way Blue see it, waitin' till *after* to pay us make sure we stick around to play. Make it feel like we done earned somethin' by the end of the night. That's the way his daddy taught him. He not seein' the side about it that make you lose your woman to some other cat. That's all Blue see is what he been taught. You just got to understand him, Sam.

P-SAM: I ain't got to understand nothin', Corn. Blue's spot ain't the only jazz spot in town, y'know? This is Paradise Valley. It ain't nothin' but jazz spots all over Black Bottom. And to tell you the truth, they doin' much better for business lately than this spot here.

CORN: This one of the first though. One of the original spots in Black Bottom. Called Paradise 'fore this lil' strip was even called Paradise Valley. Blue like to say—Paradise Valley took its name from him.

P-SAM: See? That's what I'm talkin' about. What kinda sense do that make? Paradise Valley ain't takin' nothin' from Blue. He think he the original. He ain't nothin' but everyday ordinary. Same name is a coincidence. That's all it is.

CORN: This spot was named Paradise first though.

P-SAM: What kinda coffee you be havin' in the mornin', Corn? What Pumpkin put in that toast you be havin' every day? Some kinda Blue-don't-do-no-wrong magic dope or somethin'?

(Corn laughs. Pumpkin enters with a tray of food.)

PUMPKIN: Whipped up some eggs right quick for you too. Here you go, fellas. Something to start your mornin' off nice.

(Corn grabs a plate eagerly. P-Sam doesn't budge.)

CORN: Thank you kindly, Pumpkin. Sure is nice of you.

PUMPKIN: P-Sam, ain't you hungry? The eggs is scrambled hard not soft—just like you like 'em.

P-SAM: No thank you, Pumpkin. Whatever Corn's eating, I'm gonna stay clear of.

CORN: I'll take his.

(Corn reaches over and scrapes P-Sam's plate onto his.)

PUMPKIN: Did I do somethin' wrong? I thought you mighta been hungry. That's why I whipped up some eggs too.

CORN: No Pumpkin, you did just fine. These eggs taste delicious.

P-SAM: I'm sorry, Pumpkin. I'll take that coffee though. I just need somethin' to keep me woke up. Blue got us rehearsing early and he ain't even here.

PUMPKIN: Should be back in a little bit. Just ran downtown for a sec. *(Beat)* Hey there Corn, I got a new one for you. Wanna hear it?

CORN: Love to.

PUMPKIN: You too, P-Sam?

P-SAM: Sure, Pumpkin. We got time to kill. What you got?

PUMPKIN: 'Kay. Almost got it memorized. *(Hands Corn the book of poems, open to her page)* Hold this, Corn. In case I forget.

CORN: All right. Go'on Pumpkin.

PUMPKIN:

> The heart of a woman goes forth with the dawn,
> As a lone bird, soft winging, so restlessly on . . .

Er . . . ummm . . .

CORN: Afar?

P-SAM: A who?

PUMPKIN: Oh okay—wait . . . don't tell me . . .

> Afar o'er life's turrets and . . . vales does it roam
> In the wake of those echoes the heart calls home.

CORN: That was good there, Pumpkin. Wasn't that good, Sam?

P-SAM: That was good all right. Real smart words you got there, Pumpkin. Make it sound real pretty.

PUMPKIN: They not mine. Miss Georgia Douglas Johnson. They hers.

CORN: What's that part she says here? About the heart of a woman goes forth with the dawn as a . . .

PUMPKIN: Lone bird . . .

CORN: What's that mean, Pumpkin?

PUMPKIN: I think it means . . . well . . . that a woman is just goin' off on her lonesome . . . waitin' for somebody to love her. Somethin' like that, I think.

P-SAM: Waiting for somebody to love her, hunh Pumpkin?

PUMPKIN (*Bashfully*): I think that's what it means . . . maybe.

CORN: Well I thank you, Pumpkin. For the good words and the good eatin'.

(Corn slops up the rest of his food. P-Sam watches Pumpkin take down chairs from the tables.
He joins her.)

P-SAM: Lemme help you with these chairs, now.

PUMPKIN: Oh it's all right, P-Sam. I can do it.

P-SAM: You ain't always got to call me P-Sam, you know?

PUMPKIN: I like it better than sayin' Percussion Sam all the way out. P-Sam a good nickname.

P-SAM: Yeah. Sure, Pumpkin. But it's you and me. It's all right if you just call me Sam. That's what anybody close to me call me.

PUMPKIN: I . . . feel more . . . proper . . . callin' you P-Sam.

P-SAM: Proper?

PUMPKIN: For Blue. Don't think he'll like it much, me talkin' to you improper. For a lady.

P-SAM: It ain't Blue's name. You callin' Blue, you call him whatever he say. But when you callin' my name, you can call me Sam.

PUMPKIN: Still . . .

(Pumpkin nervously moseys away from P-Sam. He watches her and smiles.)

P-SAM: You too sweet, Pumpkin. You got the perfect name for who you is.

(The door to the club opens sharply. Pumpkin jumps and moves over to the bar, wiping it down profusely.

Blue enters. He is a lion of a man, more in his demeanor than his stature. Thirties and smooth. He walks in and commands attention.)

BLUE: Where the sign go?

CORN: Hey there, Blue.

(Blue sees the cardboard sign that P-Sam had lying on the counter.)

BLUE: Who took down the sign?

CORN: We was just lookin' at it. Thought maybe it was a mistake.

BLUE: Ain't no mistake.

CORN: Sam was just lookin' at it.

P-SAM: You fired Joe?

BLUE: Joe quit. I ain't fire nothin'. He quit cuz he's a fool. Good riddance to him.

CORN: Quit? What for?

BLUE: Talkin' 'bout he want some solo time. Everybody know this is Blue's Black Bottom Quartet. My club. My band. Ain't nobody gettin' solo time but me. Don't no bassist nowhere get solo time and he think he just gonna change the rules. Joe a fool. Talkin' 'bout he gonna go'on over to the Three Sixes and get picked up over there. I told him go. Three Sixes ain't better than Paradise Club. I don't care how much money they pullin' in. Money ain't quality.

P-SAM: How we s'pose to play bop without bass? We can't play without Joe.

BLUE: We'll replace Joe. And till we do, I'm goin' on solo. And Corn, I'm puttin' you on too. You gonna do some old standards with Pumpkin for the intermission act.

PUMPKIN: Me?

BLUE: That's right, baby. Just for intermission. You gonna be on the stage and sing for me.

PUMPKIN: But . . . I—

P-SAM: What's that mean? Pumpkin and Corn doing standards. You doin' solos? Where's that leave me?

BLUE: Leave you with a roof over your head upstairs of my club free of charge. That's what it leave you. 'Less you ready to complain about that now.

P-SAM: How you gonna play solo with no rhythm section? Who's gonna do your rhythm?

BLUE: Got a guest band coming in next Friday. Just gonna play with 'em till we get back swingin'.

P-SAM: Guest band? You bringin' in somebody else to do percussion? What am I supposed to do if I'm not playin'? Sit on empty pockets till the cows come home?

BLUE: Didn't I say it's temporary? You do this till we find somebody to replace Joe. And till then, I ain't gonna charge you no rent. That's fair as I can think to make it. You know somebody else would do you that?

P-SAM: I know somebody else woulda just let Joe have his money up front and we wouldn't be worryin' 'bout none of this. We need to be out there lookin' for a bassist right now. Ain't one just gonna walk in here outta nowhere.

BLUE: Then go'on and look for one. I got other things to take care of right now.

CORN: You been downtown today?

BLUE: That's right. Some folks downtown been comin' 'round here to do some business.

CORN: Safe Eddie say they been comin' 'round by the Echo Theatre and Wilfred's Billiard Parlor too.

P-SAM: Comin' 'round for what? What they comin' 'round for?

CORN: Said they been talkin' about that plan. This new mayor 'bout to take office—Mayor Cobo . . . he done ran his campaign on it.

P-SAM: The one where they supposed to be clearin' up the slums?

CORN: Gettin' rid of the *blight* in the city. That's what he say on the radio.

P-SAM: Blight? What's he meanin' by that?

BLUE: He means these run-down buildings over here on Hastings Street. That's what he means. And I don't blame him none. Some of these places are a real eyesore. Make all our spots look run-down. I hope he get rid of it good and send them low-class niggers back to the outskirts of the city so the rest of us can finally move on up.

CORN: Them folks ain't doin' nothin' but living where they can afford. That's all. Ain't they fault some of them buildings is run-down. Half of 'em don't even own them buildings. Just payin' what they can afford. Ain't they fault.

BLUE: Fault don't matter. Long as Black Bottom stay what it is, cramped and overcrowded—we ain't never gonna have what all them white folks got. Niggers always comin' 'round here askin' for handouts and free room and board while they get on they feet. Ain't but so much favors you can do. I rely on these bastards, I'm liable to go bankrupt.

PUMPKIN: I like it here in Black Bottom. Always got somewhere I can count on folks. Know Buffalo James gonna always offer me some of his cornmeal if I run out here. Know Patty Poindexter gonna always give me a press'n'curl whether I got the money to pay her or gotta owe it to her the next time. These folks over here like family. Always got time to pull favors for family.

BLUE: Ain't nobody pullin' no more favors outta me. I been pullin' favors up to my ears and I'm goin' tone-deaf.

CORN: What was they tellin' you Blue? Them folks downtown?

BLUE: Just come askin' about Paradise. Say the land this club is sittin' on is pretty hot. More footage than the other spots around here. City wants a piece. Maybe offerin' me a pretty penny for it.

PUMPKIN: You gonna sell Paradise?

BLUE: I ain't sayin' all that. I just say they come talkin' 'bout it. So I go hear what they got to say. That's all.

P-SAM: Ain't this somethin? First you fire Joe and now you gon' put all us on the street if them downtown fellas talk to you right!

BLUE: Didn't I say I was hearin' what they got to say? Don't be puttin' words in my mouth, you hear me? And I done already told you—Joe quit!

P-SAM: Cuz you makin' him quit!

BLUE: If you don't like it, nigger, then there go the door. Ain't nobody askin' you to stay 'round here.

P-SAM: I just might, Blue. Don't go sayin' nothin' just to say it. I just might.

CORN: Ain't no need for all that. Percussion Sam and Corn the Pianoman both a part of Blue's Black Bottom Quartet and we know that, Blue. Ain't no need for nobody else to quit. We gonna find a bassist and be back in business. And till then, you go 'head and work on your solo while me and Pumpkin learn ourselves some standards.

PUMPKIN: But . . . I don't think—

BLUE: Sheet music's upstairs. I'll get it and ya'll can practice in back while I get this spot ready for dinner tonight. Ya'll learn it and be ready to go up by next Friday. And in the meantime, Sam can go'on and find us a bassist at Garfield's Lounge he wanna be so ambitious.

P-SAM: You ain't sayin' nothin' but a word.

BLUE: All right then.

(The door to the club opens. A mysterious-looking woman dressed in black enters. She wears a hat and veil. This is Silver.
Everyone stops and looks at her. She moves like a spider weaving a web. They watch her until she stops.)

SILVER: Is Blue here?

(Everyone looks at Blue. He looks at Silver questioningly.)

BLUE: I'm Blue. I know you, lady?

SILVER: Naw. But your sign in the window say you got rooms for rent. That true?

BLUE: Oh . . . yeah . . . yeah that's true. I got one-person rooms for rent. Not enough space for your ol' man or nothin'. Them kinda rooms is already occupied.

SILVER: My ol' man dead. How much you charge for your rooms?

BLUE: Five dollars a week. That include meals.

SILVER: Five dollars a week? That ain't comparable. Place up the street got rooms for three dollars a week.

BLUE: Place up the street ain't got nice hot water every day for you neither. Go'on ask folks—you think I'm lying. Lay down for a nice sleep and wake up to a roach openin' your blinds and askin' you how you like yo' grits.

SILVER: Your rooms clean?

BLUE: Pristine. Pumpkin see to that.

SILVER: Pumpkin?

(Pumpkin stares at Silver in awe . . . and suddenly snaps out of it.)

PUMPKIN: Oh yes, Missus. I keep it nice and tidy for you and I starch your sheets clean. If you need anything, you can always let me know and I'll see to it for you.

BLUE: Place up the street ain't got that for you. But you go'on stay up there if you think they better than what we got over here.

SILVER: And what about playin' that bop? You keep late hours?

BLUE: We keep as late hours as any of these other clubs in Paradise Valley. You in Black Bottom, Detroit. And this lil' strip is what we call the jazz paradise. You don't like bop or blues, you got a long way to go 'fore you find some place without it.

SILVER: I ain't said I ain't like it. I know where I'm at. *(Pause)* What if I wanna stay longer than a week?

BLUE: Long as you can pay, you can stay.

SILVER: Well then . . .

(Silver digs into her bosom and pulls out a wad of cash. Everyone watches her in astonishment. She hands money to Blue.)

That's thirty dollars. I want the month and then some . . .

(Blue counts the cash twice over . . . eyeing it widely.)

BLUE: Go'on with her, Pumpkin. Show this woman where the room at.

PUMPKIN: All right then . . . you can follow me, Missus . . . You got a name?

SILVER: They call me Silver.

PUMPKIN: Silver? Well all right, follow me, Miss Silver.

(Silver follows Pumpkin out.
P-Sam and Corn look after them.)

P-SAM: Whooo!!! You see that woman?

CORN: Seen her, I did.

P-SAM: She got some kinda walk on her, ain't she?

BLUE: She got some kinda money on her. You see her pull this out that fast? Somethin' ain't right about that.

CORN: What ain't right about it? She look right to me.

BLUE: What a woman doin' comin' here with no ol' man? You hear that? Talkin' 'bout, "My ol' man dead." Say it just like that, without no feelin' or nothin'. Somethin' ain't right about it.

P-SAM: She ain't got no man and she got a walk like that, she ain't gonna be in that one-person room too long.

CORN: She got some kinda sadness to her maybe.

BLUE: Whatever she is, she better not bring no trouble up here in Paradise. Woman like that . . . lookin' the way she lookin' . . . all on her lonesome . . . them kinda women ain't nothin' but trouble. You betta believe that.

P-SAM: Well a little bit of trouble ain't never hurt nobody really. *(Shift)* I'm gon' get on. Since we ain't rehearsing no more, I'ma go try my luck with the policy. Maybe if I bet just right, my number'll come up and I won't have to worry 'bout having no gig right now. Hmph . . . Joe quit . . .

(P-Sam heads on out the door.)

BLUE: Corn, that nigger gonna try me. I'm tellin' you. That P-Sam ain't worth the trust I'd give a honkie on a Tuesday.

CORN: He all right, Blue. We gonna find us somebody that's gonna turn things around here. You'll see.

BLUE: Yeah, I'll see. *(Shift)* Gonna get you that sheet music for Pumpkin. You got to help her sing it right.

CORN: All right, Blue. If that's what you need.

BLUE: That's what I need, Corn. She be scared and nervous . . . but you help her. I hear her humming and singing soft, and it sound real pretty. She got a voice in her. But you got to help it come out. You the only one can ease it out of her. You get me?

CORN: Yeah I get you, Blue.
BLUE: Good, Corn. That's good.

(Blue exits.)

CORN *(Softly)*: I may be the only one who do get you . . .

(Lights shift.)

SCENE TWO

Silver's room. It's rather plain, just a twin bed, a small vanity, one tall dresser. Maybe a broken-framed hanging picture. That's all, folks. Pumpkin makes the bed while Silver unpacks.

PUMPKIN: . . . and the meals regular—breakfast, lunch and dinner. So you just gotta let me know if you eatin' every night or if you gettin' your meal somewhere else. Best meal is supper. I'm usually 'lowed to give three sides 'steada two. So I switch it up. Corn hash with roast beef and string beans, cabbage, and cranberry sauce . . . or sometimes we do steak and peas with mashed potato and gravy—Blue count gravy as a side on that one—and on Fridays we usually do the fish fry with some kinda potato and greens. We got hot sauce packets but we charge a penny if you want more than two. And—

(Silver stares at Pumpkin.)

What'sthematter? Am I talkin' your ear off? Blue say I could talk a hole in your head if don't nobody tell me to hush.
SILVER: You do the cookin'?

PUMPKIN: Yes, Missus. I'm a real good cook.

SILVER: Umph. I hate cookin'.

PUMPKIN: Do you?

SILVER: With a passion. Can't stand the heat of nobody else's kitchen. I prefer the heat in the bedroom or some other places. But not in the kitchen. That's the wrong kinda heat for me.

PUMPKIN: Oh. *(Short pause)* Well it's good I'll do it for you then. No worries there.

(Silver pulls out a record player and sets it atop the dresser. She pulls out a couple of records.)

My goodness. You travel with that thing?

SILVER: Can't be one place and my music someplace else. Go crazy otherwise . . .

(Silver pulls out a silky nightgown and holds it up to herself in the mirror. Pumpkin watches in astonishment.)

This thing . . . ain't worth the rocks in my shoes. Silk my tailbone. This some kinda imposter fabric if I ever seen it. I knew that man sold it to me was lyin', but the store lights wasn't harsh as these. I can see real good now. Cheap rayon maybe. Not no silk.

PUMPKIN: I think it's pretty.

SILVER: It's yours then.

(Silver tosses it to Pumpkin nonchalantly and continues to unpack her clothes.)

PUMPKIN: Oh! No—Missus I couldn't—

SILVER: Sho you can.

PUMPKIN: But it's yours.

SILVER: Not no more. Don't like the thing.

PUMPKIN: But, I—

SILVER: So which one of them fellas your ol' man?

PUMPKIN: Oh—well, me and Blue are together—

SILVER: 'Course you are. He the one who runnin' everything. *(Shift)* So them other two fellas . . . they up for grabs then?

PUMPKIN: Well I . . . they are . . . I mean . . . I wouldn't know . . .

SILVER: That mean they are. If they wasn't, you would know. Believe me that.

PUMPKIN: What brings you over here to Black Bottom?

SILVER: Time to pick up somewhere new. I heard of Black Bottom, Detroit. 'Specially down this strip in Paradise Valley where folks got all they own business. If it's somewhere that colored folks is doing more than sharecroppin' and reapin' white folks' harvest . . . I ought to be there. They say that here's where folks sellin' automobiles and bettin' on the policy numbers and dancin' in the nighttime like they just as free as the Mississippi River. I'm here so I can get a taste of all that.

PUMPKIN: Where you come from?

SILVER: Lots of places. But Louisiana be the first.

PUMPKIN: Louisiana? Place where they got all them spirits and Negroes eatin' live chickens and drinkin' they blood?

(Silver looks at Pumpkin questioningly.)

SILVER: You ain't never been, have you?

PUMPKIN: No, miss. Never been outside Detroit.

SILVER: Well, maybe you oughta leave sometime. And when you do, try out Louisiana.

PUMPKIN: I love it here in Black Bottom. I don't never wanna leave.

SILVER: That so? Why's that?

PUMPKIN: Got roots here. And purpose.

SILVER: Got family here?

PUMPKIN: Made family here. Was sent here as a girl to stay with my aunt who run her own beauty parlor on Hastings Street. Used to work for her and attend school over there. She passed on now, and the parlor been turned into an automobile store. But I stayed around here. With different women what used to be her customers. They took care of me. Even helped to pay for my books. And eventually I met Blue.

SILVER: And the rest was history, hunh?

PUMPKIN: Yes, ma'am.

SILVER: Well, it's good you made you some roots here, but every woman got to pick up and leave after while. If you don't know that now, you gonna know it one day.

PUMPKIN (*Remembering*):
    The heart of a woman goes forth with the dawn . . .

SILVER: What's that?

PUMPKIN: A little bit of poetry. Just made me think of it.

SILVER: You a poet? Like them fellas in Harlem?

PUMPKIN: No, not me. I just like it, that's all. What you said about a woman pickin' up and leavin' . . . remind me of some poetry. It say— "The heart of a woman goes forth with the dawn . . ." I suppose that's what you doin'.

SILVER: Well, that's fancy of you. Recitin' poems like that from your memory. Maybe that's somethin' you can learn me how to do.

PUMPKIN: Oh. (*Bashful smile*) Sure . . .

(*Silver finishes putting her clothes away. She takes off her shirt and bottoms nonchalantly—leaving her in striking undergarments. She sprays herself with perfume. Pumpkin stares at her, fascinated.*)

SILVER: This fella of yours . . . he be good to you?

PUMPKIN: Blue. He's something special. Gifted.

SILVER: That wasn't my question.

PUMPKIN: I'm sorry?

SILVER: I say, he be good to you? That's important to ask a woman 'bout a man. I done learned.

PUMPKIN: He the best thing I've ever known.

SILVER: That so?

PUMPKIN: Yes, Missus. Got a gentle heart and a lion's soul. Got the will to give me everything he can. But what he really got is a gift. It make it so sometimes that's all I can see. When he play, I think he's talkin' to God and together they answerin' my prayers.

SILVER: Weelll . . . he must do you real good—up, down and inside . . . way you speak on him like ecstasy.

PUMPKIN: My goodness. You always speak this improper?

SILVER: What's improper 'bout it? I'm just speakin' straight. Ain't that what these Detroit gangsters do? Speak straight.

PUMPKIN: Why a woman need to speak like a gangster?

SILVER (*Seriously*): So everybody know she ain't to be messed with.

(*Beat.*)

I can get me one of them nice hot suppers you was talkin' 'bout this evening?

PUMPKIN: Oh . . . yes, Missus. 'Round eight o'clock. I'll be by to deliver it to you.

SILVER: That's fine by me. Now if you don't mind, I got to finish messin' with my things and get into somethin' comfortable.

PUMPKIN: Oh—right.

(*Pumpkin moves to the door with a touch of embarrassment.*)

If you need anything else, you just ring me and I'll take care of you. Phone booth is in the hallway out there. But I'm usually downstairs.

SILVER: Be sure to.

(Pumpkin opens the door.)

And don't forget this. It's yours now.

(Silver throws Pumpkin the nightgown.
   Pumpkin—clueless of what to do—nods and disappears behind the door.
   Silver watches after her for a moment . . . calculatingly.
   Then she sits down at the vanity and dolls herself up for the night.)

SCENE THREE

Afternoon sun spills through Paradise Club. Corn sits at the bar and demolishes a hearty meal.
   Pumpkin wipes down the bar and fills the liquor stock. Occasionally, she winces from a pain in her wrist. No one notices.

CORN: Pumpkin, you put your foot in this cornbread.
PUMPKIN: Not supposed to give it to you till supper, but I thought maybe you could have a light taste. For listenin' to my poetry and all . . .
CORN: You keep fillin' me up with this stuff, I listen to a hundred of your poems. Hit me.

(Pumpkin eagerly rushes to the bar and picks up a book. She passes it to Corn.)

PUMPKIN: This one she calls, "My Little Dreams."

CORN: She who?

PUMPKIN: Miss Georgia Douglas Johnson. My latest favorite. Goes like this . . .

> I'm folding up my little dreams
> Within my heart tonight,
> And praying I may soon forget
> The torture of their sight.
>
> For time's deft fingers scroll my brow
> With fell relentless art—
> I'm folding up my little dreams
> Tonight, within my heart.

CORN: What kind of fingers is that, Pumpkin? Say it scroll on the brow?

PUMPKIN: Deft. Means like, you know, how somebody got good knittin' hands? Fingers got lots of skill. That's what time got. Deft fingers. And you ever known how somebody rubbin' on your head, say a woman maybe? And she maybe smooth your eyebrow some . . .

CORN: I ain't know that in a long time. Not since my Mabel passed.

PUMPKIN: Well, that's what Miss Johnson means in her poetry. Time massaging her like your Mabel used to do you. Movin' on till it's gone and her dreams gone too. She bury them in her heart so she don't have to think on 'em or be sad no more. Like your Mabel.

CORN: Yeah. I buried her all right. I know what that Miss Johnson mean. Bury something deep inside so you can forget the hurt of not havin' it.

PUMPKIN: That's right, Corn. That's real good. You're a regular poet. An interpreter. That's what you are.

CORN: Naw, Pumpkin. That's you and this stuff. I just like to listen with you cuz it's somethin' different. We got the piano. Got the trumpet. Got the percussion. Used to have the bass. Then you come with these words and bring in another kind of music.

(The door to the club swings open. In walks P-Sam.)

P-SAM: Hey there, folks.

CORN: Hey, Sam.

PUMPKIN: Afternoon, P-Sam.

P-SAM *(Flirtatious)*: Hey, Pumpkin pie. Got a little somethin' for me to nibble on?

PUMPKIN: Today we got sandwiches for lunch. Bologna and salami. I'll go make you one.

P-SAM: What's that Corn was eating over here? That don't look like no crumbs from a sandwich.

CORN: Yes it was, wasn't it, Pumpkin? Sandwich with the works.

(Pumpkin giggles.)

P-SAM: Oh I get it. Ain't that nothin'? Corn get to taste an early dinner and all I get is a measley ol' salami sandwich.

PUMPKIN: I'll go put you some pickles on it too . . .

P-SAM: Well la-ti-da. I guess I'm s'pose to jump out my shoes cuz I get pickles.

(Pumpkin disappears into the back.)

Say, Corn, I found us somebody.

CORN: Did you?

P-SAM: String-Finger Charlie over at Garfield's Lounge. Caught his set last night and it's outta sight. Talked to him—say he lookin' to leave Percy's quintet if Blue willin' to meet his fee. Percy payin' them overtime if the set runs late.

CORN: Don't know if Blue gonna go for that now, Sam. You know he don't believe in overtime.

P-SAM: Blue don't believe in nothin' but himself. Where I'm s'pose to play, Corn? Ain't no openings for a percussion man at none of these other clubs in the valley.

CORN: You a good musician, Sam. You can get your pick anywhere.

P-SAM: Don't give me that, Corn. Ain't no place for a colored man outside of Black Bottom and you know it. I been on that other stint, playin' the white man's club in Detroit and all them other cities—entering through the back door. Carryin' my card in Harlem and if I ain't got it, I ain't allowed to make no bread or play no music. Standin' on them stages and smilin' like I'm just happy to be entertainin' these no-'count crackers that think of me as less than the spilled whiskey on they shoe.

CORN: We all been on that stint Sam. One time or another. That's the cost we pay to play.

P-SAM: Tell you the truth, Corn, Blue ain't no better. He think of us just like they do. On the bottom. Only difference is he still a nigger himself, whether he like it or not, and stingy as he is, he need us. And we need each other. That's why we got to get back in business. This the only place I can be a percussion man befo' bein' colored. You the only one can talk to Blue, Corn.

CORN: I don't know String-Finger Charlie. How good is he?

P-SAM: Seen 'im last night do this thing ain't never seen a bassman do befo'. Tap on the strings like a hammer and make two strings play by themselves. Tellin' you—this cat's outta sight.

CORN: Maybe I'll go over to Garfield's Lounge with you tonight and see for myself.

P-SAM: You do that, Corn. And then you talk to Blue. I can't be sittin' here with no money swellin' my pockets. When a Negro man ain't got no money, it's like he smell different. Negro women sniff him miles away and turn they noses in another direction. Not even the finest cologne can clean up that kinda stink. And I'm funky, Corn. It ain't right.

CORN: I'll see. That's all I can say.

P-SAM: That's all you need to say for now. *(Shift)* How that rehearsin' with Pumpkin goin'?

(Corn looks back to see if Pumpkin is near. Coast is clear.)

CORN: Terrible.

P-SAM: She that bad?

CORN: Worse.

P-SAM: Well I guess you can't have it all. Be all smart on them books, and sing like you know the devil up close and personal.

CORN: I don't know what to tell Blue 'bout it. He say he done heard her sing pretty but I ain't heard it yet. Ain't got the heart to make her feel bad. But she workin' and workin' and sound like she gettin' worser and worser.

P-SAM: Well serve Blue right, then. Put her up there and see what kinda mess it is, and then maybe he'll see the light.

CORN: I hope he see befo' Friday. He say she got a voice in her somewhere. But I can't find it nowhere.

(The door to Paradise Club swings open. Blue walks in carrying his trumpet. Zoot suit and hat, lookin' sharp.)

Afternoon, Blue. You lookin' like Sunday on a Tuesday. Where you comin' from?

BLUE: Just out takin' care of business. Where Pumpkin?

CORN: In the back fixin' P-Sam a sandwich.

BLUE *(To P-Sam)*: You pay her?

P-SAM: I thought I was gettin' room and board free till we get more gigs?

BLUE: Board ain't meals.

P-SAM: What's board if it ain't meals?! Include meals for everybody else.

BLUE: Everybody else payin'. I'm lettin' you stay up there for free. Don't mean I can afford to feed you with no money. You ain't suckin' me dry.

P-SAM: How I'm supposed to bring in money when you runnin' off musicians every chance you get?

BLUE: Don't start with me on that, nigger. I ain't startin' in with you today.

P-SAM: Listen to that. You hear that, Corn? He ain't startin' in with me. But he the one startin' everything.

(Pumpkin enters with the sandwich.)

PUMPKIN: Here ya go, P-Sam. I made it with pickles and hot sauce too.

BLUE: You charge him the penny for the hot sauce?

PUMPKIN: Well . . . no . . . not this time. We had a little extra so—

BLUE: We done been through this, Pumpkin . . . you can't keep passin' out favors like this is some kinda soup kitchen.

P-SAM: You go'on, Pumpkin. You keep that sandwich, hear? I ain't got to eat nothin' from this penny-pinchin' pistol.

PUMPKIN: Blue, sweets, if he don't eat it, it's just gonna go to waste. Might as well not let no food hit the trash. Ain't that what you told me?

BLUE: Give him the sandwich. But you got to pay sometime. This ain't no soup kitchen. You give niggers one and they want two. Tell 'em free room and they want free meals too.

P-SAM: Sam don't need nothin' for free, hear?

PUMPKIN: Here you go, P-Sam. Eat up. I made it real fine. Gonna go back and get you somethin' to wash it down with too.

(Pumpkin exits into the kitchen. P-Sam picks up his sandwich and bites into it rebelliously.)

P-SAM: Sam willin' to work for everything he got. Don't need no handouts. But you got me over here without no gig—

BLUE: Thought you was takin' care of that.

P-SAM: I am. Ain't that right, Corn?

CORN: That's right. We gonna go tonight to check out somebody s'posed to be real good.

BLUE: How that song comin' with you and Pumpkin?

CORN: Oh it's . . . goin' . . . special. Pumpkin's voice is . . . somethin' I can't even . . . explain . . .

BLUE: Good. You just gotta get her to some confidence. I can hear the music in her speak. You just gotta push it out of her. Woman like Pumpkin need a little push . . .

CORN: We gonna . . . push . . . much as we can . . .

BLUE: That bad-luck woman been down here today?

CORN: That fiiiine woman.

P-SAM: Make you wanna follow wherever she lead . . .

BLUE: Don't go followin' her 'less you wanna end up in a grave somewhere.

CORN: What you talkin' now, Blue?

BLUE: She already the talk of the town and ain't been here three days.

CORN: What they sayin'?

BLUE: Just what I was thinkin'. Woman move up here without no man got trouble followin' her. Sittin' on a stack of money. Say she killed a man for it.

CORN: Killed a man?

P-SAM: I ain't heard that. But Jimmy the Greek Johnson over at the pool hall was sayin' she done slept with over fifty men in different cities and they all disappeared.

CORN: You listenin' to Jimmy the Greek? You know he ain't never told a truth in his natural life.

BLUE: This time I believe it. I'm tellin' you. I don't trust that woman.

P-SAM: What woman do you trust?

BLUE: Don't start in on me, nigger.

P-SAM: Say they call her a witch.

CORN: Witch?

BLUE: A voodoo woman from Louisiana. That's what she is.

P-SAM: Spiderwoman. That's what they call her. Say she been to Chicago and Minneapolis and Milwaukee too. All them places, she go walkin' like that . . . some kinda sexy spider . . . lurin' fellas into her web. And then just when you get close to her . . . she stick into you and lay her poison.

CORN (*Laughing*): If ya'll don't sound like two of the silliest cats to ever play bop . . .

BLUE: You laugh if you want to, Corn . . . but you be the first one to get caught up in her web. Then you touch her one time and your longleg fall right off. Them Louisiana women got them spirits in them.

(Silver enters from the kitchen, unbeknownst to the men.)

P-SAM: You got to admit you curious about a lil' of it. But I like my longleg too much to take a bet on that. I rather try my luck with the policy.

SILVER: Afternoon, fellas.

(The men jump. Silver smiles a sexy, sinful smile. She spider-walks over to the bar and takes a seat.)

Hope I'm not interruptin' your man talk. But I was promised me a taste of early dinner and I want to cash in.

BLUE: We got sandwiches. Pumpkin be back out and take care of you.

SILVER: I look like the kind of woman eat sandwiches?

BLUE *(Glares at Silver)*: That's what you eatin' / you eatin' here.

SILVER *(To Corn)*: Say there, buttercup. You got a light?

CORN: Me?

SILVER: I don't see nobody else cute and chubby sittin' over here.

CORN *(Smiling)*: Well . . . I don't smoke none.

(Blue slides her some matches.)

SILVER: Thanks, doll.

(Silver lights a cigarette and takes a slow drag. The men watch her silently.)

You ought to have yourself a lighter. Every business owner got one of them. Personalized and inscripted. You ought to have that.

BLUE: I got what I need.

SILVER: That's what everybody think . . . till what they really need come along . . . *(Shift)* You fellas read the paper?

BLUE: You want the paper, you got to go'on over to Biddy's restaurant and spend your penny like everybody else. That don't come with the board.

SILVER: Oh, I got my paper for the day. Been doin' my reading too. See what this new mayor of yours got plannin' for this Black Bottom area. Tryin' to clean it up, I see.

P-SAM: That's right, ma'am. They lookin' for folks like us to get on outta here so they can hurry up and make Detroit bright white. But we ain't goin' nowhere . . . so you don't worry your pretty lil' self 'bout that.

SILVER: Well I just figures . . . when a city want folks to leave, they must be offerin' somethin' pretty to get rid of 'em. And you especially, sittin' on the ripest piece of somethin' over here. Say the square footage of your land bigger 'n all the other spots in this whole valley. This spot dead in the middle and in the best location.

BLUE: What of it?

SILVER: I just wonder what they offerin' for a place as hot as this.

BLUE: What's it matter to you?

SILVER: Don't matter nothin' yet. Could matter a whole lot if you was interested in sellin'.

BLUE: You think I'm gonna sell my place?

CORN: Blue ain't partin' with this club. This used to be his daddy's club.

BLUE: Leave my daddy outta this, Corn. Miss, you can keep your sidesteppin' slick talk cuz it ain't shakin' over here. Paradise Club is mine, and I ain't talkin' 'bout my plans with no simple woman.

SILVER: Cool down, sugar. I'm just makin' small talk.

BLUE: Ain't nothin' to talk about. Stuff you hearin' 'bout Paradise Club ain't nothin' but hearsay. Niggers runnin' off at the mouth cuz they ain't got nothin' better to do than worry 'bout Blue. But it ain't none of nobody's business what I do with my own spot.

SILVER: Sho, it is. What you do with yo' spot might be real influential to all others. Seem like what you do be everybody business. So you let me know if there's anything worth talkin' 'bout.

BLUE: You think you know somethin' I don't?

SILVER: I know 'bout how to run a club.

P-SAM: Where you know all that?

SILVER: Come from music. My daddy was a bluesman. Grew up 'round all this type of business. And I could tell you why that Garfield's Lounge and the Three Sixes gonna keep having way more customers than over here . . . even though you got the bigger joint.

P-SAM: Why's that?

CORN: Sam—

SILVER: Chargin' too much at the door.

BLUE: I charge what I charge.

P-SAM: What you think it oughta be?

SILVER: Should only be fifty cents. But you makin' it a whole seventy-five. Too high. Folks see that and don't care that you got the better trumpeteer or the best pecan pie. They feel like they bein' kept on the outskirts. All the other spots make 'em feel welcome. But here, it feel like everybody don't belong. Like even if we all the same people, only certain kinds get to come in and patron. You dividin' the people like pie. That's what make it not feel right.

BLUE: I ain't askin' for your business help. I been runnin' this place for five years just fine.

SILVER: Five years ain't nothin'. I seen goldfish last longer than five years. Five years still wet behind the ears if you ask—

(Blue bangs his hand on the bar. Everyone jumps a bit.)

CORN: Blue.

BLUE (Threateningly): Watch your mouth in my spot, woman.

CORN: Hey now, Blue—

(Blue walks closer to Silver.)

BLUE: Don't you think you 'bout to come in here and tell me how to run my place. You ain't been in this town five seconds and you think you know 'bout over here in Black Bottom?

(Silver remains calm. She smiles and puffs her cigarette.)

SILVER: I just thought you'd like to hear another idea, sugar. No need to get so uptight.

BLUE: You listen to me here. You come down here, you keep your mouth shut unless you wanna be out of a room. Don't think just cuz you got a stash somewhere that make you matter over here. It don't. I'll throw this money back in your face, put you out on your simple black ass, and won't think twice about it. You understand me, woman?

(Pumpkin enters from the kitchen.)

PUMPKIN: Everything all right out here? Blue, sweets, you okay?

(Blue moves away from Silver and grabs his hat.)

BLUE: Pumpkin, come on and let's get you somethin' to wear for Friday night. Gotta find you somethin' classy for when you sing with Corn.

PUMPKIN *(Hesitantly)*: But don't you want me to . . . finish gettin' dinner together for this evenin'? And I still gotta mop the kitchen and change the sheets upstairs—

BLUE: Forget about all that right now. We'll take care of that later. Just grab your coat and meet me in the back. We take the streetcar on down to J. L. Hudson's and pick you out something nice.

PUMPKIN: J. L. Hudson's? We goin' down Woodward?!

BLUE: That's right. For my woman—only the biggest and the fanciest department store in the city. Grab your coat and come on.

P-SAM: J. L. Hudson's? They only 'low niggers to clean they floors and run they elevators. What kinda nigger you think you is to go shoppin' there?

BLUE: They don't let niggers like you shop there. I ain't you.

PUMPKIN: Oh, Blue! You think we can afford it?

BLUE: Don't worry 'bout what we can afford, woman! Just come on and let me get you somethin'.

(Pumpkin rushes over to grab her coat from the rack. She lifts it and a pain stabs her wrist. She flinches.
Silver notices, as does Corn.)

CORN: You all right there, Pumpkin?

PUMPKIN: Oh, I'm just fine. Little soreness of my wrists. Get that way sometimes when I been cleanin' a lot. Just need to soak 'em in some salts and I be fine.

SILVER: Get you a box a raisins and a pint of gin.

P-SAM: Say what?

SILVER: Louisiana remedy. My grandmama taught it to me. Soak the raisins in a half pint of gin and watch all the pain go away.

P-SAM: What's the other half-pint of gin for?

SILVER: In case of anything else you need to cure. Gin make all kinda of pain disappear . . .

BLUE: Pumpkin don't need none of your backwater Louisiana hoodoo. She'll be just fine.

(Blue moves to Pumpkin's side and helps her into her coat.)

When we get back, Corn, ya'll get back to practicin'.

CORN: Sure, Blue. Whatever you say . . .

(Blue and Pumpkin exit.)

P-SAM: Say, Corn, we should head over to Garfield's 'round eight to see my man String-Finger Charlie.

CORN: I'll be ready.

SILVER: Heard they serving a sweet potato pie over at that lounge tonight that taste better than your Aunt Harriet's.

P-SAM: You want to come have a taste, baby?

SILVER: That's all right, sugar. I was plannin' on stayin' to my lonesome this evening.

P-SAM: Suit yourself, sweetheart. I'm gon' go put my bet in for the policy. You got a favorite number, baby? Maybe I'll play it for you.

SILVER: One three one.

P-SAM: One three one? How you gonna tell me something like that? One three one? You tryin' to curse me?

(P-Sam heads for the door, disgruntled.)

I'll see you later, Corn. *(Mumbling)* One three one . . . crazy woman . . .

(Silver turns to Corn and smiles.)

SILVER: What's got him so uptight?

CORN: You just gave him a number with thirteen in it. Nobody plays thirteen. It's an omen.

SILVER: Oh . . . I just gave him my old address. One three one Rue Decatur in N'awlins. Men 'round here just act so fussy 'bout every little thang.

CORN: That's just the way these fellas are. Don't pay them no nevermind, miss. I think you were mighty nice—offerin' up your address to him like that. Let him find his own good luck.

(Silver smiles at Corn. She rises from her seat.)

SILVER: Say there, buttercup . . . You're a real sweet fella. I can see that from here.

CORN: Thank you, miss. Name's Cornelius. But I like Buttercup just the same.

SILVER: Well, you can call me whatever you like.

(She heads for the door.)

Enjoy that sweet potato pie tonight. And if it's as good as they say, you let me know, will ya?

CORN: I surely will.

(Silver winks at Corn, does her spider walk, and exits. Corn sits and smiles after her.)

SCENE FOUR

Nighttime falls on the club. Moonlight peeks through the window.

In silhouette, Blue plays his trumpet. He plays a beautiful and painful melody—long, sorrowful notes.

Soft lights illuminate the rest of the club and reveal Pumpkin putting up chairs. Somewhere in his tune, she leaves one chair down near the foot of the stage, and takes a seat, listening.

Blue—in his own world—becomes too wrapped up in his pain. Suddenly he breaks free of the tune.

He stops and wipes his face . . . from sweat . . . or tears . . . or both . . .

Pumpkin applauds.

PUMPKIN: That sounded real good.

BLUE: Don't clap for that. Don't ever clap for that.

PUMPKIN: But . . . it was good.

BLUE: Mediocre. I lost my rhythm. Let it take over. Ain't never s'pose to let it take over.

PUMPKIN: That ain't nothin' but the pain swoopin' in on you. That's what makes it the most beautiful, I think. The pain is the sweetest part.

BLUE: It's weak. Need to practice more 'steada runnin' 'round this city chasin' pipe dreams.

PUMPKIN: Come 'ere.

(Blue looks at Pumpkin. For the first time, we see him soften to her. For this one moment, she is in command.
He walks over to her and kneels beside her. He grabs her waist and holds on to her.)

You look tired.

BLUE: I am tired, Pumpkin.

PUMPKIN: You can rest now.

BLUE: Ain't no rest for the weary . . . ain't that how it go?

PUMPKIN: You can rest here. With me.

BLUE: This is dead, Pumpkin.

PUMPKIN: What's dead?

BLUE: This place. Black Bottom. I'm chokin' here. I can hear it when I play my axe. Baby, I'm not right.

PUMPKIN: You sound all right to me. Just achin' inside. But ain't nothin' wrong with that. Everybody got aches. Just need somethin' soft to touch it and make it better. I can do that . . . if you let me.

BLUE: They're still here, Pumpkin. Them spirits.

PUMPKIN: What spirits?

BLUE: Spirit of my daddy. Lurkin' 'round this club. Hangin' in the walls. Hangin' in my music. Nigger won't leave me be.

PUMPKIN: Those just bad memories. You keep playing till it don't hurt no more.

BLUE: They more than memories, Pumpkin. They my daddy's demons comin' after me. I got to run from 'em 'fore they kill me.

PUMPKIN: Run where, Blue? What you sayin'?

BLUE: I'm gettin' rid of this place, Pumpkin. Gonna sell it to the city. They offerin' ten thousand for this club. That's what I been doin'. Talkin' them into givin' me what I ask for.

PUMPKIN: Sell Paradise?!

BLUE: And go to Chicago. I got these fellas comin' Friday. They got a band in Chicago and they want a trumpet man. I told 'em to come hear me play so they can see I'm the one. Say they lookin' for a songbird to sing with the band sometimes. I told 'em I got the prettiest little songbird in Detroit with me. So you show 'em your pipes and get 'em to understand, Pumpkin. Get 'em to see we belong somewhere else.

PUMPKIN: Oh, Blue—I ain't ready. I ain't no songbird. I can't barely sing in the right key—

BLUE: You got the music in you. I heard it before. You singin' to yourself sometimes.

PUMPKIN: You hear somethin' different than what it really is. I only hummin'. Carry a tune. Maybe sound good till you put me in front of folks.

BLUE: You got to work with Corn. I seen it happen before. Take your potential and turn it into power. Then you and me can make real music together . . . in Chicago.

PUMPKIN: But I love it here. In Black Bottom. I know folks here and they need me to take care of 'em. I don't wanna leave this and start over somewhere without 'em. Where I ain't got no people. Take a long time for folk to become family.

BLUE: This dead here. Don't you hear me, baby? I need you to take care of me. I'm dyin' here.

PUMPKIN: What about me?

(An odd moment. Blue looks at her curiously. Pumpkin quickly realizes her mistake. She tries to fix:)

PUMPKIN: I mean, it ain't gonna be no better in Chicago. It's pain everywhere.

BLUE: Not this kinda pain, Pumpkin. *(An admission)* I can hear her when I play, you know that? I can hear my mama cryin' sometimes and I try to drown her out. But the cryin' get louder and I can't mute it. I can't save her and she remind me over and over.

PUMPKIN: Oh, baby . . .

BLUE: I hear Daddy too. He comin' to claim me. I ain't gonna be nothin' better and he keep reminding me too. He take my music away and all I got left is chaos.

PUMPKIN: I can love all that chaos away.

BLUE: Will you, baby?

PUMPKIN: I will.

BLUE: Then you'll come with me?

(Pumpkin retreats.)

PUMPKIN: What . . . what about the band?

BLUE: This band? What about it?

PUMPKIN: Everybody here. What they s'pose to do without Paradise? This place our sanctuary.

BLUE: Sanctuary for who??? I'm tellin' you, I ain't right. The damage is in these walls. It's in this club. It's in this band. It's in this whole damn town. I don't want no parts of this no more. Detroit's gonna eat me alive. You hear me? I got to go.

PUMPKIN: Blue. I'll do anything else but I don't wanna leave.

(Suddenly, Blue grabs hold of Pumpkin's arms and shakes her.)

BLUE: Don't say that, Pumpkin. Don't say no / to me—

PUMPKIN *(Frightened)*: Blue, you hurtin' / me—

BLUE: You got to hear what I'm sayin' / got to understand me—

PUMPKIN: Please, Blue / let me loose.

BLUE: I can't stay here no more—you hear? Don't make me / stay here—

PUMPKIN: Blue / please—

BLUE: Tell me what I want to hear / need to hear—

PUMPKIN: Okay, Blue / Okay.

BLUE: Tell me you gonna come.

PUMPKIN: I'm gonna come.

BLUE: Say you won't leave me.

PUMPKIN: I won't leave you.

BLUE: I need you, Pumpkin. I need you to keep quiet and don't mention this to none of the fellas till I got the money solid. Don't want them meddlin' and tryin' to mess stuff up. You hear me?

PUMPKIN: Yes, Blue. I hear you.

BLUE: I need you in every way. Touch me like you say and soften the pain. Love it all away so I can be somebody better.

(Blue releases his grip on Pumpkin and drops his head into her lap.

She kisses his forehead tenderly.)

PUMPKIN: I will, baby. I will.

(Pumpkin touches him softly. She massages him on his cheeks, on his hands, on his eyebrows.)

For time's deft fingers scroll my brow
With fell relentless art—
I'm folding up my little dreams
Tonight, within my heart.

(Blue looks up at her and kisses her passionately. Harshly, even. Needfully.

Lights shift.)

SCENE FIVE

Late night. Corn walks into the club carrying something wrapped in foil. He puts his hat on a stand. He heads to the bar, grabs a few napkins and some silverware. Prepares the something wrapped in foil.
P-Sam enters the club anxiously.

CORN: Where'd you disappear to, Sam? Couldn't find you after the set. But you was right, that String-Finger Charlie was somethin' else.

P-SAM: Told you, didn't I? Ran off to rap with Jimmy the Greek for a minute. Had some news for me.

CORN: What kinda news?

(P-Sam looks around for privacy.)

P-SAM: Corn, I hit it.

CORN: Hit what?

P-SAM: The policy. My number came up. Straight three in a row.

CORN: Well, good for you, Sam. Got you a little bread.

P-SAM: Not no little bread, Corn. A real stash. Something to spread around and get into some serious trouble with.

CORN: You don't wanna be bettin' that on nothin' Sam. Just take your money and make you a little nest somewhere. Don't be like all these other fools done hit the numbers and run out with fur coats and that nonsense.

P-SAM: That ain't what I'm tryin' to do, Corn. I need you to talk to Blue for me.

CORN: Sam, I gotta tell ya—much as I can try to convince Blue on String-Finger Charlie, he ain't gon' be willin' to meet that fee. I can tell you that right now.

P-SAM: That's what I'm sayin' now, Corn. What kinda sense do that make? When you know Blue to be all easy about this band being out of action? Somethin' ain't right about it, and I bet I know what it is.

CORN: Don't go spreadin' stories now, Sam.

P-SAM: He's gonna sell out.

CORN: Blue got roots here. He ain't sellin'.

P-SAM: How much that city talkin' to him for, Corn? They must be offerin' him something nice. Else, Blue got another plan. But it just don't make sense. He ain't even the slightest bit concerned 'bout nothin' but playing solo next Friday. Who you know wanna go on solo that got a quartet? 'Less they fixin' to start playin' with a new one.

CORN: Sam, your mind is runnin' off with your mouth. You makin' stuff up.

P-SAM: I ain't makin' up nothin'. I'm piecing it all together. Jimmy the Greek called it. Said some of these rents over here is gettin' raised. And city payin' off the ones who own. If Blue sellin' out, what's that gonna mean for the rest of us, Corn? No steady bread. No place over our heads. You and me both . . . unless . . .

CORN: 'Less what, Sam?

P-SAM: 'Less he sell the club to me instead.

CORN: Blue ain't sellin, Sam.

P-SAM: Just listen here, Corn. I got me enough to make it worth thinkin' about.

CORN: Blue ain't sellin'.

P-SAM: That's all you can say? Blue ain't sellin'. Ain't even gonna listen to nothin' else?

CORN: Blue ain't sellin', and you or nobody else is buyin'. Don't let that Jimmy the Greek get you confused, Sam. Black Bottom ain't lettin' Blue go, even if he want it to.

P-SAM: How you know that, Corn?

CORN: Some stuff I just know.

P-SAM: Just talk to some folks around town, Corn. See if this plan to clean up the city don't mean to clean us out. Get rid of all the niggers. Just like the mayor say in his campaign—*we* the blight he talkin' 'bout. Everybody know Blue's spot is the best spot to take. They get this, they can get everybody else too. One sell out and it weaken the whole bunch. Unless 'steada sellin' to them, we sell to us. I wouldn't be nothin' like Blue. I'd take care of folks over here and give everybody solo time who want it—

CORN: You talkin' takin' over the band too?

P-SAM: I'm tellin' ya, when it's my spot, we all have a pot to piss in. I wouldn't be no cheap, hateful bastard chargin' nickels per ice cube. And I wouldn't let no crackers take from us what we done worked hard to have on our own. I ain't goin' back to playin' background for them big bands. White man say, "Wear this, play this standard, no bop. Smile like this. Sit like this. Take your meal after these folk, nigger." I ain't doin' it, Corn. If this spot was mine, we'd be the kings we supposed to be. I'd tell that new Mayor Cobo to go to hell he wanna take office and clean us out.

CORN: That's enough, Sam. This talk you doin' gonna start a mess of hearsay and send Blue into a mighty rage.

P-SAM: Corn, how long you gon' defend the devil?

CORN: I ain't defending the devil. I'm trying to keep everything smooth. You don't know what I know. You don't know the limits of a man that's on edge like I do. You ain't seen what I seen, Sam. Now I say I'll think on it. That's all I can say to you. But you got to stop this talk now.

P-SAM: You think about it, Corn. And I'll zip my lips. For now.

CORN: Good.

(Beat.)

P-SAM: I'm tempted to go spend a lil' of my winnin's on a fine woman tonight. Maybe try that spiderwoman out for size.

CORN: Not her. You leave her be.

P-SAM: Oh, don't worry 'bout me none. I ain't scared of a lil' poison.

CORN: I say let her 'lone. She ain't got no interest or cause to be talking to you.

(P-Sam looks at Corn curiously.)

P-SAM: What's it to you if I bother with her, Corn?

(Corn doesn't respond. P-Sam smiles knowingly.)

(Teasing) Oooo! You gon' git bit! She gon' put her pincers in you!

CORN: Cool it out there, Sam.

P-SAM: You wants to get bit—dontcha? Bet you headed there right now.

CORN: I ain't talkin' on it. She's a sweet woman.

P-SAM: Oh, Corn, don't go gettin' mush over this one. You walkin' a fool line. Them kinda women too much for you.

CORN: I ain't askin' for your permission, Sam. I say she's sweet and I'm done with it.

P-SAM: I bet she sweet. Sweet potato pie. Just keep yo' eyes open, Corn. You can't take no more heartbreak. If she don't know that, the rest of us do. And you think about what I said . . . about Blue . . .

CORN: I'll think about it.

P-SAM: Good. I'm gon' stay outta trouble and turn in, myself. Maybe you should too, Corn.

(P-Sam heads off.)

(Singing to himself) Sweet potato piiiieeeeee . . .

(Corn grabs the something wrapped in foil and the silverware. Lights shift.)

SCENE SIX

Silver sits in her room, playing a record on her record player: Charlie "Yardbird" Parker.
   She paints her toenails calmly.
   Suddenly, a knock at her bedroom door.
   She rises from the vanity and opens it.
   Corn stands with a bashful smile and extends the something wrapped in foil.

CORN: Sweet potato pie was too good to miss.

   (Silver smiles slyly. She takes the pie.)

SILVER: That's mighty thoughtful of you.

   (She cracks open the foil and smells.)

Smell like all kinds of sin. Can't wait to satisfy my sweet tooth.
CORN: I hope you enjoy it well. Night, miss.

   (Corn turns to leave.)

SILVER: Wait a minute there, buttercup. Where you goin' so fast?
CORN: I remember you sayin' you wanted to spend the night on your lonesome. I hear a woman say she wanna be left alone, I leave her alone.
SILVER: Well that was before you brought me some sweet potato pie. It ain't no fun to taste sin all alone.
CORN: I really ought not bother you.
SILVER: No bother at all, I say.

(Corn looks at Silver. She is the most intriguing beauty he's ever seen. He smiles shyly.)

CORN: I suppose . . . just till you finish your pie . . .

(Corn enters the room. He stands.)

SILVER: Go'on have a seat now.

CORN: Ain't no seat but the bed.

SILVER: My bedbugs don't bite nobody but me. Go'on sit down, sugar.

(Corn hesitates, but finally takes a seat on the edge of the bed uncomfortably.

Silver lifts her leg and finishes painting her toes as she talks. Corn notices the contour of her leg and then tries not to. It's impossible.)

CORN: This your record player? Brought it with you?

SILVER: Can't go nowhere without my music. A man I'll leave behind. But his music, I'll take forever.

CORN: This here one of my favorites. You play the right stuff.

SILVER: But if you a piano man, you must love some of the Duke, ain't that right?

CORN: Oh, yeah. That's right all right. He's been over to Black Bottom lots of times. Love to hang out in Paradise Valley. Even come by this club a few times.

SILVER: That so?

CORN: It is.

SILVER: What other jazz cats been through here?

CORN: Oh, the best. Mingus. Dizzy. Bird. All the greats. That's somebody I got to play with 'fore I die.

SILVER: Who's that?

CORN: Charlie Yardbird Parker. Make me wanna play till my hands fall off.

SILVER: Can't have that. A piano man's hands supposed to be the best hands in the business. Know every curve of a woman cuz the way your hands always stay curved when you play. I imagine you know how to stroke away a lot of ailment, don't you?

CORN: I suppose maybe . . .

(Silver looks at Corn and smiles. He smiles back. She stands up and spider-walks over to him.)

SILVER: Lemme see your hands.

(Silver takes Corn by the hands.)

Yeah . . . these look like they can play real nice . . .

(She strokes his fingers.)

CORN *(Nervously)*: They . . . they say you been in a lot of cities . . .

SILVER *(Calmly)*: Who say that?

CORN: Fff . . . folks . . . 'round here . . .

SILVER: I been in a few.

(Silver moves closer to Corn. She strokes his other hand softly.)

CORN: Ssss . . . say . . . you had lots of . . . mmmm . . . mmmeen . . .

SILVER: Awww . . . not many men. Not too many at all. Just . . . some . . .

CORN: Folks 'round here . . . say . . . say things . . .

SILVER: Like what?

CORN: But I don't believe none of it.

SILVER: What they sayin'? I'll tell you whether to believe it or not.

(Silver's hand moves to Corn's leg. He jumps and moves over.)

CORN: Just say . . . say you . . . got secrets . . .

SILVER: Every woman got secrets.

CORN: Say you like . . . like a spider . . . got that Louisana creole in you . . . got spirits . . .

SILVER: You ain't scared of no spiders, is you? Big ol' strong man like you?

CORN: Me?

(Silver touches his leg again softly. He is startled . . . but sits still. Allows it. Enjoys it.)

Nooooo . . . no . . . I lii . . . liiiike spidersssss . . . ever since I was a half-pint . . . collect 'em and watch 'em weave . . . a . . . web . . .

SILVER: You ever been caught in a woman's web?

CORN: Just once.

SILVER: And what happened?

CORN: Fell in love with her. Married her. But she . . . she died.

(Silver stops stroking Corn's leg and looks at him compassionately. This is a real moment.)

SILVER: What was her name?

CORN: Mabel.

SILVER: Was she pretty?

CORN: To me, she was. Most pretty thing I ever saw.

SILVER: How she die?

CORN: Had that TB.

SILVER: Shame.

(Corn looks at Silver sweetly.)

CORN: You a different kind of woman.

SILVER: Am I?

CORN: Got a bite to you. Sharp. Maybe a little bitter. But you also sweet somewhere too. I can see it in your face. Somewhere you got some sadness.

SILVER: We all got sadness. But I like to turn mine into fire, baby. What you do with yours?

CORN: Play the piano.

SILVER: I'll bet you do.

(Silver moves Corn's hand to her own thigh.)

You think you can play this? Find the notes right?

(Corn keeps his hand stiff.)

CORN: I . . .

SILVER: Cuz I need you to find all the blues, and make it sound like bop. Can you do that, buttercup?

CORN: What . . . what about yo' . . . pie . . .

SILVER: I got somethin' taste better'n that.

(Silver straddles Corn. Puts his hands on her waist.)

CORN: Whh . . . what about you? How yo' . . . husband . . . die?

(Silver moves Corn's hands to her breast. He gasps . . . overwhelmed by her allure.
She smiles slyly.)

SILVER *(Whispering)*: I shot him.

(She nibbles his ear. Corn laughs nervously.)

Kiss me, daddy.

(Corn kisses her passionately.
They fall back onto the bed.)

SCENE SEVEN

Lights up on Silver's room. It is daytime. The room is empty.
A tap-tap comes to her door. No answer. Tap-tap again . . .

PUMPKIN *(From off)*: Hello there? Missus Silver? Sheet delivery!

(No answer. The door opens slightly as Pumpkin peers in.)

Missus Silver?

(Seeing that she isn't in, Pumpkin enters, carrying a basket of laundry.)

Just gonna make up your bed for you so you have something clean to sleep on. Lord knows what kind of sinful behavior goes on in these sheets, but Pumpkin's gonna starch it all out.

(Pumpkin starts to remake the bed.
She notices some of Silver's clothing lying around untidily. She folds it and places it in drawers. Hums to herself. The melody has potential, slightly harmonious but meek.
Pumpkin notices more lingerie inside the drawers and pulls out a bit. She looks at Silver's records.)

(Reading aloud) Lester Young . . . *(Looks at the player)* This is surely a fancy record player. Hope you don't mind if I just . . .

(She puts a record on the player. Lester Young's "Mean To Me" plays.
She peeks back in the drawer and pulls out a bit of lingerie.)

My my . . . these things sure are . . . creative . . .

(She holds the lingerie up to herself in the mirror. Enjoys it— creates her alter ego.)

(Putting "on") Hey there, boys. I'm a spiderwoman, and don't none of ya'll come messin' with me 'less you wants to get bit. I'm a gangster woman from Louisiana, and I'll . . . I'll drink your blood with my chitlins! *(Laughs to herself, snorts a bit)* I'm a black widow and if you lean too close, I'll stick you right in your Mr. Longleg and suck everything out— *(Gasps with laughter, amazed at her own mouth)* I'm a . . . I'm a woman. All you fellas, stop and take a look cuz a real woman done walked in the room. Not nobody to be simple and ignored. Not nobody to be proper and hushed. Not nobody to be uprooted and . . . *(Pause)* They call me Silver.

(Pumpkin studies herself with seriousness. Something in this pretend world starts to feel disturbing.
She regroups and grabs the lingerie. She folds it hastily and tries to organize the drawer.
Suddenly she spies something and gasps.
She pulls out a gun. It shines in the light.
She freezes. Then she hastily puts the gun back and closes Silver's drawers.
She grabs her laundry basket.
Frazzled, she dashes out of the room.
The needle on the record plays on . . .
Lights fade on the room.)

ACT TWO

Lights up on Blue playing the trumpet onstage alone. The tune is beautiful but heavy. Loaded with teardrops.

Silver enters and watches him.

When he finishes, she applauds. He turns to her sharply.

SILVER: That's some real fine playin' you doin / over there.

BLUE: What you doin' down here, woman. Club is closed.

SILVER: Couldn't sleep. So I figure I ought to try goin' for a little walk.

BLUE: This ain't no place for you to wander. Go'on somewhere else.

SILVER: Well now, I figure I'm worth a little preview—don't you think?

BLUE: I say, get the hell outta here.

SILVER: My, my . . . you sure know how to play rough there, ain't it? Don't trust a woman farther than you can shove her. But I grew up in a house full of bluesmen. Brothers and a daddy. All with bigger ideas of themselves than they was ever able to be. Made 'em angry and frustrated all the time. I ain't lasted this long without knowin' how to play rough right back. *(Shift)* Say they offerin' ten thousand to folks. You heard that?

BLUE: Didn't I tell you I ain't discussing no business with you?

SILVER: Well, you told me, sho. But men who are contrary always got to say no at the first mention of something. If you smart, you let 'em get that outta the way before you ask for what you really want.

BLUE: And what's that?

SILVER: Your club.

BLUE: It ain't for sell.

SILVER: Everything's for sell. Business. Land. Soul. All it takes is the right price. I can match what this city think they gonna pay you, and add a lil' cherry on top.

BLUE: Match it? You talkin' nonsense. It ain't none of your business what I do, no way.

SILVER: I just wonder what make a person wanna leave somethin' so perfect, seem like. Got Negroes over here runnin' everything and not havin' to answer to nobody but each other. You let this Black Bottom go into the wrong hands, and the soul of this place ain't never gonna forgive you.

BLUE: You shut up now. Talkin' outta line.

(Silver spider-walks over to Blue seductively.)

SILVER: Can't. Not when I wants something. I got to move on it till I get close enough to stroke it.

(Blue grabs Silver roughly by the arm. She freezes in his grip.)

BLUE: You wanna take this club out from under me? Hunh? You might got the wool pulled over these fellas' eyes, but

I recognize a black widow any way she come. You ain't gonna stick those fangs into me and control me like some prey. You ain't worth the trust I'd give the mayor or the overseer. You out to poison our plans and I ain't gon' let you. This is my Paradise. If I leave, I'm leavin' my way. You got that, woman?

SILVER: I see it in you.

(Blue looks at her, baffled.)

Those demons. I see them closing in on you. Choking you, ain't they?

(Blue releases Silver and steps back, stunned.)

My daddy had 'em in him. Husband too. Them feelin's of bein' trapped by yo' skin. Never allowed to get beyond where you at. Turns you mad. Only place you got to escape is that horn, ain't it? But horn only make it louder. Like a dope hit. Got you flyin' and dyin' all in one. I know you, cuz you and me ain't too different. You got contempt like all mens I known. I can dance with contempt and set it aside. But you . . . it rot to the core. Fill you with demons. Turns you on yo' own kind.

BLUE: Shut up.

SILVER: But you ain't gonna get rid of 'em. They gon' get rid of you. 'Less you make amends.

BLUE: I say shut up!

SILVER: Set this place back in the right motion. Cuz if you don't, them demons gon' eat you alive. And when it done that to my daddy, *(Digging into his soul)* he lynched himself.

(Blue grabs Silver and shakes her.)

BLUE: I say shut up shut up SHUT UP GOTDAMNIT!

CORN *(From off)*: Blue?

(Corn enters the club and sees Blue's hands on Silver. Blue quickly lets Silver go.)

Blue, what's got you goin'?

(Blue is silent. Corn stares at Blue and Silver, decoding the event.)

BLUE: Nothin'. Just down here practicing.

CORN: Pumpkin worried 'bout you. Say you been down here for hours and won't go to bed.

BLUE: Ain't tired.

CORN: Still, Blue. It's late enough. *(Turns to Silver)* Maybe you should go'on to bed too, sweets. I'll come check on you in a few to make sure you tucked in safe and sound.

(Silver looks at Corn and then to Blue. She rubs her arm.)

SILVER: All right, then. *(A moment)* Night, fellas.

*(She heads out of the bar.
Corn looks at Blue sternly.)*

CORN: You too, Blue.

BLUE: Can't, Corn. I got to finish. Got to practice more. Ain't there yet.

CORN: Ain't where, Blue?

BLUE: Just ain't there. I'm gon' stay up. I need Friday to be smooth.

CORN: Blue. Pumpkin ain't gettin' no better. Might have to take her off standards. Give her somethin' else to do. I play solo.

BLUE: She got to practice more.

CORN: Practice don't mean nothin' if the music in you too scared to get free. She tryin' her best cuz she know you want her to. But it ain't what she want.

BLUE: Do somethin' else then, Corn. Just make Friday night right. I can't keep on about it. I got to finish workin' here.

(Blue walks back over to the stage with his trumpet. Corn watches him.)

CORN: Blue . . . you all right, ain't you?

(Blue ignores this and begins to play a melody.
Corn hesitates for a moment, and then goes to the piano. He joins Blue's melody. A moment of beautiful harmony.
Quickly, the trumpet goes off-tune. The music stops. Blue starts again. Corn plays again. Another quick beat of harmony. Then the trumpet goes off-tune again. The music stops.)

It'll come another day, Blue. Not tonight.

BLUE: Hey Corn . . . What you see when you look at me?

CORN: What you mean, Blue?

BLUE: Don't lie to me.

CORN: I see . . . A gifted man.

BLUE: Am I fading? Am I . . . becoming—

CORN: Love Supreme.

BLUE: What?

CORN: That's what you trying to get to, Blue. Love Supreme. That's what he was lookin' for and never found. Your daddy. But you can, Blue. Just not tonight.

(Blue takes this in. It's sobering. He turns back to his trumpet. Can't let go the obsession.)

BLUE: Go on, Corn. Leave me be.

CORN: Don't like seein' you this way, Blue. I . . . I done seen this happen before—

BLUE *(Sharply)*: I say leave me!

(Silence. Corn rises from the piano.

Blue remains. He begins to play his tune again. He is transfixed—in his own universe, impervious to Corn. The trumpet sings an unpleasant melody. Corn watches for a moment. Then he slowly heads out of the bar.)

CORN *(Softly)*: Night, Blue . . .

(Lights shift.)

SCENE TWO

Lights up on Pumpkin and P-Sam at the bar. She fills his cup of coffee. He eats toast and grits.

P-SAM: You put some cinnamon or something in these grits? They taste extra sweet this mornin', Pumpkin.

PUMPKIN: You don't like it?

P-SAM: I ain't sayin' that. Taste a lil' different. But good.

PUMPKIN: I put a dash of cinnamon and a little pinch of brown sugar.

P-SAM: You ain't gonna charge me a extra nickel for that pinch, is you?

PUMPKIN: 'Course I ain't.

P-SAM: Well, then that's all right, Pumpkin. That's all right with me. *(Shift)* You got some of your pretty words today? I could use somethin' soft like that this mornin'.

PUMPKIN: You mean it? You wanna listen?

P-SAM: 'Course I wanna listen. You think I ain't got no ear like Corn? I can hear the music in them fancy words too. Try me.

PUMPKIN: Okay. Let's see . . .

(Pumpkin grabs her book and flips through the pages. She hands it to P-Sam.)

'Kay. Hold the page right there. This one, she calls—"Calling Dreams."

> The right to make my dreams come true
> I ask, nay, I demand of life,

P-SAM: Nay? What's that word?
PUMPKIN: Just um . . . like "no."
P-SAM: Oh, all right. Go'on Pumpkin.

PUMPKIN:

> The right to make my dreams come true
> I ask, nay, I demand of life,

P-SAM: You already said that part, Pumpkin.
PUMPKIN: I was just starting over.
P-SAM: Oh, okay then . . . you got to say that, Pumpkin. I didn't know that, see?
PUMPKIN: I'm starting over.
P-SAM: Okay. I'm ready for you.

PUMPKIN:

> The right to make my dreams come true
> I ask, nay, I demand of life,
> Nor shall fate's deadly contraband
> Impede my steps, nor countermand.

P-SAM: Say it pee on what?
PUMPKIN: Impede.
P-SAM: That ain't what it sound like you was sayin'. It sounded sorta nasty.

PUMPKIN: Impede. I-M-P-E-D-E. To stop something.

P-SAM: Oh, yeah. I see that right here. I got you now. All right—keep goin'.

PUMPKIN: Sam, maybe you ought to just . . . listen. Maybe not read along.

P-SAM: I can read, Pumpkin.

PUMPKIN: Oh, I know. But maybe the words sound better when you don't read. When you just hear me sayin' 'em to you. That's the magic in it.

P-SAM: All right, then. Gimme the magic.

PUMPKIN: I'm gonna say it all the way through.

P-SAM: I gotcha.

PUMPKIN: No interrupting this time.

P-SAM *(Zips his lips)*: Locked and sealed.

(She takes a breath.)

I ain't gonna say nothin' else.

(She looks at him sternly. He realizes his mistake there. Sits quietly.)

PUMPKIN:
> The right to make my dreams come true
> I ask, nay, I demand of life,
> Nor shall fate's deadly contraband
> Impede my steps, nor countermand.
>
> Too long my heart against the ground
> Has beat the dusty years around,
> And now, at length, I rise, I wake!
> And stride into the morning break!

(Pause. P-Sam thinks for a second.)

P-SAM: Pumpkin, I ain't understand a word you just said. But I know one thing, it shoul' do sound like magic when you say it.

PUMPKIN: Thank you, Sam. Just talkin' 'bout . . . love and dreamin'. That's all you really need to know.

P-SAM: That's somethin' what makes your skin sorta blush. When you say them words.

PUMPKIN: I just like it.

P-SAM: It like you too. *(Beat)* That's what you should be doin', Pumpkin.

PUMPKIN: What's that?

P-SAM: Puttin' words together. You got a nice way of doin' it. Even if it sound confusing otherwise, you got a way to make it sound like music. I can hear it in you.

PUMPKIN: I ain't no poet. I just like to read it, is all.

P-SAM: How you know, Pumpkin? How you know what you ain't, if you ain't never tried it?

PUMPKIN: I don't know, I . . . You think I make it sound like music?

P-SAM: Like a songbird. You could be like them Harlem cats. Puttin' them words on paper and in books. Be real classy and smart. That's what you are. Ain't Blue never told you that?

PUMPKIN: I'm fine just working here. Taking care of folks. I like taking care of folks. It's what I'm good at.

P-SAM: Woman like you shouldn't have to take care of nobody. Man should be takin' care of you.

PUMPKIN: I'm okay just being here with Blue.

P-SAM: But is Blue okay just being here with you?

(Beat. Pumpkin is affected. She shifts and starts clearing P-Sam's plate.)

PUMPKIN: Gonna take this for you now, if you're done. Get to cleanin' the dishes and finishin' the laundry.

P-SAM: Why when I get to talkin' 'bout Blue, you get to talkin' 'bout dirty laundry? Why you can't just answer me straight?

PUMPKIN: I got a lot of stuff to do.

P-SAM: I see you every day lookin' just as pretty and simple as you can be, and I think of all the things I'd like to give you. All the ways you could fit right in with what I wanna do. You a go-along gal.

PUMPKIN: A go-along gal.

P-SAM: And I like that. Don't make much fuss about nothin'. Just wanna make life easy for a man. And I can do somethin' with that.

PUMPKIN: I got a life with Blue.

P-SAM: What kinda life, Pumpkin? Cleanin' his dirty drawers? You ain't got no real life with Blue. But you could have one with me.

PUMPKIN: Sam, you shouldn't talk like that.

(P-Sam moves closer to Pumpkin.)

P-SAM: I'm just talkin' the truth, Pumpkin.

PUMPKIN: But I don't love you.

P-SAM: You'll learn to.

PUMPKIN: I don't want to.

P-SAM: You need to.

PUMPKIN: It ain't right.

(P-Sam is close enough to Pumpkin to feel her breath.)

P-SAM: It ain't wrong neither. It's somewhere in between.

PUMPKIN: Sam, I can't.

P-SAM: Hear that, Pumpkin? You called me—Sam.

(P-Sam tries to kiss Pumpkin. She smacks his face.)

PUMPKIN: Damnit I say no!

(Silver enters the bar slowly.
   P-Sam takes the hit. Backs off.)

SILVER: Mornin', folks.

PUMPKIN *(Startled)*: Oh—Mornin', Missus. Was just bringing up your breakfast in a sec.

SILVER: No, never mind. I'll just have some juice right down here. That's all I need this mornin'.

PUMPKIN: Gettin' it for you right now. Bring you out another coffee too, Sam.

(Silver walks over to P-Sam and sits beside him. He slumps in his stool.)

SILVER: Doll, you look like you could use a lil' sugar in your coffee this mornin'. Need somethin' sweet.

P-SAM: I done had enough sweet for today. *(Pause)* I'll take somethin' spicy instead.

SILVER: That right?

P-SAM: Yeah, that's right, all right. *(Shift)* Say, I hear you been askin' 'round 'bout business over here. You got ambitions for Black Bottom?

SILVER: Heard that, did you?

P-SAM: I did. Notice you been talkin' with my buddy a bit. Spendin' a lot of time.

SILVER: See through walls, can you?

P-SAM: I see smiles on a face ain't smiled like that in years. Only one kind of thing be responsible for that.

SILVER: What of it.

P-SAM: Maybe you can put him up to somethin' for me. Somethin' what'll benefit us all. I done put the bug in his ear to talk to Blue for me, but I gots a feelin' you more persuasive than me. And maybe there's a shot you an' me can do some business together. If you can fancy that.

SILVER: You know, sugar . . . from what I seen—too many names on a dotted line cause too much confusion. The plans I got is for my signature only.

(P-Sam is taken aback.)

P-SAM: Oh, you too good to be partners. I get it. Well, Blue ain't sellin' this club to neither one of us without some muscle behind 'im. And I tell you this, if you ain't on this with me, then you competition. We got an order to the line sweetheart, be careful 'bout tryin' to take cuts. *(Shift)* Tell Pumpkin I said no need for the coffee. Ain't nothin' in here for me today.

(P-Sam walks off.
    Pumpkin comes in from the kitchen with juice and coffee. She notices P-Sam is gone.)

PUMPKIN: Where's Sam?
SILVER: Say he had to go.

(Pumpkin hands Silver her juice and looks at her uneasily. Silver watches Pumpkin quietly.)

Thought you might have time to teach me a bit of that fancy poetry of yours.
PUMPKIN *(Sharply)*: Can't. Busy. Got laundry.
SILVER: Oh. Well . . . *(Pause)* Maybe later then.
PUMPKIN: Can't. Busy then too.
SILVER: I see.

(Silver is onto Pumpkin as Pumpkin does a bad job of busying herself. She tries to corner Pumpkin.)

That's too bad. Maybe next time.

PUMPKIN: Um. We'll have to see . . .

(Pumpkin scurries out, narrowly missing Silver's web. Silver calls after her.)

SILVER: Hope your wrists are feeling better!

(Silver sits, disturbed that Pumpkin got away. She puts money on the bar and exits, unsettled . . .)

SCENE THREE

Dim lights up on Blue and Pumpkin in the bar. Blue plays his trumpet and Pumpkin sits, drinking tea as she listens.
Lights up on Silver and Corn in Silver's bed. They are in the afterglow of lovemaking.
Blue plays softly in the bar. The two worlds exist simultaneously. Silver smokes a cigarette. Corn caresses her.

CORN: You got the prettiest skin. Like honey—smooth. Taste like it too.

(Corn kisses Silver's arm. She smiles at him.)

And your arms. Can feel the shape of all your womanness in your arms.

(Silver blows a puff of smoke.)

SILVER: Has it been that long, sugar?
CORN: Since what?
SILVER: Since you felt the touch of a woman?
CORN: Not since Mabel died.

SILVER: That's goin' on three years now. Ain't it? How you stay away from women so long?

CORN: Thought that part was dead. Till you come along and wake it up.

SILVER: I got a way of wakin' up a lot of things in men. It ain't always good. *(Shift)* Did you do what I asked you?

CORN: I ain't talk to him just yet. He on edge 'bout this gig. After the show be better.

SILVER: Friday may be too late. He mighta already signed those papers by then.

CORN: I got to give him his chance to find what he lookin' for. Then I'll know what to do. Don't worry 'bout him sellin'.

SILVER: I know when a man is close to breakin', and I see that in your buddy.

CORN: What you askin' ain't easy.

SILVER: But it's necessary.

CORN: There's more to it than just sellin'. I knowed Blue a long time. Knew his daddy, name was Clyde Sr. What Blue don't tell nobody is he Clyde Jr. But better not call him that. He liable to pull his knife on you. Clyde Sr. gave me a shot. Let me play with the house band to keep from runnin' the streets. He made a legacy of Paradise Club, and Blue been trying to hold it together, but lately . . .

SILVER: Daddy got a cloud over him, don't he?

(In the bar, Blue's tune changes. A melody of difficulty. It grows increasingly heavy.)

CORN: Blue's daddy had that thing where his mind wasn't always right. Sometimes be talkin' to himself or to somebody who wun'nt there. But the man could play a trumpet like he was touched by God. And Blue got that same gift in him. But it come with a whole lot of extra. And that extra ate his daddy alive till he killed Blue's mama when

Blue was a young man. Said he saw the devil trying to take her, and he was tryin' to save her.

SILVER: My / God . . .

CORN: So he strangled her to death. Blue seen the whole thing. And his daddy wind up in the crazy house. That where he died. Blue been carryin' all that with him ever since.

SILVER: That kinda dead weight make a man dangerous. It can turn on you.

CORN: Blue ain't a bad man. He just wanna be mighty but the world keep him small. Cost of bein' colored and gifted. Brilliant and second class. Make you insane.

SILVER: He's divin' deeper than most. Don't you see that much?

CORN: Been seein' it for a while. He gettin' worser. But I know what he needs.

SILVER: What's that.

CORN: Love Supreme. That's what we call it when you hit that perfect note that cleans your sins, Like white light bathin' him with mercy. It's that part in the music that speak directly to God, and you ready to play with the angels.

SILVER: When you got demons that deep, they don't redeem you. They kill you to the soul. Believe me, I know. It's time for him to move on 'fore that happen.

CORN: What you want to run a club for, hunh? You stay here with me, and I'll make sure you don't need nothin' else.

SILVER: You talk like this gonna be somethin' permanent.

CORN: Isn't it?

(Silver looks at Corn questioningly.)

SILVER: Doll, listen here, I done learned from enough men not to settle my bags in anybody's heart too long. Cuz it start off good, but sooner or later I ain't gonna be able to fill all your needs. And then it's gonna be heartbreak city. I spare myself and you the pain.

CORN: What make you think I need anything else but this?

SILVER: Men always do. And I can't give it, baby.

CORN: Why can't you?

SILVER: Cuz I'm broke. And ain't no fixin' me.

CORN: I like broke.

SILVER: Not like this.

CORN: How you know?

SILVER: Cuz I'm cursed.

CORN: What you mean?

SILVER: Childless. Can't have 'em. Body just cursed.

(Blue's melody changes to a more aggressive rhythm.
Corn looks at Silver. He touches her stomach. She moves his hand.)

Ain't nothin' but dead in there, baby. Don't no life happen here. Couldn't give none to my husband and he hated me for it. Cursed me to hell, he did. And almost sent me straight there, too. But I got out of that. I'm here and I'm fightin' for my piece at life. What's a woman if she ain't bearing fruit? Ain't no other place for her in this world 'less she runnin' her own business. Got to find another way to be fruitful. I ain't gonna be nothin' frail to get preyed on. I'm gon' do the preying if it's any to be done. And this Paradise Club is ripe for the taking. So come on, baby. Tell me you gonna talk to him, so I can be something more than just childless.

CORN: And then what happens to this? Us here?

SILVER: You gon' be the headliner, baby. I'll see to that.

CORN: I wanna be the headliner right here.

(Corn touches her heart.)

Break the curse. I can do that for you, if you let me.

(Silver touches Corn's hand, then his face.)

SILVER: You must really like the taste of pain, don't you?

(He answers her with a kiss.
Blue's horn leaps in volume.
Silver and Corn fall back onto the bed as lights crossfade to Pumpkin and Blue.
Blue's final note moves from passionate to broken. He pushes again. It becomes piercing.
Pumpkin drops her teacup. It shatters.
Blue's note pierces. Pierces. Pierces.
Pumpkin rushes over to him as he blows his trumpet. She tries to stop him but he keeps on. The note pierces.)

PUMPKIN *(Screaming)*: Blue!

(She extends her arm and he pushes it away.)

(Screaming over the notes) Blue, baby! Please!

(Blue pierces more, almost in a trance. A battle between him and his trumpet. Fighting something in the notes.
Pumpkin tries to grab hold of him, tugs at his arm. His trumpet falls.)

BLUE: Noooooooooooooooo!!!!!!!!!!!!!!!!!!!!!!!!!!!!!!!!!!

(He shakes her and pushes her violently. She flies into the tables and onto the ground.)

Let her go—motherfucker! Let her go!

(He picks up a chair and throws it recklessly.
Then he falls to the ground and wails.
Pumpkin lies still. Alive and alert but frightened.)

(*Muttering*) I couldn't-could-couldn't stop stop stop it . . . couldn't-save-save-her-couldn't-fight-back-fight-back-fight him him him—couldn't-didn't-do-nothing nothing nothing

PUMPKIN (*Softly*): Blue . . .

BLUE: Killed . . . killed-her-killed-her her her I—did—I—did—was me me me

PUMPKIN: Wasn't you . . .

BLUE: Was me me me . . . I'm gone . . . gone . . . gone . . .

PUMPKIN: Blue, it's all right . . .

BLUE: I'm gone . . . gone . . . dead . . . dead . . . dead . . .

PUMPKIN: You alive, Blue, baby. You here with me. With Pumpkin.

BLUE: Pumpkin?

(*Blue stops. He looks at Pumpkin . . . like a stranger. As if it's his first time seeing her.*)

Pumpkin, I'm dead. I'm not here. They got me, Pumpkin. Stole my soul. I scream to 'em and they scream back. Won't let me forget. Won't silence. I can't hear the notes in the scale. I'm outside myself watchin', but I can't get in. It took me, Pumpkin. The madness took me.

(*Pumpkin slowly goes over to Blue. She kneels beside him.*)

BLUE: You're gonna leave me, Pumpkin.

PUMPKIN: What, Blue? Why would you think—

BLUE: You love this place more than you love me and I ain't gonna be able to stop you. I ain't gonna have nothin' left. I'm gonna die here, Pumpkin. If I don't get out soon, I'm gonna die.

PUMPKIN: If we leave here, Blue, you really think the hurtin'-a stop? I mean, ALL of it?

BLUE: It got to, Pumpkin.

PUMPKIN: Even . . . with me?

BLUE: It just got to.

(Pumpkin considers.)

PUMPKIN: Okay, Blue. I ain't gonna let Black Bottom hurt you no more.

(Blue grabs Pumpkin and falls in her lap.
Pumpkin holds him strangely, unsettled . . .)

SCENE FOUR

Silver's room. Evening light spills through the windows.
Silver listens to Dizzy and Bird on the record player.
A soft tap at the door.

PUMPKIN *(From off)*: Missus, I got your supper with me. Just gonna leave it for you out here.

(Silver goes to the door and opens it.)

SILVER: Come on in here, honey. Let me talk to you for a sec.

PUMPKIN: I got a lot of other deliveries to make. And the kitchen is a mess—

SILVER: Only for a sec? Could use a lil' girl talk—

PUMPKIN: I still gotta go straighten the bar, and then meet with Corn so I can get ready—

SILVER: I know you been through my things.

(Pumpkin freezes for a second, and then quickly enters the room—closing the door behind her.)

PUMPKIN: It was only an accident—

SILVER: 'Course it was.

PUMPKIN: I didn't mean to be inconsiderate. I just came to change the sheets—

SILVER: And listen to a little Lester Young and sort through my drawers.

PUMPKIN: I didn't—

SILVER: Relax, honey. No need to worry so. I ain't mad at you.

PUMPKIN: It was a terrible mistake and I swear I won't do it again.

SILVER: You see somethin' you like? Want it for ya'self?

PUMPKIN: Oh, no, Missus. No, I don't want to bother in any more of your things.

SILVER: You sho?

PUMPKIN: Yes, ma'am.

SILVER: Cuz I figure you musta got a lil' curious 'bout somethin'. And I can take all that curiosity away right now.

PUMPKIN: No, I'm fine. Really.

SILVER: Just let you have a lil' look-see.

(Silver pulls out the gun. It shines in the light. Pumpkin gasps.)

This what you so 'fraid of? This lil' bitty thing?

PUMPKIN *(Nervously)*: I . . . I don't need to see that, Missus. It's your . . . private—

SILVER: Ain't too private no more. Or is it? You tell me.

PUMPKIN: I ain't . . . told nobody . . .

SILVER: No? Not even yo' man?

PUMPKIN: No . . . nobody . . .

SILVER: Hunh . . . *(Pause)* Well, that's good, then. Men find out a woman got a gun, they ready to lock her in a dungeon and throw away the key.

PUMPKIN: Why you . . . why you have it?

SILVER: For protection.

PUMPKIN: Protection from who?

SILVER: Anybody. Everybody. You think a woman can move on her lonesome from town to town without the know-how to put a bullet in somebody's head?

PUMPKIN: That ain't for a lady to do.

SILVER: Says who?

PUMPKIN: That's why a woman ain't supposed to be on her lonesome. Travel with a man by your side and he be all the protection you need.

SILVER: That so? That what your man do for you? Make you feel protected and safe?

PUMPKIN: 'Course he does.

SILVER: That why you got those bruises on your arm?

(Pumpkin falls silent.)

Seem to me like you ain't no safer than me on my lonesome. In fact, I'll say I'm the better of us two. Cuz I know how to shoot straight and aim direct. And I ain't shy when I got this in my hand, neither. Ain't no wallflower. I'm front and center on the floor. And I ain't afraid to use it. That's where people get you. They see you got it but don't 'spect you to use it. But once somebody see yo' gun, they done seen all your cards right there on the table. So you either fold, or you take the win. And me, I always take the win.

PUMPKIN: What happened to yo' husband?

SILVER: That's a tale for another day.

PUMPKIN: Why you move here on your lonesome?

SILVER: I told you, he died.

PUMPKIN: How he die?

SILVER: Bullet in the head.

(Silver looks at Pumpkin—who has now scrunched herself up in a corner.)

Now gal, why you so far over there? What you so 'fraid of? Ain't you never held one of these before?

(Pumpkin is still.)

Well, goodness, come on. Let me be your first.

(Pumpkin is still. Silver laughs.)

You think I'm gon' shoot you? *(Laughing)* Don't you think I woulda done that by now?

PUMPKIN: I really . . . should be . . . going now . . .

SILVER: All right now, that's enough.

(Silver walks over to Pumpkin and grabs her hand.)

You can't be a prissy lil' thing all yo' life. Sometimes you got to learn some other tricks. Grab it.

PUMPKIN: No, Missus, I can't—

SILVER: I say, grab it!

(Pumpkin takes the gun timidly. She holds it like it smells.)

It ain't dirty drawers. You got to hold it. Give it a grip.

PUMPKIN: I don't want to.

SILVER: Here. Like this.

(Silver moves behind Pumpkin and puts her hands over Pumpkin's hands.)

You got to hold it firm. It's a delicate egg. Too tight make it bust. Not tight enough and it slip right out your hands. Got it?

(Pumpkin nods. She holds the gun.)

Now you don't wanna put your finger by that trigger too soon. Hold it up here.

(Silver moves Pumpkin's finger.)

You do it too early, and you liable to blow somebody's brains out just for sayin' good morning.

PUMPKIN: My arm feels heavy.

SILVER: You ain't used to it, that's all. When you get used to carrying it, won't feel like nothin' but another piece of you. Your best friend.

PUMPKIN: This ain't got nothin' in it, has it?

SILVER: You think I'm fool enough to give you a loaded gun?

PUMPKIN: My arm's gettin' tired.

SILVER: Hold it straight. Support it with your other hand. On the bottom. Like this.

(Silver places Pumpkin's hands properly.)

PUMPKIN: I'm breathin' funny.

SILVER: That ain't nothin' but power and nerves runnin' through your blood. Mixin' all together. Feel almost thrillin'. Like holdin' a man's Mr. Happy in your hand.

PUMPKIN: You speak so dirty!

SILVER: Feels good. Try it.

PUMPKIN: I can't.

SILVER: Just say somethin'.

PUMPKIN: Like what?

SILVER: Anything that comes out. You can say what you want with a gun in your hand.

PUMPKIN: I don't know what to say.

SILVER: Tell somebody to move out your way.

PUMPKIN: Move outta my way.

SILVER: Even with that gun you ain't scarin' nobody. Say it like you mean it.

PUMPKIN: Move outta my way!

SILVER: Good. Now tell 'em they better not mess with you or you'll shoot their balls right off 'em.

PUMPKIN: I can't say that.

SILVER: Say it now! Go'on!

PUMPKIN: Don't you mess me with me or I'll shoot you right in your—

SILVER: Balls.

PUMPKIN: So nasty.

SILVER: Say it.

PUMPKIN: I can't!

SILVER: Balls! Go'on. I'll shoot you in your—

PUMPKIN: It's too nasty—

SILVER: Scream it! I'll shoot you in your—

PUMPKIN: Balls! Balls balls balls! In your balls!

(Silver bursts out laughing. Pumpkin laughs too. They crack up for a moment.)

SILVER: My goodness! You got a dirty mouth.

PUMPKIN: I sound silly.

(Pumpkin sets the gun down.)

SILVER: Sound silly at first. But the more you believe it, the more everybody else will too. Take time, but you soon learn.

PUMPKIN: I don't need to learn. I'm not gonna be like you. Not movin' from town to town lettin' anybody in my bed who fits the season. Can't make no home that way.

SILVER: You can't make a home your way neither.

(Silver grabs Pumpkin's wrist and Pumpkin flinches.)

How many times he put his hands on you today?

PUMPKIN: I need to get goin'—

SILVER: Is it every day? Or just whenever he got troubles?

PUMPKIN: That's none of your / concern, Missus.

SILVER: Don't matter whether or not it's my concern. I know what I see. And I tell you one thing, gal. You in a heap of trouble if you think you 'bout to make a life with this man. A man with demons ain't gonna see you as nothin' but a gateway to hell. Whenever them spirits come callin', he got to fight anybody they tell him to. And if you in his way, then he gonna fight you.

PUMPKIN: Blue got troubles, yes. But every man got troubles. We take it and we ease it much as possible. That's what a woman do. 'Sides, Black Bottom is the source of most of it. Soon a change gon' come and make things better for 'im.

SILVER: Waitin' on a man to change is like waitin' for the seventh sign. When it comes, it's gonna bring a whole lotta destruction with it. I wouldn't wait for that if I was you.

PUMPKIN: He's a good man. I know you don't see that, but he is. Use' to court me at the main library on Woodward. Love goin' there to study when I was schoolin'. The architecture . . . those majestic steps. Blue come to walk me home every day after I finish my reading. Wait for me on those steps like I was royalty. He be there with his trumpet in his hand and play for me when I walk out the door. That's when I first seen it. This man has a gift. The kind that make you feel like somebody just to be close to it. Sometimes his lovin' hurts, true. But when it feels good, it feel like heaven. Even if just half as good, that's better than nothin'.

SILVER: A gift is good. But a gift can blind you. Don't get no man's gift confused with that man in the flesh.

PUMPKIN: You don't know him.

SILVER: I know men.

PUMPKIN: Blue ain't all men.

SILVER: He's a man. Men is men.

PUMPKIN: Things'll change soon.

SILVER: You'll be dead 'fore they do.

PUMPKIN: I can't move like you. It ain't me. I like soft words and taking care of folks. You got your way to make it through and I got mine. I know how to make a man feel safe and that's my trade. I'm a go-along gal.

SILVER: That ain't you. That's just the make-up you wear. You a thinkin' woman with her own words. But you play these mens just the same as me. Make 'em feel safe so they make you feel safe. But doll, ain't none of us really safe. No matter what they tell you.

PUMPKIN: Blue just ailing right now. Ain't we all?

SILVER: You want to keep ailin' with him??? Or you want it to stop? Tell me now. True.

PUMPKIN: I . . .

I want it to stop.

SILVER: Then make it.

PUMPKIN: How?

(Silver moves calmly.)

SILVER: Get you a revolver.

PUMPKIN: What?

SILVER: Or you can borrow mine.

PUMPKIN: What d'you mean?

SILVER: Woman got to put her foot down sometimes. Or it ain't never gonna stop. Sometimes, only thing can make it stop is a bullet.

(Pumpkin looks at Silver—stunned.)

PUMPKIN: You're . . . not serious . . .

SILVER: I'm bein' straight.

PUMPKIN: I would never . . .

SILVER: Keep it in your stocking. Under your pillow. In your boudoir. Wherever you can get to it.

PUMPKIN: I would never do that.

SILVER: Or carry it in your purse—

PUMPKIN: I say I would NEVER!!!

SILVER: You don't know what you would do till it's just you, him and the devil. Trust me, gal. You don't know.

PUMPKIN: Where would I even . . .

. . .

. . .

No. No, I don't want to think about this. You a filthy dirty creole woman and everything they say about you is true. You just tryin' to poison me.

(Pumpkin walks to the door and opens it. She stops and turns back to Silver.)

Yo' husband . . . How he die?

(Silver pulls a cigarette from her bosom and lights it.)

You a sick woman.

SILVER: Any man put his hands on a woman is asking to be shot. Straight between the eyes. And if you know what's good for you, you betta get your gun.

(Pumpkin, caught between astonishment and intrigue, storms out of the room.
Silver takes a long . . . long . . . long . . . drag . . .)

SCENE FIVE

A horn plays in the distance. It is Blue. He stands in silhouette, as he did in the beginning of the play. He struggles through his horn and slowly starts to find the notes. It is not perfect, but there is something on track about it. Something promising.

Lights come up on Paradise Club. The floor and bartop glisten. The place looks pristine and ready for opening.

Corn sits at the piano playing a soft tune.

Pumpkin, dressed simply, recites a poem. It is almost musical. She begins meekly, but then—as if the truth of the words over-whelms her—she gains increasing vocal power. She is half reciting, half singing. She sounds amazing.

As Corn plays underneath her, they become perfectly harmonious.

PUMPKIN:
> I want to reach you softly
> Touch you where you ail
> Lift you in your sadness
> Winds beneath your sail.
>
> I want to reach you purely
> In truth and love sublime
> I become the sun
> Come cascade in my shine.
>
> I want to reach you deeply
> My palm upon your core
> Releasing every darkness
> Until you ache no more . . .

(Corn stops. He beams at her.)

CORN: That was good, Pumpkin.

PUMPKIN: Think so?

CORN: That's the music in you. You found it. That those Miss Johnson woman's words open you like that?

PUMPKIN: Not this time, Corn. *(A small admission)* My own.

CORN: You wrote that one yourself, Pumpkin?!

PUMPKIN: Think it'll be okay for this evenin' 'stead of the standards?

CORN: I believe it's worth the try.

(Silver enters the bar. Pumpkin spots her.)

PUMPKIN: Well, then . . . I better go get dressed 'fore we open.

(Pumpkin walks past Silver briskly. Silver eyes her carefully, then turns to Corn.)

SILVER: Your playin' sound real good, sweets. You 'bout ready for this evenin?

CORN: About. Got to finish suitin' up, but I feel like Pumpkin gonna be all right—

SILVER: That's not what I mean. You know what I'm talking about.

(Pause.)

CORN: Like I told you: tonight. After. Not before. Too much going on before.

SILVER: We better hope after ain't too late.

CORN: You think about what I said too? 'Bout you and me?

SILVER: I did.

CORN: So is that a yes?

SILVER: Well . . . *(Sincerely)* it ain't a no.

(P-Sam enters the club loudly, a hint of intoxication in his walk. He approaches the bar.)

P-SAM: Well . . . look at this place. Look like a real happenin' spot tonight, don't it?

CORN: Hey there, Sam. You all right?

P-SAM: Is I'm all right? Ain't that the question-of-the-mother-fuckin'-year. Is I'm all right? Let's see there, Corn. I ain't got no gig. I ain't got no woman. And I'm drunk on some three-penny wine from Alfie's Liquor Sto'. What you think, Corn? That sound all right?

CORN: Sam, you ain't lookin' good.

P-SAM: Well, nigger, you ain't lookin' good neither. You lookin' like a backstabbing fink if I ever saw one.

SILVER: Maybe I should freshen up for the show.

P-SAM: Freshen up good, baby. Cuz Sammy know all about yo' tricks. Go'on put on some of that rose-smellin' perfume and them sugar-tastin' drawers that got my buddy here all dumbstruck.

(Corn squares off with P-Sam.)

CORN: Sam, watch your mouth there.

(Silver holds out her hand to stop Corn.)

SILVER: It's okay, sweets. We'll finish this later.

(She exits. P-Sam looks after her with contempt, then turns back to Corn.)

P-SAM: Was she worth it, Corn? Was the cootie worth it?

CORN: What you talkin' 'bout, Sam?

P-SAM: Nigger, don't be tryin' to play dumb on me. I ain't no clown.

CORN: I never say you was a clown—

P-SAM: You sold me up the river! You think I don't know?

CORN: Sam—

P-SAM: You double-crossed me, damnit!

CORN: Wait a minute, Sam. What you mean?

P-SAM: You know what I mean. That spiderwoman got your nostrils stretched so tall they blockin' yo' eyesight! You cuttin' side deals on me with her, ain't that it?

CORN: I just told her like I told you. I'm gon' talk to Blue and see if he'll listen to what you have to say. Both of you.

P-SAM: Both of us, hunh? And that's it? No leanin' him no particular way?

CORN: That's it, Sam.

P-SAM: Corn, you a lyin' monkey. I ain't never thought I'd see the day when you look me straight in the eye and lie. I guess that's what happen when you get bit by the bug, ain't it. But you done messed up now. You so busy cuttin' side deals you ain't keep yo' eyes on the prize. And that nigger sold it! Just like I say!

CORN: Sold what, Sam? Paradise??? Nawww . . . that can't be. Blue ain't leavin' this spot—

P-SAM: That's bullshit, Corn! He done already left it! Ask these other clubs—they all seen it. Blue's name on the list of sellers. Gave his word and the handshake and signin' this club over on Monday. Monday! That's three days from now. And along with him goes Percy at Garfield's Lounge, and Harold from Three Sixes. Even the Norwood Hotel gettin' bought out with this new plan. It's just like I was tellin' you. You get one—you get 'em all. And Blue done started a train wreck we coulda stopped if you'da been keepin' your ear to the ground steada up in some crazy woman's cooter.

CORN: Hold on, Sam. Monday ain't here yet. That mean he ain't signed it. A list ain't nothin' but a promise. We don't know the real plan less we hear it from Blue hisself.

P-SAM: Listen at you—hear it from Blue. You gon' trust Blue over half of Black Bottom?

CORN: If what they say is true, I got to hear it from Blue's mouth. See it in his eyes. Then I'll know what I know.

P-SAM: Then let's get it from his mouth then! Call him right now. Blue! Blue!!! Bring your sellout tail down here, nigger!

CORN: Sam!

(Pumpkin enters. She is dressed in a stunning red gown with red painted lips and a rose in her hair. She is breathtaking.)

PUMPKIN: Sam? What's the matter down here?

P-SAM: Pumpkin, this ain't none of your—

(P-Sam sees Pumpkin for the first time—fully. He is caught off guard.)

—concern . . .

CORN: It's all right, Pumpkin. Sam just a little drunk.

P-SAM *(To Pumpkin)*: You look . . . good . . .

PUMPKIN: Thank you, Sam.

CORN: Pumpkin, where's Blue?

PUMPKIN: Gettin' his suit on. Upstairs. Should be down in a sec.

CORN: I'm gonna go get him and we'll settle this once and for all.

(Corn heads off. P-Sam stares at Pumpkin, mesmerized.)

P-SAM: Pumpkin, I ain't never seen you so . . . done up.

PUMPKIN: Tonight is special, Blue say. Had to look classy.

P-SAM: You look too classy for Blue. Hell, too classy for every fella in Black Bottom. You deserve the top-of-the-line. Somewhere you can write your poems and won't have to clean one dirty dish. Get you a maid to do that.

PUMPKIN: I don't need none of that, Sam. I'm fine right here.

P-SAM: Why you fine like this, Pumpkin? Just tell me and I'll let you be. Why you won't even let me pretend to give you nothin' better?

PUMPKIN: I don't know, Sam. I don't know why I can't love you. I think you so sweet sometimes. I like to laugh with you. And I do wonder what it'll be like if I closed my eyes and just let you in. I listen to the way you drum and it sound so scattered and rough. Somehow, it works for that bop sound. But for my ear, it just don't sound like a trumpet. When I hear that horn, I get lost in its pain and its beauty. It speak to me different. I just don't know how to change what my ear is favorable to.

P-SAM: I sho wish I did, Pumpkin. I wish I knew how to turn you to my kinda sound.

(Pumpkin looks at P-Sam sincerely.)

PUMPKIN: You a good man, Sam.

P-SAM: It sound so right when you call me that.

(Pumpkin touches P-Sam's face gently. He softens to her touch. She smiles.

Blue walks in, with Corn at his heels.

Blue storms over to Pumpkin and grabs her roughly by the arm.)

BLUE: What kinda game you playin' at? You tryin' to make a fool outta me?

PUMPKIN: No, no . . . Blue, I—

P-SAM: Let her be!

(P-Sam grabs Blue's arm and turns him around. Blue snatches his arm back.)

BLUE: What the hell you want here, nigger.

P-SAM: I wanna hear you tell it, that's what. Tell Corn and everybody up in here how you sold us out.

BLUE: I ain't got to tell nobody nothin'.

P-SAM: You gon' say it, goddamnit. You gonna tell everybody how you put Paradise Club on the list to be sold for ten thousand dollars. Gonna sign it over on Monday. You tell Corn right now, nigger!

BLUE: I ain't tellin' you jack.

CORN: Blue, tell him you ain't sellin'.

BLUE: I ain't got to tell him a motherfuckin' thing, Corn. Nigger come up in here like I owe him somethin'. I don't owe nobody nothin', you hear me? I do what I wanna do cuz it's my place! Ain't nobody got to live with my madness but me, you hear me?

P-SAM: You? You you you you YOU! Everything always about YOU! But this ain't just *your* club. You might be the one to own it, but you ain't the one to make it. We all make this Paradise. You wouldn't have nothin' to stand on all this time if it wun'nt for me, Corn and Joe backing you up and makin' you sound good.

BLUE: Makin' me sound good?

P-SAM: You wouldn't have no club if it wun'nt for Pumpkin keepin' this place pristine—

BLUE: You keep Pumpkin outta yo' mouth, nigger.

P-SAM: This ain't just your club. This club belong to everybody who done had a piece in keepin' it alive. And you damn straight you owe us, nigger. You owe every moe in

Black Bottom! We the backbone of this place. And if you ain't had us, you ain't had nothin' but bricks.

BLUE: You can have all that and leave me my bricks. This place Paradise to you but it ain't to me. It ain't nothin' but a soul-stealer. You and all these bloodsuckers comin' 'round—nothin' but a bunch of worthless niggers scrapin' the bottom of the barrel and livin' on pipe dreams. You can die here, nigger. But I ain't.

P-SAM: Worthless?!

BLUE: That's what I said.

P-SAM: I'll show you worthless, motherfucker.

(P-Sam lunges into Blue. They tussle.)

CORN: Sam!   PUMPKIN: Blue!

(P-Sam and Blue are at each other's throats
   Corn tries to pull them apart and gets knocked back.
   Silver enters and jumps back with a start as the men come charging her way.
   Finally P-Sam pins Blue and starts choking him.
   Pumpkin runs out of the room.
   Corn rushes over to P-Sam. Blue struggles.)

CORN: Sam, no! Let him go, Sam. Let him go.

P-SAM: I should kill you, you sellout motherfucker!

CORN: No, Sam. Let him go.

(Corn tries to pull P-Sam off of Blue. Blue gasps and catches his breath. Corn grabs P-Sam.)

P-SAM: Get off me, Corn! Let me go!

(Finally Corn releases P-Sam, who tries to catch his breath. Blue rises quickly and charges over to P-Sam, grabbing him from behind in a headlock.
Blue pulls out a knife.)

CORN: Blue . . .

(P-Sam struggles in Blue's grip.)

BLUE: Who you gonna kill, nigger?
CORN: Blue, don't . . .

(Silver moves behind the bar and searches for some kind of weapon.)

BLUE: You wanna kill me, nigger? Hunh? Then do it. Do it right now.

(P-Sam struggles in Blue's grip with urgency, gasping.
Pumpkin runs onstage with the revolver in her hand.
Gunshot.
Everyone halts. P-Sam falls from Blue's clutch, alive and gasping.
Pumpkin holds her hand high in the air. The gun smokes.
Everyone stares at her, stunned.)

PUMPKIN: Next one won't be no warning.

(Corn moves toward Pumpkin, slowly.)

CORN: Pumpkin . . . gimme that now . . . gimme that gun . . .

(Pumpkin aims the gun at Blue.)

PUMPKIN: The devil is in you. I can . . . I can see it now. I see it.

(Blue stares at Pumpkin like she's a stranger. A betrayer.)

CORN: Come now, Pumpkin. Go'on gimme that . . .

PUMPKIN *(To Silver)*: I want it to stop.

SILVER *(Cautiously)*: Okay . . .

PUMPKIN: All the ailin', you hear me? Every last part of it. I want it to stop.

CORN: It's gonna stop, Pumpkin. We all gonna be okay, now. Just let it be . . .

(Corn reaches out to Pumpkin. She turns the gun on him.)

PUMPKIN: No!

CORN: Okay. It's okay, Pumpkin. Gimme that gun . . .

PUMPKIN: I say no! No more.

(Pumpkin waves the gun from Corn to Blue.)

I'm not leaving. Every part of this place is who I am. It's killin' you but it's keepin' the rest of us alive. I can't let you take me from here, Blue. You just ain't right. I see now. You ain't never gonna be. You already gone.

CORN: Blue, grab your trumpet.

BLUE: Say what?

CORN: Go on that stage. Play your axe. Get ready for tonight.

BLUE: I ain't—

CORN: You do it now, Blue. That's what we need right now. We need a soothin'. Ain't that right, Pumpkin?

BLUE: Corn, you talkin' crazy.

CORN: Do it, Blue. This is the moment. You got to play for your soul now.

(Blue looks at Corn. Then at Pumpkin, who keeps the gun aimed straight.)

Play like you gonna kill all them demons and open up the gates of heaven in your song. Play your axe.

(Blue slowly walks to the stage, questioning each step, unsure whether to follow . . . but something in him does. Pumpkin follows his path with the gun. Hands steady.
    Blue reaches out for his horn.
    He plays a note. Stops.)

BLUE: I'm losing it.
CORN: Nah, you ain't. I see it in your eyes, Blue. This the moment. It's gon' come right and perfect. You just got to keep playin'. Love Supreme.

(Blue considers. He tries again. Begins a tune.
    Soft at first, then increasingly beautiful.
    The trumpet sings.
    Then suddenly, a white light washes over Blue as he plays.
    Everyone stares at Blue, transfixed and mesmerized.
    Pumpkin is caught in the music. It is her prayer. She lowers the gun slowly, hypnotized.
    Blue plays a long-lasting note. It's the most beautiful note we've ever heard.
    Then finally, he stops. He is sweating. He is crying. His body shaking with pain and guilt and sorrow.
    The white light over him becomes even brighter.
    Corn nears Pumpkin, eyeing her lowered arm and gun in hand.)

See, Blue? You found it. That moment of perfect harmony. We your witnesses. Seen it all. And it's time for the madness to stop now. End on a good note.

(Blue wipes his tears. He smiles peacefully.)

Ain't that right, Pumpkin?

(Corn looks at Pumpkin. He nods at her knowingly. He steps aside from her. Pumpkin is clear, confident, resolved.)

PUMPKIN: That's right. For everybody. No more hurtin'.

(Pumpkin raises the gun at Blue.
   Gunshot.
   Blackout.)

END OF PLAY

DETROIT '67

For my mama, who first introduced me to Motown music.

For my daddy and his friends, who gave me Sly and Lank.

For my baby brother, who taught me how to love unconditionally.

And for the indestructible spirit of my Detroit people
who refuse to go up in flames . . .

PRODUCTION HISTORY

Detroit '67 received its world premiere in The Public Lab at the The Public Theater (Oskar Eustis, Artistic Director; Patrick Willingham, Executive Director), in association with the Classical Theatre of Harlem and the National Black Theatre, on February 26, 2013. It was directed by Kwame Kwei-Armah. The set design was by Neil Patel, the costume design was by ESosa, the lighting design was by Colin D. Young, and the sound design was by Shane Rettig; the production stage manager was Christina Lowe. The cast was:

CHELLE	Michelle Wilson
BUNNY	de'Adre Aziza
LANK	Francois Battiste
SLY	Brandon J. Dirden
CAROLINE	Samantha Soule

Detroit '67 was produced by Detroit Public Theatre (Courtney Burkett, Sarah Clare Corporandy, Sarah Winkler; Producing Artistic Directors) on May 13, 2016. It was directed by Kamilah Forbes. The set design was by Michael Carnahan, the costume design was by Dede Ayite, the lighting design was by Jen Schriever, the sound design was by Justin Ellington and the projection design was by Alex Basco Koch; the dramaturg was Lauren Imwold. The cast was:

CHELLE	Michelle Wilson
BUNNY	Jessica Frances Dukes
LANK	Amari Cheatom
SLY	Brian Marable
CAROLINE	Sarah Nealis

Detroit '67 was developed with the support of The Lark Play Development Center (John Clinton Eisner, Artistic Director).

CHARACTERS

CHELLE (MICHELLE), black woman, late thirties. Strong, steadfast, firm, and not easily impressed. A widow, mother and sister. A loving heart beneath her pride.

LANK (LANGSTON), black man, early thirties. Cool, loving and charismatic. A dreamer. Has a special effect on women—but not a womanizer. Chelle's younger brother.

BUNNY (BONITA), black woman, mid to late thirties. Fun, spunky, sexy and joyful. A friend and sometimes a lover. Never lets nothin' get her down.

SLY (SYLVESTER), black man, late thirties. Hip, slick and sweet-talking. An honest hustler and numbers man. Fiercely loyal. Lank's best buddy.

CAROLINE, white woman, late twenties to early thirties. Beautiful, quietly strong, troubled, soft and mysterious. A world of danger behind her eyes.

Detroit, Michigan. July 1967.

A " / " indicates where the next line of dialogue begins.

ACT ONE

Lights up on the basement of a two-story home. It is an unfinished basement, but efforts have been made to make it look inviting. A little balcony with stairs spills from upstage right. A board, some cabinets and a couple of stools makeshift a bar.

Pictures of Motown artists adorn the walls. Proud posters of Joe Louis and Muhammad Ali. Somewhere else, a photo of Malcolm X. A big tack through Malcolm's forehead.

A big old freezer leans against the upstage-left wall. Somewhere else, a washer, dryer and sink. A few clothes hang on a line.

A string of Christmas lights lies on an old, shabby couch, which sits in the middle of the floor. Next to it, an old recliner. Crates covered by cloth make a coffee table. A couple of pipe poles stand as pillars on both sides of the space. Height markings are somewhere on the wall. A name in cursive. A drawing of a huge four-pointed star. A huge black fist. A very bad and lumpy portrait of a brown girl.

Behind the couch against the wall is an old record player. It plays the Temptations' "Ain't Too Proud to Beg."

Chelle sings along as she works to untangle the Christmas lights. Suddenly the record skips.

CHELLE: Dang it!

(She hurries to the record player and moves the needle past the skip. Goes back to singing. It skips again.)

Not this part . . . come on!

(She goes to fix it again.)

(To the record player) You gonna behave now?

(She waits. Watches. It seems cool. She goes back to untangling the lights.
    The record player skips again.)

Dang it! *(Plays with the needle)* You got something against David Ruffin? Hunh? What's the matter? *(Waits for an answer from the player)* Ohh . . . you wanted to see him in concert? Honey, me too. I was mad he didn't show up. He can sing you outta your drawls, you let 'im. But that's no reason to mess David all up right now. He ain't a bad man. Just a little troubled, maybe. But troubled don't make you bad. Can't nobody sang like him . . . Hell, can't nobody sang like none of the Temptations. They all got voices of honey you ask me. So don't go scratchin' up on David just cuz you mad. You let David play.

(She puts the needle back on the record. It behaves.)

That's better. Got us a party happenin' this weekend, and I need you to act right. All right now?

(Somehow, the player agrees. Be imaginative.
    Chelle continues untangling the lights. The task is creating much displeasure.)

Lawd . . . come on thangs! *(Tangles them more)* Dang it!

(A colorful knock at the top of the stairs.)

BUNNY *(From off)*: Hey hey hey! You want some comp-naay?
CHELLE: I'm down here, Bunny! Come on in . . .

(A firecracker of a woman, Bunny, comes on down the steps. It is an art for her. She wears a one-piece jumpsuit, bangles every-where, and the highest of high-heeled shoes. Face fully beat with fake lashes'n'all. Middle of the day? No matter.)

BUNNY: What's happenin', mama? Heard ya'll was fixin' up for a party this weekend. Movin' the party to ya folks place, hunh?
CHELLE: Tryin' to.
BUNNY: Ya'll been quiet for a few weeks since ya'll took the party outta Lank's old crib.
CHELLE: Took us a minute to get him settled back over here, that's all. Now that Daddy done joined Mama up that stairway to heaven, we figure it make more sense for him to move back in.
BUNNY: Well the folks been askin' me where to go. I been sendin' 'em over to the Dukes—hate to say.
CHELLE: You ain't!
BUNNY: I had to Chelle! Now you know I love you like potato salad, but folks pay me to send 'em to the happenin' places. They want an after-hours joint, I gotta send 'em somewhere. With ya'll off the scene, Dukes done tight-ened it up. Even got that new hi-five record player.

CHELLE: You mean hi-fi?

BUNNY: Whatever.

CHELLE: We just had to finish squarin' up this business with Mama and Daddy's money. Took a lil' minute. Them lawyers'll try to trick you out of your own inheritance, I swear.

BUNNY: I told ya'll to talk to my man Stubby. He woulda gave ya'll a good price.

CHELLE: I told you I didn't want no lawyer named Stubby. Sounds short and fat and unprofessional.

BUNNY: Fine then. You go'on over to Hamtramck and get you one of them Steinbergs or them Zielinskis—or how you say it. See if they don't charge you both your arms and your legs. And probably your mama's legs too.

CHELLE: Not Mr. Furman. We got us a deal. I told him to work with me on these legal fees and come time for him to need a car, I got Sly on the job. Get him somethin' for a real good deal. He seem to like them odds. So he took care of us just fine.

BUNNY: You say so. (Beat) You having Christmas in July?

CHELLE: Naw, girl. Help me with this string, will you? I'm trying to untangle this mess so we have some kinda decorations. Lank supposed to be out getting us some more bulbs for 'em, cuz half of 'em done burned out. Had these since we was little ones. Every time I leave Lank in charge of wrapping 'em, this is what I end up with. Tangled mess.

(Bunny helps Chelle untangle the lights.)

BUNNY: That brother of yours shoul' got his own way of doing things, don't he?

CHELLE: You can say that again.

BUNNY: What ya'll gonna spend your folk's money on? A new car? Some baad threads?

CHELLE: Julius's college tuition is all I care about. You know that much. Use the inheritance for that, and pay off this house note with the parties. That's all I need.

BUNNY: Oooo girl, if I had me any kind of inheritance, I'd see the world. Tellin' you, I'd be in Rome and Paris and all them high'n'mighty places with my mink coat and my painted nails and my tea and crumpets—or whatever them folks be havin'. I wanna be just like them white gals we be seein' at the picture show. Sittin' back on one of them satin sofas, fannin' myself and readin' magazines till my man come back home from makin' his thousands to scoop me up and lay me right.

CHELLE (*Laughing*): You always lookin' for somebody to lay you right!

BUNNY: That's right, honey. 'Cept these niggers 'round here ain't bringing back no kinda thousands. Hell, they ain't even bringin' back no hundreds. 'Less them fools done hit the numbers and picked up a big ol' stack from Sly, only thing they comin' to lay is they hair to the side with that conkaline!

CHELLE: You a mess!

BUNNY: That's why I got to do for myself, now. Keep my ear to the ground and tell folks where to get things. Go here for the best hairdo in the city. Go there if you need a new auto part. Go up if you want some good blow. Go down if you want some good bump. Go to the side if you want some down-home cookin'. Go crooked if you wanna shoot the dice. Go left if you want the cheapest threads. Go right if you want the finest wine. And go to Twelfth Street if you wanna partaaaaaay . . . And if you ain't lookin' for none of that, then what the hell you doin' in Detroit?

CHELLE: You just better be tellin' folks to come on through to 1568 Clairmount from now on, cuz the Poindexter parties are back in the neighborhood!

BUNNY: Well all right. We been missin' ya'll parties.

CHELLE: These parties gon' be better than the rest. I gave Lank some money to go'on out and pick up some new 45s.

BUNNY: Ooooh . . . who you gon' get? I hope he pickin' up some more Temptations.

CHELLE: You know we got the Temps.

BUNNY: And some of that Marvin Gaye? Cuz I can work my best hip roll to his voice. It just go together the best. Like his voice got some kinda magnetic pull and my hips got the charge.

CHELLE: Got Marvin. And Martha and the Vandellas. And I still got the Miracles. I'm gon' put on a good one for you right now.

(Chelle rushes over to the record player and sets up her 45. The Miracles' "Shop Around" plays.)

BUNNY: I love me some of the Miracles, too. That Smokey'll make you throw ya drawls on stage. I wanna hit him smack in the face with mine, I ever get the chance.

CHELLE: You so nasty, Bunny.

BUNNY: That's why they call me Bunny, baby.

(The record suddenly skips—deflation.)

CHELLE: Dang it!

BUNNY: Awww nawww nawww . . . That ain't never gonna do . . .

(Chelle rushes over to fix the record.
    A slam upstairs. Moments later, Lank enters the basement, carrying a box of goods down the stairs.)

LANK: Bring that next one down here, Sly!

SLY *(From off)*: Behind ya in a sec! Gotta turn off the truck!

(Lank drops the box in the middle of the floor.)

CHELLE: You got the stuff!

(Chelle rushes over to the box to look through the goods.)

BUNNY: Hey there, daddy.

LANK: Miss Bonita—Bunny herself. Lay some on me, mama.

(Bunny plants a sultry kiss on Lank's cheek. He taps her on the bottom. Chelle pulls out some posters, a velvet painting, a neon light that says OPEN, *some pathetic party favors.)*

CHELLE: Where's the bulbs for the lights?

LANK *(Vague)*: They in there.

BUNNY: You gon' save me a dance this Friday, sugar?

LANK: I got my slowest one saved for you, Bunny girl.

BUNNY: I done told the folks ya'll startin' things 'round midnight. That way they don't have to wait for the clubs to close if they don't want to. Ya'll can get the jump on folks.

CHELLE *(Head in the box, displeased)*: Yeah, cuz Bunny been sending folks over to the Dukes these days.

LANK: You ain't!

BUNNY: Just till ya'll ready to come back out right.

LANK: Oh we ready, baby. We ready. You gon' see in one second.

CHELLE *(In the box)*: These all the bulbs? This itty-bitty pack? This ain't enough for the whole string. And what's with this tacky lookin' neon sign? Where's this thing supposed to go?

LANK: They was . . . throwin' that away down at Roscoe's Liquor Store. Got a nice color to it. Thought we could use it for somethin' . . .

CHELLE: Color! We have plenty of color with my Christmas lights.

LANK: Awww Chelle, don't start wrinkling your forehead, now. I got plans that's gonna make our parties outta sight!

CHELLE: Where's the drink coasters I asked you to get? I don't see them in here nowhere.

(Another door slam upstairs.)

And tell Sylvester to Stop Slammin' My Doors!

(Sly enters the basement carrying another box.)

SLY: Hey hey there sweet Chelle. What's happenin' Bunny?

BUNNY: Hey Sly.

(Chelle rushes over and starts going through the box before Sly can finish setting it down.)

SLY: Whoa . . . pedal and ease there, mama.

CHELLE: I better find my coasters in here.

LANK: You gon' find somethin' better than them coasters.

SLY: That's right, all right . . .

(Sly looks at Lank inquisitively. Lank shakes his head no. Chelle pulls out an 8-track cartridge. She looks at it strangely.)

CHELLE: What the hell is this?

BUNNY: Oooo, I seen one of them before. They got 'em down at Lucky's.

CHELLE: Where're my 45s? You supposed to be gettin' that lil' Stevie Wonder. That Junior Walker everybody talkin' about. The Elgins. The Four Tops.

LANK: I told you not to sweat it, Sis. I got it taken care of. Come on, Sly. Let's bring it down.

SLY: You got it man.

(Sly and Lank head up the basement stairs.)

CHELLE: Bring what down? You better be bringin' down my 45s.
I gave enough money for all the songs on my list.

BUNNY: Somethin' tells me they ain't givin' two shits 'bout your
list.

*(At the top of the stairs behind the door, Sly and Lank begin
maneuvering something.)*

LANK *(From off)*: Pick it up with that hand.

SLY *(From off)*: Nah nah nah . . . I need to hold this part with
that hand. You grab this part.

LANK *(From off)*: Naw, man! That don't make sense. I need to
hold this part right here.

SLY *(From off)*: Cool, man, I got it. Just grab that one.

LANK *(From off)*: I got it. Just don't drop that thing. Cost us a
fortune.

SLY *(From off)*: I got it, man. I got it. Just go'on . . .

*(Seconds later, Sly and Lank emerge onto the balcony carrying
speakers and a music system.)*

CHELLE: That don't look like no 45!

LANK: This here's somethin' better than them 45s. This here's
an 8-track player.

BUNNY: That's right! That's what it's called. Seen a commercial
for it on TV while back.

CHELLE: Langston Hughes Poindexter! Tell me this ain't how
you done spent all that money I gave you.

LANK: Now cool out for a minute, Chelle. Just listen. This here's
gonna be the answer to all our problems. Tell her, Sly.

CHELLE: Naw Sly, don't tell me.

SLY: It's true, Chelle. The 8-track player supposed to be better than a record player. You can get one in your car. You can move this thing around with you. And they say—you play some of that Smokey on this thing—his voice sound more velvet than it do right now.

BUNNY (*Intrigued*): They say that?

SLY: That's what they say, now.

CHELLE: Hmph—don't look like much to me.

LANK: Is you crazy? Look at this thing, Chelle. Ain't it beautiful? Even light up when the song play.

CHELLE: It's ugly. And weird. Look too technical. My record player plays and you can hear the needle movin' through the song. The way it dance up against the vinyl real close . . . that's what I like. Not no 8-track.

LANK: Give it a chance, Chelle. I'ma set this up with Sly and then we gonna play you somethin' on it. You'll see. It sounds much better than that ol' record player.

CHELLE (*Faint*): Daddy gave me that record player.

LANK: Won't be no scratchin' on a 8-track. Song play all the way through—smooth.

BUNNY: Now that sound like somethin' you need.

LANK: Dukes ain't got nothin' like this. We'll shut them down so quick, folks'll be like—Dukes who?

SLY: It's true, Chelle. Right now, Dukes ranked number one for after-hours joints in Detroit. But you tell folks you got somethin' new to listen to that Motown on, they gonna be pushin' to get through. Believe it, woman.

CHELLE: How much it cost?

LANK: Money ain't no object when it comes to quality. Tell her, Sly.

CHELLE: Naw Sly—don't tell me nothin'! You done spent it all, didn't you? All the shoppin' money I gave you—gone, ain't it?

LANK: You see this quality?

SLY: Top-of-the-line quality.

BUNNY: Look like a fine quality to me.

CHELLE: Well I guess it ain't nothin' left to say since the amen corner done spoke. Forget my lil' record player then. I keep it to myself . . .

(Chelle moves away and goes through the boxes. Sly looks at Lank and motions for him to tell Chelle something. Lank mouths, "Not yet." Chelle is oblivious. Bunny notices, but merely shakes her head and says nothing.)

BUNNY: Ya'll stand to make a killin' this month offa these parties. Folks been hittin' the after-hours joints more since some of the vets done come back home from 'Nam.

LANK: Heard Otis Jones done come back home. Say he been talkin' to himself sometimes on the street.

CHELLE: Poor Otis.

SLY: That's why folks need a good place to get a drink and have a good time and leave that Vietnam blues back overseas.

CHELLE: Don't say it that way, Sylvester.

SLY: I'm just sayin' what it is.

CHELLE: Just don't say it that way. Make it sound like we doin' more than we are. We just trying to make a lil' money the way we know how.

LANK: Sly know that, Chelle.

SLY: We all know it, Chelle.

CHELLE: That's all. Not tryin' to mess these vets up more than they been already.

LANK: Ain't nobody messin' nobody up. We here to make people feel good. Make some extra money to keep my nephew in that Tuskegee Institute. I told Julius—he gonna be like one of them airmen. That's what he promised me.

SLY: A young colored brother from Detroit in school down there in Tuskegee . . . that's somethin' to make folk feel real good. I'll drink to that one myself—hell . . .

BUNNY: He gon' study all through the summer too?

CHELLE: Say he wanted to stay down there and work during the summer. *(Beat)* I think it's a girl.

LANK: That's my nephew.

BUNNY: Just like his uncle.

LANK: Watch your mouth there, woman.

SLY: You, uh . . . you gon' be needin' some real money to keep him down there, ain't you?

CHELLE: With these parties . . . we should be all right. Keep Julius down there till he graduate. My boy is gonna go all the way.

(Sly looks at Lank again. Lank finally nods and mouths, "Be smooth." Sly adheres.)

SLY: Say there . . . uh . . . Lank . . . you know Shepling's Bar on Twelfth Street gettin' sold?

LANK *(Feigning surprise)*: That right? Old man sellin' it?

SLY *(Feigning casual)*: Yeah, that's right. Movin' to the suburbs. Peanut said white folks all over town been tryin' to sell they property and move on out.

(Bunny senses they're up to something and watches with amusement.)

LANK: Tryin' to get away from all these niggers movin' in, hunh?

BUNNY: Well where they goin'? Cuz if it's nice, I got news for 'em. Niggers gon' find it.

LANK: Niggers deserve nice stuff too. Hey Sly . . . how much he sellin' for?

SLY: Say he takin' bids. Folks that can come up with five grand can get in on the bid.

LANK *(Overly surprised)*: Five grand? That's it? *(Beat)* But what about the license? That's what run your well dry.

SLY: Say he gonna sell the license too. Bid on the table is fifteen grand—license included.

LANK *(Overly excited)*: License included?!? What's he playin' at?

SLY: Peanut say he talkin' straight.

LANK: Straight away? Fifteen grand? Whoo . . . that's somethin'!

(Lank looks at Chelle.)

Ain't that somethin' Chelle?

CHELLE *(Nonchalantly)*: I guess so . . . for somebody who want it. *(Beat)* Not me.

LANK: Well you know, Sly . . . me and Chelle got that much to put in if that's what he's playin' with.

CHELLE: Oh no we don't.

LANK: Sure we do. Say Sly . . . we got that much from the stash Daddy left us.

SLY: Say what? Ain't that a coincidence? I was just sayin' what I was sayin' without knowin' nothin' bout that . . . That's funny . . .

(Lank looks at Chelle. She stops rummaging through things and studies him closely.)

CHELLE: What the hell's goin' on?

BUNNY: Some funny shit, fa sho . . .

LANK: Nothin' funny. Just thinkin' 'bout this bar Sly done brought up. That's all.

CHELLE: Sly done brought up . . . Hunh . . . What you got up your sleeve?

LANK: Why you always think somethin's up my sleeve, Chelle?

CHELLE: Cuz when it come to you and Sly, it always is. *(Beat)* This 8-track machine ain't just for no basement party, is it? Ya'll done bought all this stuff for some kinda scheme!

LANK: Awww, Chelle . . . *(Beat)* Okay, looka here . . . Me and Sly . . . we been thinkin' 'bout how it'd feel to be legit. Thinkin' . . . we could get us a piece of Shep's bar and start to build somethin' for ourselves. Found this stuff for a good deal—thought it'd be great for a bar!

CHELLE: So that's why you done changed all the decorations? For some bar?!

LANK: Not just some bar. A bar of our own.

CHELLE: No, Lank.

LANK: Whoa there—think about it for a sec, Chelle.

CHELLE: Nothin' to think about. I just say no.

LANK: Now hold on just a minute. It'd be somethin' to be legit. Wouldn't it Sly?

SLY: Do better than dodgin' these pigs every second. They been cracking down on the after-hours spots, y'know. Trying to catch everybody operating without a license. Get us for throwin' dice or smoking a joint—whatever they can. Dukes almost got raided couple weeks ago, but Peanut came in and told us the Big Four was 'round the corner. Niggers was runnin' this way and that 'fore they could shut everything down.

BUNNY: That Big Four been serious 'round Twelfth Street too.

SLY: When it's time to clean up the city, the ghetto be the only place they come lookin' for trash . . .

LANK: I'm tired a bein' treated like trash. Four pigs rollin' together to pick out niggers one by one. I can think of a whole lot more need to be cleaned up on these streets than us.

BUNNY: Wish they'd clean up them potholes on Grand Boulevard. Damn near flipped my car last week—hole was so wide.

SLY: They wanna clean somethin', why don't they clean up them pigs that come down here droppin' that dope off on the corner? I seen 'em talkin' to Otis a few times. I know what kinda game they playin' . . .

LANK: Pickin' out niggers ain't gonna do nothin' but lock away a whole lotta potential. Put us to good use, this city be full of all kinds of production. I'm tired of bein' laid off at that plant and runnin' joints outta my basement like I got somethin' to hide. Like the only way I can be somethin' is underground. I'm ready to be aboveground just like them white folks. Ain't no tellin' what Detroit could be if we was all put to good use. We could make some kinda . . . what's that word when things is all copacetic and beautiful? Like perfect, damn near?

SLY: Utopia.

LANK: Utopia. Detroit could be some kinda . . . what's that place Malcolm went? Side by side with them other . . . y'know . . . Muhammad folks?

SLY: Mecca.

LANK: Detroit could be some kinda mecca . . . that's what it could be. Colored folks moving this city forward. Get us some business of our own—make them stop treatin' us like trash to be swept away. I'm tellin' you, we get a chance to get above ground, Detroit'll be a mecca.

BUNNY: Honey, if you can make Detroit that kinda place, I'll marry you.

LANK: You better go'on and pick out your dress then, baby.

CHELLE: And you better come on and help me finish gettin' this place ready. We need this joint jumpin' by Friday. Let them Dukes know the Poindexters are back on the spot.

BUNNY: Midnight good?

CHELLE: That's good to me.

LANK *(To Sly, aside)*: You gettin' in on that bid fa sho?

SLY: Like I told you—I'm gon' try. My number hit the other day, so I got me half. If you could pull the other half . . . then that'd be somethin'.

LANK (*Hushed*): Lemme talk to her.

SLY: You said it, my man.

BUNNY: See ya'll good folks later. Got to catch up with my ol' man.

LANK: Awww, don't tell me that, now. You breakin' my heart, baby.

BUNNY: Don't worry honey. There's plenty of Bunny to go 'round.

(*With a luxurious twirl, Bunny heads up the stairs and out of the basement.*)

SLY: I'ma go'on too. But I'll catch you at Lucky's, Lank. See you soon, sweet Chelle.

CHELLE: Goodbye, Sylvester.

LANK: Later, Sly.

(*Sly exits up the stairs. Chelle goes through the box. She pulls out 8-track cartridges with disapproval.*)

There you go. That's that Mary Wells you been wanting.

CHELLE (*Firmly*): On 45.

LANK: You gon' like this better. Trust me.

(*Lank starts to set up the 8-track player.*)

Listen here, Chelle. This bid on the bar . . . this ain't a bad thing, y'know.

CHELLE: No, Lank.

LANK: Now just hear me out, will you? I got enough friends over here to make this spot happenin'. We won't be wall-to-wall up in here. Got space for more folks. Won't be competing with them Dukes no more. Our own spot— that'd be somethin'.

CHELLE: That ain't the somethin' I want, Lank. Put Mama and Daddy's hard-earned money on the line just to keep hustlin'? Cuz that's all a bar is. A hustle on the books.

LANK: That's all any kinda business is.

CHELLE: I don't wanna be hustlin' forever.

LANK: What you wanna do, Chelle? Sit on the money till we rot?

CHELLE: I just wanna have somewhere for Julius to return and call home. These parties are temporary. Survivin'. This house and this life is all I need. I don't wanna take on nothin' that could make us lose it.

LANK: Don't you see I'm tryin' to make things better? Invest this money so it grow into somethin' more. For you and Julius. Be the man for him that his Daddy woulda been— was he alive.

CHELLE: I know, Lank. You been a good fill-in for my Willie and I love you for it. But I don't love no bar. I don't wanna lose my son's future to no bar. Too shaky. I want him to have something solid.

LANK: Me too.

CHELLE: Then promise me you won't blow our money on this deal.

LANK: Come on, Chelle.

CHELLE: Promise me we gonna hold this house and this family together. Promise me that, Lank.

LANK: All right, Chelle. Never mind the bar.

(Beat.)

CHELLE: I'm gon' go up to the corner store and get us some liquor for the shelf. Where the keys?

LANK: Upstairs on the counter.

CHELLE: Be back in a few. *(Beat)* I'm gon' see 'bout this Mary Wells when I get back. Bet it ain't better than my 45.

(Chelle heads up the basement stairs. Lank, alone, goes to his 8-track player and plugs it in.
    He picks up a cartridge and smiles.)

LANK *(To the cartridge)*: We'll show her, Mary . . .

(Mary Wells' "What's Easy for Two Is So Hard for One" plays.
    Lights fade on Lank and his 8-track.)

SCENE TWO

Night falls on the house. The basement is dark and still. Suddenly, the door cracks open. A peek of moonlight from the balcony.
    Shuffled footsteps come down the stairs . . . followed by muffled voices.

SLY: Where to? Not there —wait—to the left some —on my foot not— gotdamnit—nigger, my foot!

LANK: Over here. Right there—okay—hold on— what's that—whose foot is that?—move over more!

LANK: Put her on the couch.

(Lank and Sly carry a large covered figure over to the couch and plop it down.
    Lank goes over to a lamp and flicks it on.
    Sly stands over the unknown figure and stares.)

SLY: She's still out.

LANK: Check her pulse?

SLY: Don't need to. She's breathing. I can see that much. She's breathing.

LANK: Thank God.

(Lank walks over to the concealed figure and pulls back the cover. Caroline, a young white woman, lies motionless.)

SLY: Say Lank, I'm gonna need a joint for this one.

LANK: You know Chelle don't like smoking in the house.

SLY: I think I'ma need a pass on this one.

LANK: How 'bout a drink instead? Some gin in the cabinet.

SLY: I'm already over my limit . . . but . . . what the hell . . .

(Sly goes to the bar and fixes himself a drink.)

LANK: She bleeding anywhere?

SLY: Don't think so.

LANK: Gotta make sure.

(Lank moves around Caroline carefully. He touches her lightly. She stays motionless.
Sly gulps his drink.)

SLY: She knocked out cold.

LANK: You said it.

SLY: Maybe she might need some kinda ice pack or somethin' for her head. Right there in the corner. Look like some dried blood.

LANK: Yeah . . . yeah . . . I think we got that . . .

(Lank goes over to the freezer and pulls out a box of frozen veggies. He brings it back and starts to set it on Caroline's forehead.)

SLY: Whoa—hold on there. You might wanna cover it with somethin' first. She get freezer burn or somethin'. Have a pack of vegetables stuck to her face.

LANK: Wouldn't want that . . .

SLY: There go a towel over there.

(Sly points to the sink basin.)

LANK: Right.

(Lank rushes over to get the towel. He wraps the box of veggies and comes back over to Caroline. He sets it on her face. She flinches but doesn't awaken.)

It's all right, miss. It's okay . . .

(Lank lifts the box.)

Maybe I should leave her be.

SLY: Maybe. *(Beat)* What you gon' tell Chelle?

LANK: The truth. Ain't nothin' else to tell her.

SLY: The truth? Hell . . . I'd like to know the truth myself. Truth ain't comin' till that woman wake back up.

LANK: I pray to God she wake back up.

SLY: We must be two of the craziest niggers in Detroit right now—get ourselves involved in this mess.

LANK: Mess found us. What else could we do?

SLY: I go listenin' to you . . . that's my problem. Shoulda left her out there and kept rollin'.

LANK: You listenin' to me? I couldn't tell . . .

SLY: Yeah nigger, I'm listenin' to you. You the one think you some kinda Negro Messiah. Every time I turn around, you tryin' to part some seas or walk on water or some shit. How I get into it—where I fit in this mess—I don't know.

How I let you make me bring this white girl back here, I don't know! I must be drunker than I thought.

LANK: Awww man, I ain't make you do nothin'. A man can't make no other man do nothin'—he a real man. You got hands and feet ain't you? Drove the truck here, ain't you? You in this just as much as me.

SLY: How am I in this as much as you? I ain't the one grab her!

LANK: No—you the one sat there till somebody tell you what to do.

SLY: Tell me what to do?! I got feet and hands ain't I?

LANK: I ain't so sure.

SLY: Ain't nobody tell me what to do. *I* tell me what to do.

LANK: Well okay then, you said it.

SLY: Say what?

LANK: You did this cuz of you. Not cuz of me. Just like you said.

(*Beat.*)

SLY: Nigger don't be tryin' to slick-talk me when I been drinkin'!

(*A door creaks at the top of the stairs. Chelle enters the balcony sleepily.*)

CHELLE: Lank? Sly? Ya'll all right down there? I heard ya'll comin' in . . . woke me up . . .

LANK: We all right Chelle. Go'on back to bed. We all right.

(*Chelle catches a glance at the couch. She sees that someone is sprawled out on it.*)

CHELLE: Who's that . . . what's goin' on down there? Can't none of ya'll drunk friends sleep here tonight . . .

LANK: It's nothin' Chelle—go'on back to bed now.

(*Chelle peers farther over the balcony. She comes down the steps.*)

CHELLE: Lank—I don't want none of your women over here tonight neither. We done talked about this—

(Chelle stops. She sees Caroline—passed out.)

What the . . . hell?

LANK: Chelle, relax now.

CHELLE: Relax—my ass!

SLY: Hold on a minute, Chelle.

CHELLE: Hold on—nothin'!

LANK: Gimme a chance to explain.

CHELLE: You better start explaining real good. What the hell is this white girl doin' down here? You done went stupid?

LANK: Hold on, Chelle! It's not what you thinkin'—

CHELLE: Well tell me what it is then! Cuz I'm thinkin' you and Sly done lost ya'll everlasting minds! Bringing this girl at this hour—

SLY: We got a reason for that, Chelle.

CHELLE: I ain't hearin' no reasons! Somebody better tell me what's what.

LANK: We found her, Chelle.

CHELLE: Found her how? Where was you lookin' for her at?

SLY: Wasn't lookin' for her. Just found her when we was leavin' Lucky's place. Stumbling on the side of the road and lookin' real bad.

CHELLE: What make you pick her up and bring her here?!

LANK: She been hurt up. Somebody done hurt her up good.

(Chelle goes over to Caroline quickly. She pulls the cover back farther and sees the bruises along Caroline's face. Swollen eye, dried blood by her temple, greens and yellows staining her face.)

CHELLE *(Gasps)*: Good Lord. She look terrible.

SLY: Did a good number on her, whoever they is.

CHELLE *(Leaning down to Caroline's chest)*: She breathing. Thank God. *(Beat)* Ya'll didn't . . . ya'll ain't messed with her—

LANK: Come on, Chelle.

CHELLE: Just have to ask. *(Beat)* What happened to her?

LANK: Caught a glimpse of her when we was leaving Lucky's. Stumbling 'round on Chicago Boulevard. Lookin' like she might fall right into traffic.

CHELLE: Lord . . . she probably done got robbed. What was she doin' on Chicago?

SLY: Thought maybe she was drunk and done forgot where she was. I seen that a few times.

LANK: Slowed down to ask if she was okay. That's when we saw her up close. Lookin' in bad way and not really all there. Mumbling somethin' to herself. Not really makin' a lot of sense. I leaned out to ask her if she needed a ride and that's when she looked at me . . . dead in my eye—in this way like . . . like she knew exactly where was she was for a second. Like she heard me for the first time. And she said, "Get me outta here." Real serious—like that. Dead in my eye. Then she got faint, like she was gonna drop right where she stood. I jump out to grab hold of her . . . helped her into the truck to drop her off somewhere, and she just pass right out. Couldn't get her back up.

SLY: So this . . . this nigger say—

LANK: Say to Sly, we better bring her back here. We leave her down there, whoever done this may be comin' back to finish the job.

CHELLE: Her face—sweet Jesus. It look like it's been some-body's punching bag.

LANK: Way she looked at me . . . dead in my eye like that . . . *(Beat)* I dunno . . . just messed with me . . . Had to do somethin'.

CHELLE: You get her some ice?

SLY: Took a pack of vegetables in the freezer.

CHELLE: She gonna need some ointment for this gash. Sly, run up in the bathroom and get me some ointment out the cabinet.

SLY: Whatever you say.

(Sly wobbles upstairs.)

CHELLE: So where we gonna take her?

LANK: Ain't nowhere to take her. Just figure we let her stay here tonight. Figure the rest out when she wake up.

CHELLE: We can't keep her here.

LANK: What else you wanna do, Chelle? Leave her in a alley?

CHELLE: I ain't sayin' that, but she can't stay here!

LANK: What's it gonna hurt—one night?

CHELLE: What you think gonna happen when this white girl wake up in a house full of colored folks in the ghetto? You think she gonna be thankful and happy you saved her when she see all these gashes on her face? You think she gonna be able to distinguish one colored fool from the next?

LANK: How you know it was a colored fool?

CHELLE: I pray it wasn't. But if it was . . . we all in trouble. Even if it wasn't . . . all she got to do is say it was, and we all in trouble.

LANK: I know that, Chelle. Don't you think I know that?

CHELLE: If you know that then why is she still layin' on this couch? Let's get Sly, and let's go drop her down off at the hospital.

LANK: They takin' names down at the hospital. 'Less we just dump her at the door and keep rollin', they gonna have our names. See our faces. They wanna pin somethin' on two colored men, they just got the names and faces.

CHELLE: Then drop her off and let's keep rollin'.

LANK: Chelle! I ain't gonna do that, now. Have some kinda heart.

CHELLE: I got a heart! I got a mind and a gut too. And they all throwin' up caution signs every whichaway.

LANK: I say she can stay here through the night, Chelle. We can do that much.

(Sly reenters with the ointment.)

SLY: Found some ointment. Some bandages and tape too.

(He hands them to Chelle. She begins applying the ointment to Caroline and bandaging her up.)

So where we gonna take her?

LANK: She stayin' here for the night.

SLY: That right?

CHELLE: That's what Lank say.

LANK: She stay till the morning, and we help her get on her way.

SLY: That's what you say, then that's what it is.

(Sly heads to the stairs.)

I'ma go'on home then. Catch you when the sun come up . . .

(Sly stumbles on the stairs. Lank hurries over and helps him.)

LANK: Gimme them keys, man. I got the wheels.

(Chelle continues to bandage Caroline . . . carefully, meticulously.)

Be right back, Chelle. You got this?

CHELLE: I guess I do, don't I?

(Lank helps Sly up the stairs. They disappear behind the door.
Chelle finishes bandaging Caroline. She stands and studies
her quietly for a moment.

She grabs a pillow and props up Caroline's feet. Then she covers
her back up, heads to the stairs . . . looks back with reluctance . . .
Shaking her head, she goes up the stairs.

(Softly) Good Lord, don't let it be no niggers . . .

(She hits the light and disappears behind the door.)

SCENE THREE

Daylight. Sun spills through the small windows. Caroline lies sleep-
ing on the couch.

She turns once. Then again. Then violently. Finally she jerks out
of her sleep.

Beat.

Caroline looks around at her surroundings. Slowly, she rises
from the couch and surveys the basement. She sees the pictures of
Motown artists. Muhammad Ali. Joe Louis. Malcolm X. The four-
pointed star on the wall. The black fist. The portrait of the lumpy
looking brown girl.

She freezes, slightly bewildered, slightly intrigued.

She passes a mirror on the wall. Looks at her reflection and gasps.

She studies herself in horror. She lifts her bandages. Sees her
bruised eye, her swollen jaw. She touches her face gently, pressing at
the pain and wincing.

The door at the top of the stairs opens and Lank emerges. Caro-
line halts.

LANK: Hey there, miss. I guess you're up now, hunh?
CAROLINE: Who are you?

LANK: I'm Lank. Brought you some breakfast. My sister made it, not me. Some eggs and toast. She can burn . . . my sister can . . .

CAROLINE: Lank?

LANK: That's right. This is our house. Me and my buddy Sly . . . we picked you up last night . . . standing out there off Chicago Boulevard . . .

CAROLINE *(Sobering)*: Oh. Fuck. Right.

(Lank sets down the tray.)

LANK: We didn't do nothin' . . . just found you stumblin' 'round and brought you back cuz . . . you was hurtin'. You was needin' some help, remember?

CAROLINE: Yeah . . . Yeah, thanks um . . . shit.

LANK: I can call somebody for you. Call you a cab or drop you somewhere. If you just tell me where I can take you . . .

CAROLINE: No! Uh, thanks but . . . no . . . thanks. *(Ob16)* Where am I?

LANK: You over here on the West Side. Twelfth Street and Clairmount. You ever been over these parts before?

CAROLINE: Twelfth Street. Sometimes. *(Quickly fixing)* Not really though. Not much. But yeah—no.

(He offers the toast again.)

LANK: Some food. That's what you need. Somethin' on your stomach.

(Caroline looks at the food, at Lank.)

Go on.

(Caroline politely pinches a piece of toast and nibbles.)

CAROLINE: Good jam.

LANK: My sister makes it from scratch. Jars it.

CAROLINE: She's good.

LANK: She knows it too.

(Caroline laughs faintly.)

She ran out to the bank. She'll be back in a few. Maybe she can get you some of her clothes to put on. Help you get cleaned up some. You got some family? Somebody I can call for you?

(Caroline stops nibbling.)

CAROLINE: No, I'm all right. That's okay. *(Shift)* I should . . . um . . . I should give you something for your help and everything . . . *(She looks around herself)* I'm just gonna get my um . . . my purse?

LANK: Purse?

CAROLINE: It's gone? My purse.

LANK: I didn't see you with no purse, ma'am. Sorry.

CAROLINE *(Panic)*: Shit! Motherfucker!

LANK: Whoa—miss . . . if it's some money you need—some fare or somethin', my sister and me—we can help with that.

CAROLINE: Yeah?

LANK: Yeah, if you needin' somethin' . . .

CAROLINE: Yeah . . . *(Then quickly)* No, uh . . . Mister . . .

LANK: Lank, remember. Name's Langston . . . but folks 'round here call me Lank.

CAROLINE: Riiight Langston. Yeah, okay, um . . . thank you for the food and for your help.

LANK: You gonna be okay?

CAROLINE: The bathroom. I need the bathroom.

LANK: 'Course. There's one in that washroom right there. Got some towels in there too, you need one.

CAROLINE: Great, thanks.

(Caroline exits. Lank watches after her for a moment.
The door to the basement opens. Chelle comes down the stairs.)

CHELLE: She woke up yet?

LANK: In the next room washin' up.

CHELLE: She tell you anything? Who she is? What done happened?

LANK: Ain't said much yet. Just gettin' her bearings. Don't think she has nobody, Chelle.

CHELLE: What you mean? She didn't give you no people to call?

LANK: Say ain't nobody to call. I think she in trouble.

CHELLE: Oh Lord . . . that mean we in trouble with her. You ain't get her to tell you nothin'?

LANK: She worried about somethin'. Ain't sure what. Or who. But that trouble from last night ain't over. That's all I know.

CHELLE: I don't want that trouble followin' her here, Lank. We gotta find out who her people are and get her back to them. That's what we gotta do.

(Caroline reenters looking mildly cleaned up. Her face is cleaner,
her hair a bit tidier. She stops when she sees Chelle.)

CAROLINE: Thank you folks for your help and the good jam . . .

CHELLE: No problem, miss. My brother Langston is gonna take you to the hospital to make sure you're okay.

CAROLINE: Oh no . . . that—thank you—that won't be necessary . . .

CHELLE: Well where can we take you, honey? You got a sister or some friends somewhere? Somebody wondering where you are?

CAROLINE: No I . . . I'll just . . . I'll be fine . . .

CHELLE: You sure, miss?

CAROLINE *(No)*: Of course . . . I just . . . I'll just be out of your hair now . . . But thank you again for all your trouble . . .

(Caroline walks over to the stairs, then stops suddenly.)

Say listen, you wouldn't have—or know where—I could rent a room . . . work for my board . . . for a few days or so?

(Lank and Chelle look at each other.)

LANK: You need some room and board?

CAROLINE: Just . . . I don't have anything . . . my purse is gone, you know . . .

CHELLE: We could pull together a few bucks for you, miss—

LANK: I told her that—

CAROLINE: I just need somewhere to room for a week or so . . . just until I can leave. Pay for train fare—

CHELLE: There's Algiers Motel not far—

LANK: Won't let you stay on credit.

CAROLINE: I won't be trouble. I'd work for it. Doesn't matter where. As long as it's safe.

LANK: You can stay here, miss—

CHELLE: Lank—

LANK: If you need to.

CAROLINE: I would work—

CHELLE: We don't have no work—

LANK: We got us a bar needin' some upkeep. Doing some renovations around here. Maybe you could help with that—

CHELLE: And what we gonna pay her?

LANK: Tips.

CAROLINE: I know how to work a bar. I could do that.

CHELLE: Work for us?

LANK: Why not? My sister been needing some hands on that bar. But just so you clear, miss—it ain't during regular hours.

CHELLE: Lank!

CAROLINE: Oh that's all right with me. I'm used to a lot of irregular.

LANK: Good then. It's a deal. You help us out . . . you stay right here on this couch. Folds out into a bed if you like. You stay here till you got enough to pay for that train fare.

CHELLE: A week. That's all it take. No longer.

CAROLINE: A week—yes. That's great. That'll do.

(Beat. Chelle silently fumes. Lank extends his hand to Caroline.)

LANK: Welcome to the Poindexter house, Miss . . . Miss?

CAROLINE: Caroline.

LANK: Caroline. Welcome. We good people here. Hard workin', hustlin' people. You gonna be just fine. That's my sister, Michelle.

(Caroline nods. Chelle remains stern.)

She's gonna take you upstairs—get you some clean clothes to put on.

CAROLINE: You don't have to—

LANK: It's fine. Ain't that fine, Chelle?

CHELLE: Oh yeah, it's fine all right. *(Beat)* Go'on up them stairs. To the right, down the hall. I'm right behind you. Gonna pull some laundry for you.

(Caroline moves up the stairs.)

CAROLINE: Thank you both. Really. You're good folks.

(Caroline slowly disappears behind the door.)

CHELLE: You done went plain stupid.

LANK: What I tell you? She in trouble, Chelle.

CHELLE: You damn right she in trouble! Can't figure out whether she comin' or goin'. Lookin' like a wild animal that done went astray.

LANK: You ain't see her like I seen her. Standin' on the side of that road—lookin' me in my eye like the devil himself come to claim her. I just can't send her back out there just yet. Can't have that on my soul . . . She just need a little help, is all. A little help and a little time.

CHELLE: A week, Lank. And her time run out. You hear me?

LANK: A week, Chelle.

CHELLE: And this one, Lank . . . she ain't for touch. You understand?

LANK: Come on now, Chelle. That's not what this is about. I'm just being friendly. That's all.

CHELLE: I know you, boy. I know your kinda friendly. And I say—keep your friendliness to yourself . . . or this gonna be a short week.

LANK: Go'on help her get into somethin' clean, Chelle. Help her out, will you?

(Chelle eyes Lank firmly. Then she turns, grabs some clothes from the line and heads up the stairs.)

CHELLE *(Muttering)*: Done invited a white girl to the joint . . . tonight's gonna be some kinda party . . .

(The door closes.
Lank remains . . . contemplative for a moment. He looks at the tray of half-eaten food. He lifts it and carries it up the stairs.
Lights fade.)

SCENE FOUR

"Dancing in the Street" by Martha and the Vandellas plays.
Lights up on the basement in full pre-party mode. Chelle moves quickly about the space, filling bowls of nuts and setting out napkins. Lank stacks up cartridges by the 8-track player, which lights up as each song plays.
Bunny sits on a stool and rocks to the music.

BUNNY: This is my jam! Oooo Lank, baby—this 8-track player is sounding real good!

LANK: Didn't I tell you, woman?

(Chelle looks at an empty bowl.)

CHELLE: Who ate the nuts that quick?

(Bunny points at Lank as he devours a batch of nuts in his hand.)

Lank! That ain't for you! You eatin' 'em all up before the guests even get here.

LANK: What? I'm testin' 'em out!

CHELLE *(Yelling)*: Caroline! We gonna need some more of those cashews! And you finish mixing that punch?

CAROLINE *(From off)*: Almost!

BUNNY: This some shit I just can't believe.

CHELLE: Don't even mention it, Bunny.

BUNNY: Ya'll got a white girl over here in the ghetto runnin' 'round under ya'll like some kinda maid? This some shit'll make ya mama and daddy raise right back out they graves. Everybody gonna wanna see some of this.

LANK: Not a maid, Bunny. She's just helpin' us out. That's all.

BUNNY: What you know about her? Who's her people?

CHELLE: Ain't said. She been keepin' real quiet and polite all day. Too polite.

LANK: She still a little shook up, that's all. Just trying to get on her feet.

BUNNY: Well whatever she doin'—it's enough to have this place packed tonight. Word done got out quick. Folks can't wait to get served by a white girl over here! White girls can get the joint jumpin' every time. You even mention some kinda blue eyes and niggers will stop what they doin' to get close enough to have a gaze. Swear it—white girl is a natural aphrodisiac.

CHELLE: Hush, Bunny.

BUNNY: You'll see what I mean.

(The basement door opens. Sly enters with a bag of liquor. He is dressed to the nines—party suit and all.)

SLY: Heard there was a happenin' party this way tonight!

(Lank peers inside Sly's bag.)

LANK: You brought some sip? What's the word?

SLY: Thunderbird.

LANK: What's the price?

SLY: Thirty twice.

LANK: My maaan . . .

(Lank slides sixty cents to Sly.)

BUNNY: Look at you, Sly . . . You done bought some new threads.

SLY: Told ya'll my number hit.

BUNNY: How you the numbers man and your number hit? What kinda gamblin' rig is that? That sound like some jive if I ever heard it.

SLY: I don't cheat, now. Just cuz I run around collectin' bids don't mean I can't bid too. I ain't no psychic. Can't tell which number'll hit. Everybody know I'm true—black not blue. I came lookin' my best for you tonight, Chelle.

CHELLE: Go'on somewhere, Sly.

SLY: Don't be mean, woman. I came all past the pigs flashin' their lights in my face just to be up in your fine, fine place.

BUNNY: They came messin' with you?

SLY: Stopped me over there on La Salle. Askin' my plans for the night. Like I need some kinda pass to walk the streets that say: No, Mister Pig, I ain't goin' to get high or drunk without makin' sho the fine city of Detroit get to tax it for they profit.

LANK: They follow you?

SLY: Told 'em I was on my way home from Lucky's. Soon as they fixed to get in my face, radio went off. Heard somethin' 'bout a tussle near the freeway and they took off. But not before they told me to make sure my nigger ass went home and didn't come back out.

CHELLE: Listen to how they talk.

BUNNY: Boys in blue.

SLY: Talkin' ain't the half of it. 'Specially 'round this way. Sniffin' out these joints and bustin' nigger ass like it give 'em a special kinda high. Like it's recreation, damn near.

BUNNY: Tried to grab me up last night leavin' my ol' man's. Say women like me up to no good.

I know what they meanin'. But honey, if I was a streetwalker it wouldn't be over here on no La Salle. Pig wouldn't be able to afford my kinda price.

CHELLE: You ain't sass him, did you?

BUNNY: Honey naw. Way they been swingin' them clubs lately . . . ain't no kinda chivalry in them ass whoopins. Men. Women. Don't seem to matter.

LANK: Well I ain't standin' 'round waitin' to get my ass busted. I tell you that much. Ain't so long you can hit folks 'fore they start to hit back.

CHELLE: Hush that kinda talk, Lank. We just got to make sure folks keep a low profile coming over here and mind themselves. Don't want none of ya'll getting in no trouble on account of us trying to have a good time.

SLY: Don't worry. Won't be nobody in else in threads this fine. That's how come they pulled my card. Said—that brother is lookin' too happenin' in that suit. He must be trouble. Ain't that right, Chelle?

CHELLE: Move on, Sly . . .

LANK: Ay Sly, I got me this velvet painting I wanna hang up. Come help me with it.

CHELLE: Not that ugly thing—Lord.

(Sly follows Lank to a corner. They create space for the painting. Caroline enters with a bowl of punch, carefully descending the stairs.)

CAROLINE: High Five Punch—coming up.

CHELLE: Did you put enough Kool-Aid in it?

CAROLINE: I think so.

CHELLE: Four packs. And then you gotta drop the Silver Satin in it on a five count.

CAROLINE: And four cups of sugar. I believe I did it right.

CHELLE: I'll taste.

(Chelle pulls out styrofoam cups.)

BUNNY: Caroline, you ever tasted Silver Satin and Kool-Aid?

CAROLINE: No ma'am, can't say that I have.

BUNNY: Ma'am? Who you callin' ma'am?

CAROLINE: I'm sorry . . . did I say something—

CHELLE: Just called her old. *(Sips the punch)* Not bad.

BUNNY: I'm a young Bunny rabbit.

CHELLE: With a fast rabbit tail.

BUNNY: Just call me that and we be fine.

CAROLINE: Sure thing.

BUNNY: You must be from elsewhere. That must be it. *(Beat)* Where you from?

(Chelle raises a brow. They watch Caroline.)

CAROLINE: Outside of here a ways. *(Quick subject change)* You know what I have had? Bali Hai. It's really something delicious.

BUNNY: Bali Hai? What you know about Bali Hai?

CAROLINE: I know that if you drink it back in three sips, it goes down smoother than oil. Tastes like you swallowed silk.

BUNNY: Umph . . . that's right—it does . . .

CAROLINE: Michelle, should I start putting the chips in the bowls?

CHELLE: Sure. They're upstairs in the kitchen.

CAROLINE: Got it.

(Caroline drifts up the stairs. Bunny watches her disappear.)

BUNNY: She a nigger lover.

CHELLE: Bunny! What you talkin'?

BUNNY: I'm tellin' you . . . she is.

CHELLE: Girl, you too much for me.

BUNNY: You hear that? Bali Hai? What's a white girl doing drinking Bali Hai? That's some ghetto smooth if I know anything 'bout liquor. She got some colored taste in her or she knows her liquor. It's one or the other, or both. I can tell you that much . . .

LANK: Hey—you two chicks . . . quit all that yakkin' over there.

SLY: Looka here, looka here.

(Sly and Lank hang up the velvet painting. Two naked black women laid out. Chelle scowls. Bunny smiles.)

CHELLE: If that ain't tackier than my thumb, I don't know what is.

BUNNY: I think it's sexy.

LANK: Every colored brother in Detroit oughta have himself one of these hanging in his house.

SLY: Every colored brother in Detroit oughta have himself the real thing at home . . . ain't that right, Chelle?

CHELLE: Hush up, Sylvester.

LANK: Can't nobody look at this and not feel like dancing up on a woman—close.

SLY: You can say that again. Get you the right song? Whoooo . . .

LANK: I got it.

(Lank goes to his 8-track player and shuffles through the cartridges.)

SLY: All through high school—'member them parties they was throwin' right before we was all headin' off to service? You 'member them?

LANK: Do I?

SLY: Movin' in on Marietta Wilson . . . just waitin' for the chance to ask her to dance.

(Lank puts on the tape. Smokey Robinson and the Miracles' "Oooo Baby Baby" plays.)

I'd move in slow . . . pretend I was shy.

(Sly demonstrates on Chelle. He takes her hand. She shoos him.)

CHELLE: Go'on now, Sylvester.

SLY: Just groove with me, baby.

(*Chelle tries to fight, but the song and the moves are too entrancing. They dance.*)

I remember what it would be to dance up on some mama, holdin' onto her like she was gonna go outta style if you let her go.

(*Caroline reenters at the top of the steps with a bowl of chips in her hands and looks on silently.*)

LANK: Mine was Damita Bell. She had that flip thing with her hair. I'd get nice with the DJ . . . slip him a dime. That way, he let me know just when my song was 'bout to play. Then soon as the record spin—there goes my hand in hers 'fore she had time to say no.

(*Lank scoops Bunny's hand. She goes along without protest.*)

But I was never one of them shy brothers. I make your body feel all the layers of the tune.
BUNNY: Yeeees daddy . . . that's right, you do . . .

(*Lank grinds on Bunny. Their dance is much more down'n'dirty than Chelle and Sly's.*
Caroline watches distantly. She enjoys the scene . . . and Lank.
Chelle drifts into Sly's arms. Relaxed. Free, if only for a moment.
Caroline giggles with amusement.
Chelle is brought back to reality. She pulls away from Sly, who works hard not to let her go.)

CHELLE: Go'on now, Sylvester. Lemme go.

SLY: Come on, sweet Chelle. Why you don't never let me keep you in my arms for a time?

CHELLE: Go'on now. Let go a me.

SLY: Say now, woman. I know I smell good. Don't you wanna be close to this sweet cologne I done bought with my new money?

CHELLE: I say let go. Leave me be. I got work to do.

(Eventually Chelle wins. She moves toward the bar. Sylvester absorbs the rejection. Beat.)

Come on down, Caroline. You got the chips?

CAROLINE: Sure . . . I just didn't want to disturb—

CHELLE: You wasn't disturbing nothing. Folks'll be showing up in a few. *(Looks at the bowl)* Oh naw . . . that ain't the right bowl. We gonna need somethin' bigger than that. And some more cups. And I need to write out the prices next to stuff 'fore folks think this is some kinda charity liquor. You can help me with that too. And Bunny—

(Bunny and Lank continue to groove, unconcerned with anything else.)

Lank! Ya'll need to finish stockin' this bar.

(Slowly and reluctantly, Lank pulls away from Bunny.)

LANK: I'll be back to finish my dance later. You make sure don't nobody fill my card.

BUNNY: You at the top, baby.

(Lank taps Bunny on the bottom and heads over to the bar.)

I'll come up there with ya'll, Chelle. Tell Bunny what you need her to do . . .

CHELLE: Well good . . . in that case . . . you can start with the chip dip. It's gonna need some dill . . . And maybe show Caroline how to mix that next batch of Kool-Aid . . .

(Chelle, Bunny and Caroline head up the stairs and disappear. Sly joins Lank at the bar, stocking the liquor.)

SLY: You talk to Chelle some more 'bout Shepling's bar?

LANK: Yeah man. I tried to convince her. She ain't movin' on the subject.

SLY: Peanut say that property could be goin' up if we don't move fast. Say them Italian mobster boys, them Greek boys, them Jewish boys . . . they all been lookin' to buy up some of the empty properties in the city. We don't buy this stuff up, won't be no colored folks owning nothin' over here.

LANK: They gonna hijack our idea and leave us out!

SLY: That's what I'm sayin' to you. Unrest happening every-where, even down at the plants. Peanut say colored men startin' to organize and let folks know they ain't takin' the short end of the stick no more. We got to do the same over here 'fore we lose everything we got.

LANK: I hear you, man. But what I'm gon' tell Chelle?

SLY: Tell her the truth . . . after. *(Beat)* Shep be at his bar tomor-row mornin'. We can get the jump on them other boys. *(Shift)* Maybe Chelle wrong this time.

(Loaded beat.)

LANK: In the morn. You and me. We goin' down to Shep's . . . and we gonna get that bar . . .

SLY: My maaan . . .

(Sly pats Lank on the back.)

LANK: Just got to figure out how to tell Chelle . . .

(The sound of cars pulling up to the house.)

CHELLE *(From off)*: Hey Lank! Turn on that music! The folks is here!

LANK: I got it! *(To Sly)* Here goes nothin' . . .

(Lank puts on an 8-track. The music swells . . .)

SCENE FIVE

Lights up on Chelle. She stands at the bar and counts out money.

CHELLE *(To herself)*: Ninety-seven, ninety-eight, ninety-nine . . . two hundred.

(Caroline enters from the washroom, drying her hair.)

We did good last night.

CAROLINE: Did we?

CHELLE: Sure enough. You worked this room like a little butterfly. Luring them fellas into your cocoon. Got Harold and Peanut spending more money in this place than I've ever seen.

CAROLINE: Just doin' my part . . .

CHELLE: You served up those drinks faster then Lank ever could. I should keep you around and send him on.

(Caroline laughs. Chelle looks at her.)

How's that gash coming?

CAROLINE: Oh. *(Beat)* It's fine.

CHELLE: Healing okay?

CAROLINE: I suppose so.

CHELLE: You ought to keep putting that ointment on it 'fore it gets worse.

CAROLINE: Oh right . . . Okay . . .

> (Beat.
>> Chelle counts out money and hands it to Caroline.)

CHELLE: Here you go . . . Twenty dollars. From the tip jar, like we agreed.

CAROLINE: Thanks.

CHELLE: I'm goin' out to run a few errands for tonight's joint. You hear Lank come in, just tell him for me.

CAROLINE: I'll let him know.

CHELLE: Don't know if it's my decorations or Lank's 8-track player or Mama and Daddy's house . . . or you . . . But one of them four is real good for business around here . . .

> (Chelle folds her money and puts it in an envelope.)

Be back soon . . .

> (Chelle exits up the steps. Caroline looks around herself. She counts her money again.)

CAROLINE: Fifteen . . . twenty . . .

> (She moves to the clothesline and finds a safety pin. She pins the money to the inside of her bra. She is meticulous. She's done this before.
>> Caroline looks around the basement, slightly bored. She heads to the 8-track player.
>> She filters through the tapes and chooses Marvin Gaye. "How Sweet It Is (To Be Loved by You)" plays.

Caroline dances to the song with reckless abandon.
She finds a pole, goes to it. Dances with it like a lover.
Lank opens the door to the basement and stands at the bal-
cony. Caroline dances—oblivious. Lank watches with a smile
and enjoys Caroline's moves.
Finally, she turns and sees him staring.)

LANK: Hey there.

(Beat. Caroline is frozen. Marvin sings on. Lank smiles. Caroline
moves over to the player and stops the tape as Lank approaches.)

CAROLINE: Shit—I'm so sorry / for bothering with—
LANK: No need for sorry / you ain't did nothing—
CAROLINE: I shouldn't have / been messing in your things—
LANK: It's all right. / I'm not protesting—
CAROLINE: I'm so embarrassed.
LANK: Don't need to be embarrassed. Just dancing.
CAROLINE: I had no business in your music. I was just . . . curi-
    ous—that's all . . .
LANK: Curious is okay with me. I like curious. *(Beat)* You like
    Motown?
CAROLINE: Yeah . . . I like it . . .
LANK: Yeah? Who you diggin' on?
CAROLINE: I don't know, um . . . all the groups you have here.
    Temptations. Four Tops. Gladys Knight and the Pips.
LANK: You know about Gladys Knight and the Pips?
CAROLINE: Sure. The Supremes. Martha and the Vandellas.
LANK: You diggin' on Negro music?
CAROLINE: Somethin' wrong with that?
LANK: Maybe not. *(Beat)* What you dig about it?
CAROLINE: Depends on who's singing.
LANK: What about the Temptations?

CAROLINE: The Temps? Their dance moves—total synchronicity. Their harmony . . . their bass . . . it's what all music should be made of . . .

LANK: Mary Wells.

CAROLINE: Voice like cashmere. Real sweet sounding . . .

LANK: Listen at you!—Marvin Gaye?

CAROLINE: Now Marvin is something altogether different. His voice can just sort of . . . pull on you . . .

LANK: How you mean?

CAROLINE: Like . . . I don't know . . . like tug at someplace deep in you. Somewhere no one else can touch and just . . . moves you in a way you didn't even know you could be moved, you know?

LANK: Yeaaah . . . moves you real good . . .

(Beat. Getting a lil' hot in here.)

CAROLINE: Yep it's . . . good music . . .

(Lank approaches the fuse box, opens it.)

LANK: Hope I'm not intruding on you . . .

CAROLINE: Not at all . . .

LANK: Just wanna check the fuse box. Almost shut the party down last night when I blew that fuse. Worst thing in the world is to be the DJ when the music stops playing before quittin' time. Folks'll be ready to chop off your neck.

(Lank flicks switches on the fuse box. He goes to the 8-track player.)

Think I'm gonna change that extension cord, too. 8-track player is a new breed. My sister don't get that. I try to tell her, this is changin' the way we hear music. And we got to change with it. *(Beat)* You heard the difference? The cassette sound? Real smooth, wasn't it?

CAROLINE: It was. Sounded really good last night. Folks were dancing so hard, I swear I saw the walls sweating.

LANK: Yeah . . . now that's what a party is supposed to do. You ever dance till the walls sweat?

CAROLINE: Not dance . . .

(Beat. Getting even hotter. Need to cool down.)

LANK: I wouldn't have picked you for a lover of Negro music.

CAROLINE: What's wrong with Negro music?

LANK: Nothin's wrong with it. Just seem like you'd listen to those ol' classical cats. Beethoven or Chopin. Them piano dudes.

CAROLINE: What's a Beethoven?

LANK: What's a Beethoven?!

(Caroline laughs and shakes her head. Lank looks at her.)

Ohhh . . . I see . . . You pullin' my leg. Havin' a little fun with me . . .

CAROLINE: Maybe.

LANK: So you like Negro music. I like Negro music. But only one of us is a real Negro.

CAROLINE: Maybe.

LANK: Maybe?

(Caroline laughs and shakes her head again.)

Ohh . . . you like to joke a lot. Like to play with me, hunh?

(Caroline shrugs. Lank looks at her, intrigued. She returns his look. Quick beat.

Lank finishes at the fuse box. He moves over to the 8-track player and changes the extension cord.

Caroline moseys across the basement floor. She brushes past the walls. The little brown girl. The four-pointed star. The black fist.)

CAROLINE: Who's the artist?

(Lank looks up. Caroline points to the star.)

LANK: Artist? . . . You mean that thing?

CAROLINE: It's interesting.

LANK: Chelle drew that . . . long time ago. My ol' man—he used to have me and Chelle down here all the time. Gave us permission to write on the walls. "Mark your territory," he used to say. So . . . we did.

CAROLINE: She like stars?

LANK: Did she? Would make stars outta everything. Christmas lights. Dominos. Pencils. Whatever.

CAROLINE: And this?

(Caroline points to the lumpy-faced brown girl.)

LANK: That's supposed to be Chelle. I drew it for her. Six years old. Tryin' to be thoughtful. But she started crying and told Mama I was trying to make her look ugly on purpose. She tried to make me wash it off . . . but Pops convinced Mama it was art, and that we'd laugh about it one day. *(Beat)* Chelle still ain't laughed yet.

CAROLINE: You draw the fist too?

LANK: Nah. Pops drew that. Said it was Joe Louis's fist. Said the Brown Bomber was gonna always be a champ in this house. "That black fist is gonna set us free." That's what my ol' man would say.

CAROLINE: You were close to your folks.

LANK: Pretty tight-knit. Whole family. You?

CAROLINE: No, I . . . no. My folks split when I was a kid. We don't really talk much. I'm kind of a loner.

LANK: Oh . . .

CAROLINE: But your folks . . . they gave you lots, hunh?

LANK: Didn't have much, but they had this house. That's one thing they had. Both of 'em—hard workers. Mama would fry hair right upstairs in that kitchen—

CAROLINE: Fry hair?

LANK: You know . . . with the hot comb on the stove? *(Beat. Nothing)* Anyway, Pops was an auto man. Ford Motor Company. Served 'em till his death half a year ago. He tried to get me in there . . . but that auto stuff ain't for me. I ain't never been one for a whole lotta up and down when my heart is into somethin' else.

CAROLINE: Somethin' else like what?

LANK: Doin' for myself. Finding somewhere to really be somebody and have something that no one can take from me. You know?

CAROLINE: Yeah, sure . . . *(Beat)* But how . . . I mean . . . how do you get that, you know?

LANK: Me—I bought some property over here. Gonna open up my own business.

CAROLINE: Yeah?

LANK: That's the plan. Just hopin' it's the right one. Ain't settle in me easy yet.

CAROLINE: Maybe that's good. If it was too easy, it probably wouldn't be worth much. At least you got a plan. That's good to have. Keeps you believing in something.

LANK: What you believe in?

CAROLINE: I . . . *(Beat)* I don't really know anymore. Things I thought I believed—changed. It's like I woke up and suddenly I'm not the same person I thought I was. I'm just in this moment and . . . everything before it is

bullshit. *(Beat)* It's good you found something for yourself. I wish.

(Lank looks at Caroline.)

LANK: Say—what happened to you?
CAROLINE: Oh . . . um . . .
LANK: Somebody hurt you.
CAROLINE: Langston, I—
LANK: Lank.
CAROLINE: Lank. I just . . . think it's best to leave that night in
     the past.
LANK: You sure it's gonna stay there?

(Beat. Lank approaches Caroline slowly.)

When I saw you out there that night . . . somethin' hap-
pened. I saw you look at me. Heard you without no words.
You know what I mean?
CAROLINE: You heard me . . .
LANK: It don't make a lotta sense, I know . . . me bein' what
     I am and you—but in that moment, all the trouble could
     come on me ain't matter. Only thing mattered was that
     I felt you needin' somethin'. Couldn't pull away.

(Lank steps closer to Caroline. She inhales.)

CAROLINE *(Nearly breathless)*: What'd you feel . . .

*(Lank doesn't answer. Instead, he takes another step closer. They
stare at each other for an extended moment . . . dangerously
close . . . on the brink of a kiss . . .*
     The door to the basement flies opens as Chelle enters.)

CHELLE: Hey Caroline—is there any more ice in that freez—

(Caroline quickly moves away from Lank.
Chelle stops when she sees Lank and Caroline alone. The silence is revealing. Chelle looks to Lank with instant disapproval. Her eyes bore holes through him.
Uncomfortable silence. Air. Tension. Thickness. Long, long beat.)

CAROLINE: I . . . think we're out of ice . . .

(Chelle's eyes remain on Lank. She makes no contact with Caroline as she answers.)

CHELLE: Freezer in the garage . . . got plenty . . .
CAROLINE: Should I go out back and bring some in?
CHELLE: That'd be good . . .
CAROLINE: No problem . . .

(Caroline walks past Lank and moves toward the steps. She passes Chelle, who remains focused on Lank.)

Be right back . . .

(Caroline leaves.
Chelle glares at Lank for like an eternity. Disapproval and disgust shoot from her eyes.
Lank feels the impulse of shame at first, but then suddenly looks back at Chelle defiantly.
Finally, Chelle turns and leaves.
Lank remains still . . . contemplative.)

SCENE SIX

Nighttime in the basement. Caroline lies on the couch, sleeping restlessly. Indistinct voices of a crowd are heard from outside.

Caroline abruptly awakens.

Beat. She sits in the silence, restless and uneasy.

Suddenly, the faint sound of an alarm. A police siren moments later.

Caroline listens to the sounds for a moment in stillness. As they increase in volume, she moves toward them with concern.

Lank bursts into the basement. He halts when he sees Caroline awake.

LANK: Oh—hey . . .

(Lank heads down the stairs carefully but deliberately. He begins to search for something.)

CAROLINE: Hey.

LANK: Sorry to wake you. Need to grab my flashlight.

CAROLINE: It's okay—I wasn't . . . Everything okay?

LANK: Nah—it's a lot of trouble going on out there.

CAROLINE: What kind of trouble?

LANK: One of the joints up the street got raided. Cops went in there beatin' on folks and bustin' ass. Folks out there mad as hell and now that joint is on fire.

CAROLINE: What? Oh God . . .

LANK: They sayin' they 'bout to head to some of the businesses down the block and raise some more hell. *(Beat)* I got to get on down there.

CAROLINE: You don't think that folks'll—

LANK: Not if I can help it.

*(Lank begins to search through some boxes.
Chelle enters the basement in her robe.)*

CHELLE: Lank, you hear all that noise outside? Them ain't still folks from our joint, is it?

LANK: No, Chelle. It's a bunch of trouble. Leave it be.

CHELLE: What took you so long to drop everybody home?

LANK: Dukes' spot is on fire.

CHELLE: What?!?!

LANK: Couldn't hardly get the truck past for all the commotion. I got to go get Sly and get on down there.

CHELLE: Go'on down there for what?! Ain't no need for you joinin' in that business!

LANK: I ain't joinin' in Chelle. *(Shift)* Where the flashlight? I always put it in this box!

CHELLE: Lank you better stay here and don't go gettin' involved in this mess.

(Lank feverishly searches through more boxes. Drawers. Shelves.)

LANK: I'm already involved, Chelle. *(Shift)* Found it. Where the batteries?

CHELLE: Lank—

LANK *(Snapping)*: Chelle, where the batteries?!

*(Chelle—startled—jumps to search for the batteries.
Caroline—also frightened—jumps to help.)*

CHELLE *(Nervously)*: Lank—you better tell me what's going on. Why you gotta go out there and get involved in this craziness?

(Lank stops. He looks at Chelle squarely.)

LANK: Because I got to protect our business, Chelle. Me and Sly . . . we done put up the money for Shepling's.

CHELLE: You did what?!

LANK: I was gonna tell you after the deal was final. I swear I was.

(Caroline pulls batteries from a box.)

CAROLINE: D batteries. These work?

(Lank nods and grabs the batteries.)

CHELLE: You gave up our money?!

LANK: I had to act fast, Chelle.

CHELLE *(Stunned)*: You . . . you just gave it up? All of it?

LANK: I did what felt right to me, Chelle. Okay?

CHELLE: No! It's not okay!!! You gave your word. You looked me in my face and gave your word! Didn't belong to you! Belonged to *us*!!! And you just throw it all away?!?!

LANK: I ain't throw it away, Chelle! I'ma take care of it! *(Beat)* I ain't got time to stand around and feel bad about it. I got to try and convince these folks not to burn us down.

(Lank grabs a bat from a corner and heads up the basement stairs.)

Damn!

CHELLE: Lank—

LANK: Just stay here. I'ma make this right.

(Lank disappears. Chelle is left with Caroline—dumbfounded. Blackout.)

ACT TWO

Lights up on Chelle hanging clothes on the line and tending to the laundry.

    Bunny tap-taps at the basement door and peers in.

BUNNY: Hey, Chelle—you doin' all right?

CHELLE: I'm doin'.

BUNNY: Honey, you hear about all this craziness goin' on since last night?

CHELLE: I heard.

BUNNY: Girl, Lucky's is on fire now.

CHELLE: You kiddin' me?!

BUNNY: Naw . . . I ain't. Folks been goin' and goin' last few hours. Ain't stopped. Folks sayin' them pigs went into the Dukes' and started all kinds a hell. Beat on Buddy Johnson so bad his head damn near cracked open. Even had Martha Briggs on the floor . . . kickin' her in the stomach and everything.

CHELLE: Jesus.

BUNNY: Girl, the folks is so mad about these pigs . . . they think they fightin' back.

CHELLE: What kinda way is that to fight back? Runnin' 'round burnin' up the city? That ain't hurtin' nobody but us.

BUNNY: What you doin' down here with your laundry? Ain't you been outside to see what's what? Twelfth Street lookin' like some kinda smoke bomb been set off.

CHELLE: I don't wanna see. Besides, Lank said to stay put while he run to check on . . . this damned bar. If I don't keep busy with somethin', I might lose my mind.

BUNNY: Girl, me too. My mama and 'nem done left and went over to Toledo to stay with my Aunt Bobbie. They ain't even wanna stick around to see what's gonna come from this mess. *(Beat)* Let me help you. I got to keep busy too.

(Bunny picks up some laundry and begins pinning it to the line.)

CHELLE: Took me three tries to get through to Julius this morning. Some of the phone lines is down.

BUNNY: You ain't worryin' him none, I hope. It's best he stay right on down there at that school.

CHELLE: He doin' real well. Say he met him a girl. She from Tennessee. She got more brains than even him, he says. Gonna bring her home for Christmas.

BUNNY: If Detroit still standin' by Christmastime . . .

CHELLE: I just don't wanna think about it . . . let's talk about somethin' else . . .

(Bunny looks around.)

BUNNY: Where the white girl?

CHELLE: Upstairs in the shower.

BUNNY: Well lemme tell you . . . I done put out to my fishes and somethin' done bit back. I got some news 'bout your lil' hired help.

CHELLE: You done found something 'bout her? From who?

BUNNY: Stubby.

CHELLE: Aww—girl!

BUNNY: Now you know he do the books for some of them businessmen downtown that run all those nightclubs. He say a white girl who used to work over at the Red Stallion come up missin'—'bout three–four days ago now.

CHELLE: Red Stallion? That dancin' club? One where the women be on stage in all that frimpy underwear?

BUNNY: That's what Stubby say.

CHELLE: Girl, get on. Stubby got the wrong white girl. Caroline don't hardly look like nobody's dirty dancer.

BUNNY: Ain't said she was one of the dancers. Just say she used to work over there. That's all Stubby say.

(Chelle is momentarily quiet.)

CHELLE: What else a woman do at the Red Stallion besides dance?

BUNNY: Waitress. Work the bar and the patrons. Trust me, I know.

(Chelle looks at Bunny incredulously.)

Don't look at me like I got some kinda titty in the middle of my forehead. I know cuz I hear stuff . . . not cuz of nothin' else!

CHELLE: If she workin' at that club, she workin' around all them dirty men who go there.

BUNNY: Say she used to fool around with this big-time cop who hung there sometimes. Both white and colored men get down in there . . . colored men with money, anyway. Bet she be servin' up some Bali Hai. You can take a colored outta the ghetto but you can't get rid of his nigger taste. She probably make a full hundred on a good night.

CHELLE: She makin' money like that, what she need to stay here for? Stubby tell you anything else?

BUNNY: That's 'bout as much as I could get outta him 'fore the pigs showed up—nosin' around. I split.

CHELLE: They got business with Stubby?

BUNNY: Ain't sure. But I tell you this much, if that white gal come up missin', she got the law lookin' for her fa sho. Must got somethin' to hide . . .

(A bang at the basement door.)

SLY *(From off)*: Chelle? You home?

CHELLE: I'm down here, Sylvester!

(Sly opens the door and enters hastily. He looks worn and disheveled. His clothes are a mess. His face is sleepless. Chelle and Bunny gasp at the sight of him.)

SLY: I was hopin' ya'll was gonna be here.

BUNNY: Sly, what's the matter with you? You look a mess!

CHELLE: Where's Lank?

SLY: Chelle, listen here. We done got into some trouble.

CHELLE: What kinda trouble?! Where's my brother?

SLY: They took him downtown.

CHELLE: At the jailhouse?!?!

BUNNY: He got arrested?

SLY: Big Four came up on us at Shepling's. Saw us down there checkin' on the space and accused us of tryin' to loot.

BUNNY: Oh naw!

CHELLE: Did ya'll show 'em your papers and prove that it was your spot?

SLY: Wasn't nothin' to show yet. Still got to get the papers changed in our name.

CHELLE: Did ya'll explain that to them?

SLY: They wasn't listenin' to all of that, Chelle. They come on us shinin' flashlights in our faces tellin' us to get the hell outta there. So Lank, he got a lil' too angry. He started shinin' his flashlight right back.

CHELLE: No!

SLY: They grabbed us, Chelle. Threw us both in the car and took us downtown. Peanut came to bail us out. But they wouldn't let go a Lank. Say we gotta pay more for his bail and Peanut ain't have enough. Wouldn't give Lank his phone call or nothin'.

CHELLE: They got my brother! Lord—we gotta go get him!

BUNNY: You need some more money?

CHELLE: I got it . . . upstairs . . . I got a lil' stash.

SLY: Come on. We take my pickup.

BUNNY: I'll wait here for ya'll.

CHELLE: My brother . . . goddamnit . . . not my brother!

(Chelle and Sly rush up the stairs and out.)

BUNNY: Stay clear of that fire out there!

(Bunny sits alone for a moment, unsure of what to do. She moves to the 8-track, picks up cartridges.
Caroline enters the basement.)

CAROLINE: Where's Michelle going? Is everything okay?

BUNNY: Naw . . . it ain't . . .

CAROLINE: What . . . did something happen?

BUNNY *(Ignoring her)*: How the hell you work this player . . .

CAROLINE: What's going on?

BUNNY: Don't you worry. They'll be back. Just a big mess outside. Negroes mad. Po-lice mad. Even white folks mad. *(Beat)* Just tell me how to play this thing 'fore I get mad too and start breakin' shit up in here . . .

CAROLINE: Where's Lank?

(Beat.)

BUNNY: He's in jail. They gone to bail him out.

(Bunny looks back through the 8-tracks and selects one.
    Caroline quickly moves to the couch. She lifts the pillow and pulls out her stash.
    Then she rushes back up the basement stairs.)

Where you headin'?

CAROLINE: I . . . sorry I have to go . . .

BUNNY: It's a real mess out there, girl . . . you crazy?

CAROLINE: Sorry—I just have to go . . .

(Bunny attempts to refute her, but doesn't get the chance. Caroline is already out the door.
    Bunny looks at the 8-track player with frustration. She tries to work it to no avail.
    The room closes in on her. She looks for a release.
    Finally she whacks the player with her hand angrily.)

BUNNY: Gotdamnit, play me some music!

(Bunny screams in frustration.
    Lights out.)

SCENE TWO

Late night in the basement. The lamp is on. Bunny lies asleep across the couch—wildly. Legs going every whichaway.

"My Baby Loves Me" by Martha and the Vandellas plays on the 8-track player.

Chelle enters the basement, followed by Lank. There are visible bruises on his face. Greens. Blues. Yellows. Dried blood by his temples.

CHELLE: Come on and rest up while I put somethin' on that gash.

(Lank follows quietly. He sits on a chair next to the sofa. Chelle goes to the 8-track player and turns it off.)

LANK: What'd you do that for?
CHELLE: Too loud.
LANK: Was just fine to me . . .

(Chelle goes to the freezer and digs through it. Bunny moves in her sleep and slowly wakes up.)

BUNNY: Ooo . . . what time is it? I passed out . . .
LANK: It's late.
BUNNY: Ooooh Jesus—what'd they do to you?

(Bunny takes a good look at Lank.)

LANK: Sssssshhhhh . . . you don't wanna know . . .
CHELLE: Put their goddamn hands on him. That's what they did.

(Chelle brings over a steak and places it over Lank's eye. He flinches.)

BUNNY: What they charge you with?

LANK: Didn't end up chargin' nothing. Said I was comin' down there to rob the place and they would hold me till I cracked. But when I didn't, one of 'em finally called Shep and he told 'em the truth.

BUNNY: Damn baby, they roughed you up pretty awful . . .

LANK: Jefferson . . . the one named Jefferson, I think . . . he was the real bastard. Mad at me for bein' a uppity kinda nigger. Motherfucker musta had steel or iron in his boot. Shit hurt worse than any kick I ever felt.

CHELLE: I can't even listen to this no more.

LANK: Sorry, Bunny. Chelle get sensitive about it.

BUNNY: Honey, me too.

(Chelle wrings out a cloth and wipes Lank's temples.)

CHELLE: These cops coulda killed you. They been known to shoot us for less. And you sittin' up here shining your light in that officer's face like it's some kinda game.

LANK: That's what you think this is Chelle? You think it's a game to me?

CHELLE: I think you act outta impulse without thinkin' nothin' through. Just like puttin' our money into this damn bar—

LANK: Awww—I knew this was comin'—

CHELLE: Damn right it's comin'! You had no right to take that money—

LANK: Money belong to me too—

CHELLE: Mama and Daddy scraped to earn that. Broke they backs to give us somethin' to stand on, not for you to throw into some foolishness—

LANK: It's not foolishness—

CHELLE: —without gettin' no papers—

LANK: Got to get the papers transferred. This is how it works over here—it ain't by the books but it's legit—

CHELLE: —without tellin' me the plan . . . You just blow it all on some ol' white man's word like some kinda fool!

LANK: I'm not a fool, damnit! I listen to you, all we ever gon' do is be quiet and safe and never have nothin' better than what we got!

CHELLE: You always tryin' to have somethin' better! But what Mama and Daddy gave us is already fine without you tryin' to change it or replace it. Ain't nothin' wrong with what we got!

LANK: Ain't said it was nothin' wrong with it! But life ain't just about keepin' what you got. It's about buildin' somethin' new. You gon' see that Chelle.

CHELLE: I'm gon' see Mama and Daddy's hard-earned money go right down the toilet cuz of your selfishness! That's what I'm gon' see!

(Beat. Silent fuming. Bunny remains quiet and observant.)

BUNNY: Well ya'll—much as I love me a good ol' family throw-down . . . I better get on to my ol' man. He probably think I'm layin' up with some other moe by now.

CHELLE: Where's Caroline?

BUNNY: Oh yeah . . . she took off.

LANK: Took off? You mean, she left?

BUNNY: Ran outta here like the devil was chasin' her.

LANK: She comin' back?

BUNNY: She ain't say. But them bus and train stations full of folks tryin' to get outta Dodge. She be real lucky to hop on somethin' tonight.

CHELLE: Maybe it's for the best.

LANK: Maybe she come back.

(Bunny walks over to Lank and touches his face tenderly.)

BUNNY: I was real worried about you, honey. You just . . . you be careful for me . . .

(She kisses him sweetly on the forehead.)

CHELLE: Bunny, you need me to call Sly to give you a ride? They still settin' fires out there.

BUNNY: Oh naw, honey. I took the ol' man's car. That Cadillac across the street . . . that's me . . . *(Smiles)* Bunny be just fine . . .

(Bunny exits.
Lank and Chelle are quiet. Lank moves over to the couch and stretches out for a moment. Chelle straightens up for a moment.)

CHELLE: You goin' to bed? Get you some rest.

LANK: I'm just gonna stay down here for a minute.

(A moment.)

CHELLE: She may be gone, Lank.

LANK: I'm gonna stay down here. Listen to me some music.

CHELLE: What is it you seein' in her?

LANK: What's that?

CHELLE: You think I don't notice? How you lookin' at her. How you dance close to her flame. You think I don't see?

LANK: Chelle, you just bein' paranoid.

CHELLE: Ain't never see you look that way at Bunny. You toy with her like she's your plaything. But you ain't doin' that with Caroline. You treat her like somethin' to be taken serious. I don't know what you doin', but it's something more dangerous. That's all I know.

LANK: She's all right, Chelle.

CHELLE: She's a white woman, Lank. Maybe you ain't noticed, but I have.

LANK: I noticed, Chelle.

CHELLE: That's what I'm afraid of. It's like . . . you get around her and you get further and further away from reality. Forgettin' who you are and what this world can do to you. You come in here with your new 8-track player and your new bar and this white woman, and you think you somebody you ain't.

LANK: Why can't I just do what I do without it bein' about somethin' else? Hunh? Just for once?! *(Sudden twinge)* Sssssssstttt . . .

(Chelle jumps to his aid. She gently tends the wound. Beat.)

CHELLE: Gonna need some time to heal.

LANK: I know.

CHELLE: Ain't seen your face like this in a long time.

LANK: I know.

CHELLE: Not since you was like . . . seven or eight. You got into that fight with Patrice Cooper. You remember that?

LANK *(Laughs faintly)*: Yeah. She clobbered me good.

CHELLE: I didn't care that she was littler than me. I was ready to come down there and knock that brat into the middle of next week.

LANK: You musta knocked her into the middle of next lifetime, cuz I don't think I ever saw her around school after that.

(They laugh for a moment.)

CHELLE: When I'd get mad at you about somethin', Daddy always reminded me that you were my little brother and it was my job to defend you to anybody who tried to mess with you.

LANK: Yeah, that's Pops.

CHELLE: It was my job to love you best. That's what he'd say. *(Beat)* Lank, this is you and me. All of this. That poster of Joe Louis. That ugly picture you drew of me. That pole I used to dance with and pretend it was my boyfriend. Daddy's black fist. Those dashes on the wall where you tried to prove to me you were growing. And now, even that ugly velvet painting . . .

(Lank is about to object . . . then concedes.)

This is always gonna be you and me. We stuck together by the root. You my baby brother. You and Julius . . . you the only two guys in my life that matter anymore. And I'm not gonna just sit back and let you get beat up by nobody. Not Patrice Cooper. Not the pigs. Not even yourself. *(Beat)* I love you best. Just like Daddy told me to. Ain't nothin' can come along and be better than that . . .

(Chelle gives Lank a kiss on the forehead.)

Don't be up too late. You need to rest . . .

LANK: Night, Chelle . . . I be fine.

CHELLE: Night, Lank.

(Chelle leaves the basement.
Lank moves to the 8-track player. He plays "People Get Ready" by the Impressions.
Lank sits and enjoys.
The basement door opens. It's Caroline.
Beat. They stare at each other for a moment.)

LANK: I thought you left.

CAROLINE: I did.

LANK: You went lookin' for me?

CAROLINE: I ummm . . .

LANK (*Disappointed*): Oh.

(*Beat.*)

When you leave?

CAROLINE: Tomorrow night.

LANK: What's the rush?

CAROLINE: It's just better if I leave. Would've left tonight but I . . . (*Pause. A moment of truth*) *You* . . .

(*Beat. Caroline sees Lank's bruises.*)

God . . . what . . . did the . . . cops do that?

LANK: Yeah . . . they like to play rough with my kind . . .

CAROLINE: Shit . . .

LANK: This bar I got goin' . . . they didn't believe I was gonna be the owner. They beat on us to keep us aimin' low. Soon as we aim high, they know Detroit gonna be a nigger city and not theirs. I'm gonna show them what's what when I got my own spot.

(*Beat. Caroline stares at Lank with concern.*)

CAROLINE: Lank?

LANK: Yeah?

CAROLINE: I think you should be careful.

LANK: What d'you mean?

CAROLINE: I know these kind of men . . . crooked law men . . . And they're not easy to cross. Believe me, I know.

(Pause. Lank studies Caroline intently.)

LANK: How you know?

(Caroline is silent.)

That night . . . those were cops. That's who hurt you?

CAROLINE: I was involved with one. Met him at my job. Cocktail waitressing at the Red Stallion. He was always my biggest tipper.

LANK: Why would he . . .

CAROLINE: I wanted him to settle down but . . . that was never his plan. *(Beat)* Threatened to tell his wife. That's why he . . .

LANK: Huh.

CAROLINE: I was with him sometimes when he'd take money from folks. Criminals. On the payroll of some of the worst kind of men. Illegal businesses. There's plenty of it in Detroit . . . not just on this side of town. I was with him when he'd ride around in certain parts . . . looking for folks to . . . give a hard time. One time I saw him beat this . . . colored man . . . said he looked up to no good . . . beat him so bad his face looked . . . distorted or . . . something . . . like a monster. That's how I'd picture him in my mind sometimes. A hideous monster. *(Beat)* Maybe he even deserved it. I thought that sometimes too . . .

LANK: Deserved it? That's what you think?

CAROLINE: No, I don't—umm . . . *(Beat)* You tell yourself things so you don't feel . . . so you can go to sleep at night. Otherwise, you'd never . . . sleep at all . . .

LANK: He so low-down . . . why'd you dig on him?

CAROLINE: I don't know what to say. I could say he took care of me. That's partly true. With money mostly. Security. But there was another part . . . the part that hurt but . . . still felt good enough. Like he was at least there . . . a constant . . . for a while anyway. And I could take the hurt that came with him much more than having nothing at all. Cuz having nothing . . . that's complete bullshit. Bullshit way to live.

(Lank stares at Caroline.)

You think I'm scum, right?

LANK: You're not those folks.

CAROLINE: How can you be so sure?

LANK: I ain't sure. I just . . . got a feeling . . .

(Beat.)

CAROLINE: That night I was with him . . . at a motel as usual. I was sick of it. We got into an argument. And he hit me . . . a lot. Passed out drunk. So I split . . . fast as I could. Pain was so bad I couldn't think. If you hadn't stopped for me . . .

LANK: But I did. Found you. Kept you safe.

CAROLINE: I know. I'm safer here than anywhere I've been in my whole life. *(Beat)* But you're not. Not if I stay. The things I've seen . . . if they find even a thread between us, it'll bring you a whole new kind of trouble, Lank. I can't stay here.

LANK: Where you gonna go?

CAROLINE: Across the border. Windsor. After that, wherever the feeling takes me.

LANK: What about the feeling right here?

(Beat.)

CAROLINE: That night you said you felt me needing something . . . what was it?

LANK: Somewhere to be . . .

(Caroline smiles faintly.)

CAROLINE: Yeah . . . *(Beat)* You know . . . you have this way of seeing things inside that just . . . makes people wanna be better. *(Pause)* If we both find wherever that place is . . . to really be somebody . . . I hope we'll see each other there.

(Beat. Lank studies Caroline.)

LANK: Say . . . you wanna hear a song?

CAROLINE: Yeah . . .

(Lank goes to the 8-track player.)

LANK: I don't want you to say nothin' much, okay? Just listen to the words.

CAROLINE: Okay . . .

LANK: Close your eyes.

(Caroline does.
Gladys Knight and the Pips' "Everybody Needs Love" plays.
Lank sits and closes his eyes also.)

You feel that, Caroline?

CAROLINE: Yeah . . . I do . . .

(Lights fade on Lank and Caroline.)

SCENE THREE

Chelle cleans the basement, sweeping, dusting corners and cobwebs.
From outside, the occasional sound of a tank rolling by. It jars
Chelle each time.
"It's the Same Old Song" by the Four Tops plays on the record
player. It skips a couple of times. Chelle smoothly moves the needle past
the skip and continues cleaning.
Sly enters the basement with a newspaper in his hands.

SLY: Hey there, Chelle. Where Lank?

CHELLE *(Dryly)*: He's not here, Sylvester.

SLY: We got us a meeting at Shep's today. Four o'clock. Furman got somebody bringing us the papers in our name. I figured I'd stop by to see if he wanted to go over there together.

CHELLE: Well he's not here.

SLY: I'll wait for him. Better I don't be hanging around out there. *(Beat)* You know where he is?

CHELLE: No. *(Beat)* Woke up this morning and he wasn't here. Just me cleanin' and Caroline up there fixin' a bite. No Lank.

SLY: Hope he ain't go down by Grand Boulevard. Folks is gathering to throw rocks and all kinds of stuff at them police. Mayor Cavanagh got them big tank boys rollin' in. Say he done called in the National Guard.

CHELLE: Heard it on the radio this mornin'. Had to turn it off.

SLY: What you turn it off for? You ain't scared is you, baby?

CHELLE: You wanna talk about scared? I stepped out on the porch this morning to a cloud of smoke. Look like we in some kinda war picture. Mean lookin' guards come down this street, hunting us like we're the enemy.

SLY: Don't you be scared, Chelle. It's gonna get cleaned up soon. President Johnson himself gettin' involved. Say so right here in the paper.

(Sly holds out the newspaper to Chelle.)

(Reading) "Governor Romney today asked for five thousand regular army troops to reinforce seven thousand National Guardsmen and two thousand policemen in quelling Detroit's race riot." See there? These pigs can't control us good enough. Gotta bring in the army for some order.

CHELLE: Race riot? That's what they sayin' this is?

SLY: That's what they say so. Makin' like we just hate honkies and burnin' shit up. But I wish they'd come askin' me some questions. I tell 'em—if this is about niggers hatin' honkies, then you tell me why white folks down there gettin' they lootin' in too. Naw . . . this is about pigs hatin' niggers. That's what this fire is about. *(Beat)* Be glad when we get this bar though. Soon as this stuff clears, it'll be good to start over.

CHELLE: Start over . . . hmph . . . that's what you call it.

(Chelle moves away from Sly and continues cleaning.)

SLY: Why you bein' so mean to me today, Chelle?

CHELLE: I'm busy, Sylvester.

SLY: I know why you bein' mean. You mad about me and Lank and this bar.

CHELLE: Well if you know everything, then what you askin' me questions for . . .

SLY: Come on, sweet Chelle. Don't be such a bitter candy.

CHELLE: Don't call me "sweet Chelle."

SLY: I always call you "sweet Chelle."

CHELLE: And I always hate it.

(Beat. Sly is hurt. He tries to recover.)

SLY: It was partly me, I'll admit. I wanted him to join me on this thing. Me and Lank, we like brothers, y'know.

CHELLE: He's my brother.

SLY: I just . . . I just know we both tired of all this hustlin'. Dough that comes fast one day and don't come at all the next. Got you dressed nice enough to smile at some fine woman this day, and dressed like a wino on Woodward the next. We just tired of the up and down. Of not havin' nothin' we can really put our hands on. Put our time into. That ain't a bad thing to want, is it now?

CHELLE: What if it get burned to the ground by these fools out here? Ya'll even been thinkin' 'bout that? You sign this deal and then you lose everything. What about that, hunh?

SLY: We been thinking 'bout it Chelle. We done put up signs say "Soul Brother" in the window.

CHELLE: So did Teddy Rollins and they still burned him down.

SLY: Teddy ain't us. Folks 'round here know us. They know what we tryin' to do. I done got a lotta folks over here some of they best stuff. Helped 'em find cheap cars. Take their numbers and give 'em a chance to have some extra money in their pocket that ain't gonna get taken by Uncle Sam. We good to our folks, and that counts, Chelle. But even if it burn to the ground . . . we still did somethin'. We tried.

CHELLE: You and Lank . . . ya'll both go dreamin' with your noses wide open. So wide I could run one of them tanks outside right through your nostrils.

SLY: You know your problem, woman?

CHELLE: I'm sure you gonna tell me.

SLY: You don't never let nobody hold you long enough to believe in nothin'.

CHELLE: Move on, Sylvester.

SLY: Naw Chelle, I mean it. See . . . you so worried about gettin' to tomorrow, you don't never conceive of the days and weeks and months after. Tomorrow's all right. Keeps you livin'. But if you look far enough ahead, you start to see tomorrow ain't all there is. It's plenty of days after that. And when you got somebody close to you . . . somebody to hold onto and slow dance with . . . you wanna believe in everything. You wanna believe stuff can happen that'll make you smile. You wanna dream . . . And even if the dream don't work out . . . even if it don't last . . . at least it felt real good tryin'.

CHELLE: I ain't said it was nothin' wrong with ya'll dreamin'.

SLY: You ain't said it was nothin' right with it neither. *(Beat)* It'll be somethin', Chelle. We gonna make you a believer. I been thinkin' of names to make it sound good. Sound like a place even you gonna wanna visit. Call it . . . Sly and Lank's Feel-Good Shack. That's the one I settled on. 'Course, Lank probably gonna want his name first . . . but see, that'll just mess up the good rhythm of it. Lank and Sly's Feel-Good Shack don't really make you feel that good.

(Sly moves close to Chelle.)

First night we open, I'm gonna play a special song for you.

CHELLE: Move on from me, Sylvester.

SLY: What's your favorite? Miracles? Temps? Cuz mine . . . it's the Four Tops.

CHELLE: I don't care what your favorite is.

SLY: You say you don't . . . but I think you lyin'.

(Sly touches Chelle on the arm.)

CHELLE: How many times I got to tell you to get on?

SLY: Tell me you didn't like my slow dance.

CHELLE: Sylvester, I ain't in the mood.

SLY: Tell me you didn't like for just one minute . . . my arms holding you tight . . .

(Chelle shakes her head no. Sylvester moves closer to her . . . pulls slowly and carefully on her arm. She moves toward him in spite of herself.)

Lemme hold you, Chelle.

CHELLE: Go'on now, Sly.

SLY: I like it when you call me Sylvester. Can't nobody say my name like you. *(Mocks her)* "Go'on Sylvester," "Don't slam my doors, Sylvester," "Don't touch me, Sylvester."

(Chelle laughs faintly, in spite of herself.)

CHELLE: I don't sound like that.

SLY: "Don't feel so good, Sylvester."

CHELLE: I don't say that!

SLY: "Don't be so handsome, Sylvester."

CHELLE: Now you just talkin' crazy.

SLY: "Don't love me, Sylvester . . ."

(Beat.)

CHELLE: I don't . . . I don't say that.

SLY: You know my favorite Four Tops song?

(Chelle shakes her head no. Sly grabs her into a slow dance, singing badly but sincerely.)

Now if you feel that you can't go on
Because all of your hope is gone
And your life is filled with much confusion

Until happiness is just an illusion
And your world is crumbling down, darlin'
Reach out . . . Come on girl, reach on out for me . . .

(Chelle stops dancing and looks at Sly.)

I sound good to you, baby?

(Beat.)

CHELLE: Yeah, Sylvester. You sound real good . . .

(Chelle smiles. Sly smiles back and holds her. They slow dance in silence for a moment.)

SLY: We can be somethin', Chelle. You an' me. I can make you feel like things is all right, even when they ain't. And you can do that for me. We can be that to each other.

(Chelle pulls away.)

CHELLE: I got to finish cleanin' up, Sylvester.

(Lank comes into the basement with haste.)

LANK: Sly?! There you are. We got to go'on over to Shep's now.
SLY: It's almost four? *(Checks his watch)* Oh yeah . . . yeah, I'm ready.

(Chelle cleans and tries to mask her worry. Sly notices Lank's urgency.)

What's the word?
LANK: Some boys in blue . . . Peanut say they been nosin' 'round over there. Askin' folks our whereabouts.

SLY: What they nosin' 'round for? Place is ours, fair and square.

LANK: Don't know but we got to go see. Somethin' givin' me a funny feelin' about it.

SLY: What kinda funny feelin'?

LANK: Think we better get over to our spot.

CHELLE: Lank . . . Sylvester . . . please . . . don't get into nothin' this time. Please . . .

LANK: We be fine, Chelle. Gonna get our papers and we be fine.

SLY: That's right, sweet Chelle. Don't worry your pretty face, baby. You just save Sylvester a dance for later. Reach on out for me, and I'll be there . . .

(Lank and Sly head up the steps. Sly looks back at Chelle.)

Four Tops. You an' me?

CHELLE: Fine, Sylvester.

(Lank and Sly disappear. Chelle sweeps and sweeps and sweeps . . .
The sound of a tank rolling by.
She stops sweeping and looks at the basement door.
A moment of worry.
Lights fade.)

SCENE FOUR

Lights up on Chelle and Bunny. Two half-empty glasses of wine sit before them.
The occasional sound of tanks in the background.

BUNNY: Summer's usually my favorite time in Detroit. Julys been the best. Got my first kiss in July over on Belle Isle. Right by the beach—me and Greg what's-his-name. He was fifteen and I was only twelve. We met at the family reunion. Hadn't never seen him before but me and all the other cousins thought he was all kinds of fine. Had peach fuzz and everything. Shit drove me crazy. So while everybody else was building sand castles and buryin' each other alive . . . we stole away behind the rec building and that's when we went for it. Kissin' like crazy. Let him put his tongue in and everything. Tasted like saltwater. But it was all right. Sweet but a little nasty. Just how I like it. Even let him touch me on my butt and hold it real tight. *(Beat)* Hope he wasn't a cousin.

(Chelle laughs. Bunny does too.)

After the reunion was over . . . I didn't see him no more. Didn't come back to Detroit the next time the reunion was here. All I got left to 'member him by is that saltwater taste I get in my mouth when I think of July in Detroit. *(Beat)* Wonder what my July memories are gonna be like now . . .

CHELLE: July's always been a time for barbeque and streamers. Daddy used to always let Lank light some kinda firecracker in the yard. Sound like somebody shootin' at us. Used to hate the sound. *(Beat)* Now I miss it. *(Beat)* Before Willie died, we used to take Julius and go'on down to the park and watch the fireworks off the river. I like that much better than the firecrackers in the yard. Felt more put together. Gave us something to do as a family. Grab the bucket of chicken and blankets, find us a spot on the lawn, and stay for the whole day till the show started at night. That used to be my favorite family time. Me and my fellas. Nothin' was better.

BUNNY: You always got your fellas.

CHELLE: I guess.

(Caroline enters the basement.)

CAROLINE: Oh . . . hey there ladies. Sorry to interrupt.

BUNNY: Just biding our time till Lank and Sly get back here.

CAROLINE: Just came to ask what you'd like me to do with the clothes you loaned me. They're all washed and folded upstairs.

CHELLE: Your train leave soon?

CAROLINE *(Nods)*: Before dawn.

CHELLE: That's good. You can keep that blouse and those shorts if you wanna. Don't hardly fit me no more anyway.

CAROLINE: Sure okay, thanks.

(Chelle reaches into her bosom and pulls out some bills. She approaches Caroline.)

CHELLE: Here's a little something extra. Give you some cushion. Pin it somewhere mysterious.

CAROLINE: Appreciate it. *(Shift)* Is Lank around?

(Chelle looks at Caroline and raises a brow.)

CHELLE: No. He's gone.

CAROLINE: I'll . . . stay awhile. Don't have to be at the station till an hour before.

CHELLE: May be out for a bit.

BUNNY: Way them cops over there nosin' around, could take more than a bit.

CAROLINE: Cops? You mean . . . to calm the riot?

BUNNY: Sound like they doin' more than that. Few of 'em snoopin' 'round Lank and Sly's bar.

CAROLINE: Few of 'em? For what?

BUNNY: Who knows? Cops is cops.

CAROLINE: Oh God . . .

(Caroline stares at Chelle and Bunny . . . considers . . . then:)

You've got to stop him.

CHELLE: Stop who from what?

CAROLINE: You've got to reach Lank. Tell him to stay away from there.

CHELLE: What are you talking about?

CAROLINE: The cops . . . I tried to tell him they're dangerous—

CHELLE: What are you tellin' me girl? You got police after my brother?

CAROLINE: No! I tried to warn him to be careful. There are important officers trying to keep me quiet—

CHELLE: Keep you quiet? They the ones did that number on you?

CAROLINE: They don't want me around. Not with everything I've seen—

CHELLE: And they messin' with Lank? Do they know you staying around these parts?

CAROLINE: I don't know for sure, but if Lank gets mixed up—

BUNNY: Lord, Chelle! Them cops been talkin' to Stubby!

CHELLE: You got these bad men after my brother?

CAROLINE: I'm trying to get out of here before things get worse. I tried to tell Lank—

CHELLE: You ain't tried hard enough! Been so busy cuddlin' under him you ain't worry 'bout nothin' else.

CAROLINE: Cuddling under him?

BUNNY: Chelle, it's okay.

CHELLE: Naw—it ain't okay! Ever since this girl been here it ain't been okay! I knew she was keepin' somethin'!

CAROLINE: Listen Michelle, I'm not trying to cause you any trouble—

CHELLE: All you been this whole time is a bunch of trouble! If you in bad with the cops, then we in bad with the cops. It's that simple. Messed up in something and now you puttin' it on my brother.

CAROLINE: I'm not putting anything on your brother!

CHELLE: Like hell, you ain't. You think I don't see it?

CAROLINE: See what?

CHELLE: The way you slide under Lank's nose like a perfume. Tease him with your scent so you can play him for the fool. Make him believe you an' him is the same. But you ain't the same.

CAROLINE: You don't know what you're talking about.

CHELLE: I know exactly what I'm talking about.

CAROLINE: I'm sorry that being here has caused you trouble. Believe me. But that's not my intention. Lank sees that.

CHELLE: Lank got a lotta blind spots. I got twenty-twenty. I know what it mean to have somebody like you get into his skin. He start believing things in this world is different than they really are. He start believing it's possible to be you. To live like you. To dream like you. And it ain't.

CAROLINE: How do you know it's not possible?

CHELLE: Because I do! I been living like this a lot longer than you have. Just cuz you hanging 'round over here don't mean you know what it's like to be us.

CAROLINE: I never said I did. But I know what it's like to be me! To never have a family or a place to call home. You have that, at least. You have something here . . . with each other. Something I never had with anyone . . . until Lank—

CHELLE: You ain't got that with Lank.

CAROLINE: You don't know what I have with him.

CHELLE: Oh, I know. You and him can pretend to be cut from the same cloth all you want. But outside this basement tell a different story. Lank got his eye on the sky but Detroit ain't in the sky. It's right here on the ground. A ground with a lot of dividing lines. We on one side and you on the other.

CAROLINE: And what about when the lines are blurred? When you feel something that can't be cut up or divided? When you know you belong somewhere even if people tell you you're not allowed? That's where we meet, Lank and me. Somewhere outside of all the zones and restrictions. Some place where we're not stuck. Maybe that's a place you refuse to go, but that's where someone like Lank and someone like me are exactly the same. And if you don't want to see that, maybe *you're* the one with the blind spot!

CHELLE: I'm the one with the blind spot? *(Beat)* You can run out of here right now. Leave town with these cops chasing you. They can harass you and bruise you and even try to kill you. That may make you the same. But if you survive it, you can leave. You can disappear and reappear wherever else you want, in any zone you choose. Live a new life without permission or boundaries or some kinda limits to your skin. Can Lank do that? Can any of us? Everywhere we go, the lines is real clear. Ain't nothin' blurred about it. You might dream the same. You might even feel the same heartbreak. But till *he* have the same *title* to this world that you got, you and him ain't gon' never be the same! And that ain't blindness tell me that. That's twenty-twenty.

(Loaded beat.
    Finally Bunny attempts . . .)

BUNNY: The train station got seats . . . a waiting area . . . even got a TV down there . . . some pop machines . . . You be real comfortable . . .

(Silence.)

CAROLINE: Sounds like it'll be a fine place to wait.

(Beat. Caroline heads to the stairs.
    She stops, her heart in her throat.)

Please at least . . . tell Lank for me. Just tell him . . .

(Bunny nods.
    Caroline heads up the stairs and out the door. The sound of tanks accompanies her exit.
    Beat.
    Bunny goes to Chelle and touches her softly on the arm.)

CHELLE: Whose fault is it, Bunny?

BUNNY: Whose fault is what?

CHELLE: This gap I feel in my heart? Is it Caroline's? Or Lank's? Or Willie's? Or Sly's? Or Mama and Daddy's? Whose fault?

BUNNY: I don't know, honey. Maybe none of 'em. Maybe all of 'em. What's it matter?

CHELLE: I don't hate her.

BUNNY: I know.

CHELLE: Can't say I love her none either.

BUNNY: I know that too.

CHELLE: Sometimes I just see the way my brother lookin' at her . . . and it makes me mad.

BUNNY: I know. *(Beat)* Thought it would make me mad too . . . but . . . it don't really . . .

CHELLE: Why don't it? He take to her a certain way. Look at her like she's somethin' special. More special than anything he's ever known. And it makes me mad, Bunny. Makes me mad he don't look at you that way . . .

BUNNY: Me? I don't take Lank no kinda serious. Why you fussin' over me?

CHELLE: Cuz you and me . . . we close to the same. And I wanna know why he don't see that somethin' special in us? In what we come from and all we been given? I see him lookin' at her, and it makes me feel like we ain't enough. Like he sees somethin' better in her than he sees in us. Throw us out like a scratched record. But ain't we got no value?

BUNNY: 'Course. A lil' scratch give you character.

CHELLE: Lank don't see it like that.
BUNNY: Well . . . maybe he don't have to. *(Beat)* Way I see it, I'm always gonna be Bunny. Had a fast tail since saltwater Julys in Detroit. And Lank . . . he slow. He like to play fast, but he ain't fast enough for me. I'm like lightnin' . . . and he's like . . . some kinda quiet creek. I love him, I do. Love him like I love a creek on a hot day. Any water will do . . . *(Beat)* Now if Lank get that, he all right by me. But maybe he never get that and he still all right by me . . . cuz I'm always gonna be Bunny, regardless. And you always gon' be Chelle. You got to let Lank be Lank . . . whatever that is . . . It's all right . . . whatever you are . . . that's all right, too . . .

(Chelle smiles and touches Bunny's hand on her shoulder.
The basement door opens.
Lank comes in wildly disoriented. Blood on his shirt. He stumbles down the stairs.)

CHELLE: Lank! Jesus—what happened to you?
BUNNY: Baby—what'd they do?
LANK: He's . . . he's . . . they . . .

(Chelle rushes over to Lank and tries to help him to the couch.)

CHELLE: Come down here—you been / hurt?!
LANK: No!

(He holds her off.)

BUNNY: Lank!
CHELLE: What happened to you? / You bleedin'!
BUNNY: Somebody hurt you, baby?
LANK: They um . . . they . . .
　　. . .
　　. . .

CHELLE: They what? What'd they do?!

BUNNY: What happened honey? Jus' take it / slow

CHELLE: They hurt you???

LANK *(Carefully)*: They come up on us—the pigs—

CHELLE: Come up on / you how?

BUNNY: Honey you scarin' / me.

LANK: —come to burn us out / but we got 'em—mother-fuckers . . .

CHELLE: They burn the / bar?!?!

BUNNY: Where's Sly, Lank?

(The sound of tanks rolling by.)

LANK: He . . .

    . . .

    . . .

    . . .

CHELLE: Lank, you really scarin' me. What happened?

(Pause.)

LANK: Tanks come 'round the corner—

CHELLE: What / tanks?

BUNNY: What'd they do?!

LANK: Those goddamn tanks . . . goddamnit, Sly!

CHELLE: Where's Sly, Lank?

LANK: I told him . . . I told him stop runnin'—I told him

CHELLE: What do you—   BUNNY: No—
    What are you—????

LANK: I told him . . .

CHELLE: Where's Sly, Lank?

BUNNY: Chelle—

CHELLE: What'd they do?!?! Where is he???

BUNNY: Chelle.

LANK: He's . . . they . . .

—

—

(Chelle looks at Lank in horror.)

CHELLE: No.

LANK: He's . . . dead.

CHELLE: No!

BUNNY *(Breathless)*: Oh God . . .

LANK: They . . .

CHELLE: No!!!!

LANK: They killed him.

BUNNY: No.

LANK: They killed / him!!!

CHELLE: Stop it! Stop it!!! Don't say that!!

(Chelle collapses and wails.
Lank stumbles and clings to anything. The couch. The crates.
The chair. The rail. The floor. Whatever will hold him.
He finally releases. A wail. A scream.)

LANK: They killed SLY!!!!!!!!!!!!!!!!!!!!!!!!

(Blackout.)

SCENE FIVE

Chelle sits by the record player, alone. No music. She sips coffee deli-
cately. A gust of wind could knock her over.
Lank comes through the basement door. He is cleaned up. Fresh
shirt. He comes down and watches his sister for a moment.

Silence.
Lank goes over to the bar. He pours a drink to the brim.
He holds his glass up to the sky. Pours a little back into the sink,
in a reverie.
Beat.
Lank sips.
Chelle remains stoic.

CHELLE: Julius call this mornin'.

LANK: That right?

CHELLE: Say he heard the U.S. Army was up here now and they been quellin' this fire. He sayin' he want to come back home to check on us.

LANK: You tell him we fine. Just stay at that school where he safe from all this.

CHELLE: I told him to stay put. I told him we . . . fine . . .

LANK: You tell him 'bout . . .

CHELLE: No . . . not now . . . not like this . . .

(Beat.)

LANK: Caroline ain't come back?

CHELLE: She . . . gone. Said to tell you goodbye . . .

LANK: Well I guess that's it. You wanted her gone so she gone.

CHELLE: It wasn't safe, Lank.

LANK: I know, Chelle. *(Beat)* I know you . . . you see her and you see me and you ain't like it. And I don't know what to say 'bout it. When I talked to her I just felt like all the rules put on me cuz of this or that or where I'm from or what I am . . . it was possible to break 'em all and still have somethin' . . . *(Pause)* But I guess that wasn't real. The rules is the rules, and soon as you step outside the space you been given, it don't do nothin' you think it's gonna do. You thinkin' it's gonna open the world up. All it do is upset the world and set it on fire. All it do is make you lose your best buddy.

CHELLE: Lank . . .

(Lank holds in a wail.)

LANK: I lost him, Chelle.

(Beat.)

I was there with him, till the end. There when we signed the papers in our name. There when he went runnin' after them pigs who showed up tryin' to burn us down. Tryin' to send us a message for bein' uppity. There when we chased after 'em. There when them big tanks rolled 'round the corner. He ain't seein' what I see. Told him stop. Don't run after. He ain't see 'em rollin' up. Them soldiers that come to back up the police for the riots.

Saw niggers chasin' after cops and decided the niggers were the ones to shoot. And I was there when they shot him, Chelle. There when he fell. Went back to him and lifted him in my arms. Felt his blood soak my shirt. Saw his chest open—

CHELLE: Don't, Lank.

LANK: I was there, Chelle. Till the end. *(Beat)* He was my best buddy.

CHELLE: I know, Lank.

LANK: And he's gone.

(Beat.)

I messed up, Chelle. Was tryin' to really be somethin' . . . but it's just like you say . . . nothin' but foolish . . .

CHELLE *(Softly)*: Since when you listen to anything I say?

(Chelle falls silent. She moves over to the 8-track player and picks up some tapes.)

How you play this thing?

LANK: Want me to show you?

(He starts to approach her. She holds out her hand to stop him.)

CHELLE: No I . . . wanna do it myself. Just . . . tell me . . .

LANK: Turn the cartridge face up. Have the closed part facing you. Leave the open side to the machine. And push it in.

(Chelle does so.)

CHELLE: Then what?

LANK: You turn on the power.

(She scowls at Lank. Pause.)

CHELLE: I figure that much.

LANK: Well . . . why ain't you doin' it then?

CHELLE: When I'm ready.

LANK: Ready for what?

CHELLE: Just when I'm ready.

(Beat.)

You gonna put this 8-track player in that bar of ours?

(Lank looks at Chelle in surprise.)

LANK: Ours?

CHELLE: It'd be nice for us to have some music. Some way for people to dance and feel good.

(Lank is somewhat breathless. He tries to question her, but the words fail him. She answers the gesture:)

Lank . . . it don't always make sense to me how you walk through life. Don't match how I see the world and know to get through it. But I suppose it don't have to. You start somethin', you got to finish it. Nothin' wrong with drea-min', Lank. *(Beat)* It's still standin' ain't it?

LANK: Yeah . . .

CHELLE: Well then . . . Don't be talkin' like it's some kinda ashes. Hear me?

LANK: Yeah . . . *(More solidly)* Yeah . . . *(Pause)* Lank and Sly's Feel-Good Shack . . . I'ma tell all the folks that come up in there how it came to be. How Sly was the mastermind. How we stood our ground through the fire, even if the rest of Detroit is nothin' but dust. We got somethin' we started and we gonna finish it. That's what I'ma tell folks.

CHELLE *(Softly)*: Good . . .

(Lank grabs a hat and heads for the stairs.)

LANK: I got to go get the truck. Get his sister. Take her to see his . . . *(Beat)* Be back this evenin'.

CHELLE: All right.

(Lank heads up the stairs.)

You tell them folks . . . when they ask. You tell 'em Syl-vester wasn't no looter. Tell them he was a businessman. A dreamer. That's what he was . . . what you both are . . .

LANK: I will . . .

CHELLE: And you . . . call the place Sly and Lank's, will you? Lank and Sly's Feel-Good Shack just don't make you feel as good . . .

(Lank stares at Chelle. A moment. A smile? A tear? Something in between . . .)

LANK: Sly and Lank's Feel-Good Shack . . . yeah . . . *(Solidly)* Yeah . . .

(Lank disappears behind the door.
    Chelle sits for a moment. Stands. Goes to the bar. Pours herself a drink. Sips.
    Goes to 8-track player. Turns on the power.
    The Four Tops' "Reach Out, I'll Be There" plays.
    Chelle sways her hips slowly.
    She moves over to the pole. Grabs a pillow. Something to indicate companionship.
    She begins to sing along through her tears . . .)

CHELLE *(Singing)*:
    Now if you feel that you can't go on
    Because all of your hope is gone
    And your life is filled with much confusion
    Until happiness is just an illusion
    And your world is crumbling down, darlin'
    Reach out . . . Come on girl, reach on out for me . . .

(Chelle reaches out her arms.
    She dances freely . . . lovingly . . . even nastily . . . but definitely free.
    Lights fade on Chelle.)

END OF PLAY

SKELETON CREW

This is for my Auntie Francine, my grandfather Pike,
my cousins Michael Abney and Patti Poindexter, my Uncle Sandy,
my friend David Livingston, my relative Willie Felder,
and all of the UAW members and autoworkers whose passion for
their work inspires me. And this is for the working-class warriors
who keep this country driving forward.

This is also for the politicians, financial analysts,
and everyday citizens who echoed the negating sentiments,
"Let Detroit Go Bankrupt." Yep, this is for you too, damnit.

Skeleton Crew received its world premiere at the Atlantic Theater Company (Neil Pepe, Artistic Director; Jeffory Lawson, Managing Director) at Stage 2 Theater on January 6, 2016. It was directed by Ruben Santiago-Hudson. The set design was by Michael Carnahan, the costume design was by Paul Tazewell, the lighting design was by Rui Rita, the original music and sound design were by Robert Kaplowitz, the original songs were by Jimmy "J. Keys" Keys, the projection design was by Nicholas Hussong; the production stage manager was Laura Wilson. The cast was:

FAYE	Lynda Gravátt
DEZ	Jason Dirden
SHANITA	Nikiya Mathis
REGGIE	Wendell B. Franklin
PERFORMER	Adesola Osakalumi

Skeleton Crew transferred to the Linda Gross Theater at the Atlantic Theater Company and opened on May 13, 2016 with the same cast and production team.

Skeleton Crew was developed at The Lark Play Development Center (John Clinton Eisner, Artistic Director) as part of the 2014 BareBones Workshop, with the following cast: Lynda Gravátt (Faye), Jaime Lincoln Smith (Dez), Nikiya Mathis (Shanita) and Wendell B. Franklin (Reggie). It was also developed at the 2014 Sundance Institute Theatre Lab (Philip Himberg, Artistic Director). It was awarded the 2014 Sky Cooper American Play Prize at Marin Theatre Company (Jasson Minadakis, Artistic Director; Michael Barker, Managing Director).

CHARACTERS

FAYE, black, mid to late fifties, working-class woman. Tough, a lifetime of dirt beneath her nails. Somewhere, deep compassion.

DEZ, black, mid to late twenties, working-class man. Young hustler, playful, street-savvy, flirtatious. Somewhere, deeply sensitive.

SHANITA, black, mid to late twenties, working-class young woman. Pretty but not ruled by it. Hardworking, by the books. Believes in the work she does. Also, pregnant. Somewhere, a beautiful dreamer.

REGGIE, black, late thirties, white-collar man. The foreman. Studious, dedicated, compassionate. Somewhere, a fire brims.

Detroit, Michigan. A stamping plant. Winter, somewhere around year 2008.

A " / " indicates where the next line of dialogue begins.

This play operates in realism with touches of the magical/ ethereal. The moments where the mechanical intrusion of the story peeks into the transitions should not feel like cool tricks separate from the base of the play. They are part of the storytelling of automation. They are part of the omnipresence of the plant without overwhelming the realism of the play. I guess simply put, my ask would be however your production imagines this automation (shadow puppets, choreography, video, a combo of all), that it doesn't become a shtick, but instead continues to add to the fullness of the plant so that even though we're only seeing the breakroom, we're also seeing the whole factory deteriorating.

The language of the play must also drive. These characters have a banter with each other that is so natural and second nature that they can almost finish each other's sentences. As much as possible, breaks or pauses between text or within passages of text should be avoided until written in. There are silences in the ellipses or pauses that are written into the text such that they make an impact.

ACT ONE

In darkness, smoke comes out of a stack. Auto plant machinery hums and rattles. Hip-hop drum beats (J Dilla inspired) blend into the rhythm—a cacophony of working-class hustle. Echoes of sighs. Machinery hums, hums, hums. J Dilla beats rock, rock, rock. They blend together until we are almost bopping our heads to it . . . a factory-line hymn . . .

In silhouette: the drone of workers on the line, operating stamping machinery. No clear people, just shadowed workers misted by the smoke.

The background sounds fade out.

Lights rise on the breakroom of a stamping plant. Harsh fluorescent lights bleach the room. There are posters on the wall of various cars and SUVs. Pictures of various auto parts—shocks, sparkling engines, etc.

A table and some chairs sit in the middle of the room. A raggedy couch. Crates hold random kitchen supplies—plasticware, ketchup packets, etc. Somewhere, a microwave and refrigerator.

Most important in the room: a bulletin board, covered in notices and papers. Larger than them all are two signs, posted on top and on bigger paper.

One, handwritten, says, UNIT MEETING THURSDAY. DON'T MISS IT AGAIN YA'LL. *The other, also handwritten, says, NO SMOK-ING* FAYE.

Faye, with a heavy walk and weathered from the day, comes into the breakroom and goes over to her locker. She takes off her sweatshirt, leaving her in a white T-shirt and hard yellow boots that are dirty and worn. She moves past the NO SMOKING *sign, looks at it blankly.*

Faye pulls out a cigarette from her bosom. She lights it and puffs. Dez enters, wearing gloves and a vest.

DEZ: Cold then a bitch today, ain't it?

FAYE *(Puffing)*: Shiiitt.

DEZ: Told them fools something ain't right with the heat in here. Upstairs could give a damn less.

FAYE: Reggie bringing in a heater today, supposed to.

DEZ: Reggie supposed to been brought in a heater—days ago. Head somewhere else.

FAYE: He got a lot on his mind lately.

DEZ: He ain't the only one.

(Dez opens the fridge and pulls out a dilapidated sandwich. He looks at it pitifully, then bites into it anyway. He looks at Faye squarely.)

You ain't cold?

FAYE: I got a heat you don't know shit about. Leave me 'lone.

DEZ *(Laughing)*: Awww hell, Faye. You on that over-fifty-pause?

FAYE: You better leave me 'lone—talking 'bout over fifty.

DEZ: You hittin' my mama status. It's 'bout to get serious.

FAYE: I told you don't mess with me boy.

DEZ: I know how ya'll do. Be in the dead of winter, and she talkin' 'bout—"Dez, roll the car window down." I'm like— hell naw, Ma! Why I gotta freeze in the middle of January just cuz you in yo' own personal July?

FAYE: I hope yo' mama slapped you good. Ain't s'pose to bother a woman battlin' her own heat.

DEZ: You know you ain't supposed to be smokin'. You ain't see Reggie's sign?

FAYE: This what I think of Reggie's sign.

(She blows a circle of smoke.)

DEZ: You know he gon' trip. Can write you up.

FAYE: Bet' not.

DEZ: You think you a OG, don't you?

FAYE: I'm is, fool. Been on the line longer than you been born.

DEZ: You swear.

FAYE: 'Fore you knocked up yo' first girlfriend in the back of somebody's Ford.

DEZ: You know I ain't never knocked up nobody in no nothin'.

FAYE: Been puttin' in my time 'fore you even knew what a stamping plant was, fool. I'm yo' elder up in here. Bow down and lick the dust off my Tims.

DEZ: You better go'on somewhere with that.

(The door to the breakroom opens. Shanita enters, wearing goggles. She is visibly pregnant. She heads straight for the fridge. Dez smiles at her.)

Hey baby.

SHANITA: Shut up, Dez.

FAYE: She gon' file a sexual harassment report on yo' tail. And I'ma throw the book at you.

DEZ: Psshhhh . . .

SHANITA: Who had some of my salad dressing?

DEZ: Wasn't me.

FAYE: Me neither.

SHANITA: I put my name on it. Big letters: S-H-A-N-I-T-A. Who the hell can't read?

(Shanita sits down in a huff and tends to her salad.)

FAYE: Ya'll and these damn signs.

DEZ: What you eatin' salad for? I like my women with meat on their bones.

SHANITA: Boy you swear to somebody's God that I want you. *(Shift)* Faye, you smokin' in here?

FAYE: For five seconds.

SHANITA *(Indicating her pregnant belly)*: Ahem!

FAYE: I'm sorry I'm sorry.

(Faye puts out the cigarette.)

Shit. Ya'll the ones invadin' my lil' hideaway. Ain't nobody stopping you from eatin' in yo' cars with the rest of them fools. *(Mumbling)* Worryin' 'bout me 'steada all that dust out there swimming in yo' lungs.

SHANITA: I wear my mask. And I'm not stepping off the line until I absolutely have to. Get the most of my benefits. *(Shift)* Thought you quit, anyway.

FAYE: That patch is a damn lie. All these programs are. You quit when you're ready to quit. Till then, you just a nicotine tease. Flirt with her till you kiss her right down to the ash.

SHANITA: You better quit, Faye. Don't know nobody that invincible they can battle breast cancer and still be smokin' like it ain't no thang.

DEZ: Faye like flirtin' with death.

FAYE: Been this way over fifty years, don't see why I gotta change now.

SHANITA: What's your son got to say about that?

FAYE: Not a damn thing.

SHANITA: Stubborn.

DEZ: As a mule.

FAYE: Ya mamas. *(Shift)* How's production comin' on the 3-line?

SHANITA: Slow. Since we done lost half the crew, I don't know how Reggie expect us to meet deadline. I'm already workin' overtime four days this week. My feet swellin' as it is.

DEZ: Want me to rub 'em?

SHANITA: Want me to kick you?

FAYE: I'll take yo' overtime. And Dez too, if you want.

DEZ: Not me, naw. You know I'm saving up.

FAYE: You still talkin' 'bout starting that repair shop?

DEZ: Found me a garage over on Six Mile. All I gotta do is save me enough to buy it outright. Few more months of overtime, I'm in there.

FAYE: And then what? You quit?

DEZ: You mean if we ain't next to get dropped? It's dead flies all around this plant, Faye. I ain't waitin' 'round till I get swat.

FAYE: Anywhere else you go you get swat there too, shit. Ain't nothin' new.

SHANITA: You got to make yourself irreplaceable. That's what I'm doing.

FAYE: How you figure you irreplaceable? I been from stamping doors to installing shocks to them seven years I spent sewing interiors. It ain't nobody in this plant more irreplaceable than Faye Davison.

SHANITA: I'm talking work efficiency and ethic. I don't complain. Got the least write-ups. Do a lotta overtime.

DEZ: And you fine' then a mug. *(As in "muthafucker")* That make you irreplaceable as hell to me.

SHANITA: And that's sexual harassment number five thousand and sixty-two.

DEZ: I notice you keepin' count.

SHANITA: And anyway, I'm in good standing with the union.

FAYE: Everybody in good standin' with the union, except for Dez.

DEZ: Dues too damn much.

FAYE: You youngins don't have no respect for the blood been spilled so yo' ass have some benefits.

DEZ: What benefits? I don't hardly see no benefits.

FAYE: Was a time when you wasn't even allowed in the union, dummy. Wasn't nothin' but the mule of the industry doin' the shittiest labor you could think of. And now here you are, *choosing* yo' trade and thinkin' you got that shit all by yo'self.

DEZ: Faye, don't start all that with me. You bastards pull money outta my paycheck every month, for what? Only thing the UAW do for me is force me to strike when I don't even want to. Rather stack my paper and build my own enterprise. I done paid enough dues in my life already, I ain't tryin' to pay to nobody else. Them union suckers might get my money, but I ain't got to smile and grin while I sign the shit over. I feel like grittin' my teeth, I'm grittin' my teeth.

FAYE: You ain't seen no UAW strikes till you done lost a few teeth to assholes trying to break yo' line and fight you down into the gutter. I can always demonstrate upside yo' head if you need to know how it went.

SHANITA: Knock him out real good, Faye.

DEZ: Awww baby, you ain't got to knock me out. You can just have your way with me.

SHANITA: Boy, please.

(The door to the breakroom opens. Reggie enters, with a neat haircut, neat pants and a white-collar button-down shirt. He rolls in a space heater.)

REGGIE: Faye, there you are. I was looking for you.

FAYE: For what? I still got a half hour left to my break. Tell them fools on 16-line to take a chill pill and let me rest my dogs.

REGGIE: Wanted to chat with you for a sec.

SHANITA: Finally, a heater!

REGGIE: Smell like smoke in here.

SHANITA: You know who that was.

REGGIE: How big I got to make the sign?

FAYE: Bigger.

DEZ: You got more overtime for me?

REGGIE: I might be able to find something. But Charlie and Bo put in before you.

DEZ: Charlie and Bo been gettin' overtime all week. What about me?

REGGIE: What about you? You want me to throw them to the side cuz you took too long to ask?

DEZ: Don't mean you gotta let them have all the overtime. Ain't s'pose to be no monopolies on overtime.

REGGIE: Don't start fussing with me, Dez. I don't need your insubordination today.

DEZ: Insubordination?

SHANITA: Dez can have my overtime. I was gonna tell you anyway. Had to take a doctor's appointment this afternoon. Only time I could get in.

FAYE: Gonna find out the gender?

SHANITA: Not sure yet. Think I wanna be surprised.

REGGIE: Fine. Dez, you're on. I'm done with it. *(Shift)* I'm gonna plug this up, but then you ain't gonna be able to use the microwave. Can't use too much wattage in this outlet. Gonna have to pick and choose.

DEZ: If that ain't hood-rigging, I don't know what is.

REGGIE: Gotta take what we can get.

FAYE: That's a company heater? Or you brought that from home?

REGGIE: Just take the heater.

FAYE: Foremen ain't responsible for bringing in personal heaters to keep the breakroom warm.

REGGIE: Just take the heater.

DEZ: Ay Reggie, I heard they closed down Kemp.

REGGIE: Where'd you hear that?

DEZ: Bony J.

REGGIE: News from Bony J always comes crooked and on the diagonal. You know not to listen to rumors like that.

DEZ: Nah nah, he showed it to me in *Plant Closing News.*

SHANITA: It's in the newsletter?

DEZ: Think I'm lyin'?

REGGIE: I guess they went on ahead with it then. Thought they got revived when that new Chrysler came out. Kemp was the number one company for exporting their shocks.

DEZ: They doin' 'em within now.

SHANITA: That make us the last small factory standing now, ain't it?

FAYE: Shoul' do.

REGGIE: That 16-line is gonna be a massive undertaking. They gonna have to bring in rigging crews from all over. If you start hittin' the gym more, Dez, you can go'on down there and find you some pickup work.

DEZ: Psshhhh—too bad I could give a damn less watching another plant turn into a ghost town. I'm straight on that.

FAYE: You 'fraid of ghosts?

DEZ: Them assembly-line ghosts? Hell yeah.

SHANITA: Shut up, Dez.

DEZ: Say them empty plants a breeding ground for 'em. You can hear the echoes of machines just runnin' and runnin' in the hollow space. Them fools that be goin' down there playin' in the ruins; dumb-ass white boys come over from Windsor and Ohio to stand in front of those empty plants and take pictures like it's some kinda cabaret step and repeat? Heard that be the last picture they ever take. Some of them jokers never make it back out. The old gas vapors swallow them whole. Disappear.

SHANITA: That's stupid.

REGGIE: Even more stupid is the press operator that goes around spreading that mess.

DEZ: You ain't got to believe me. I know what I know.

FAYE: And that ain't much.

DEZ *(Checking his watch)*: Shit, my break almost over and I ain't even get to make good on my promise to Bony J. S'posed to catch him for a game of bones and take his money right quick.

REGGIE: You know you're not supposed to gamble on work grounds. I could write you up.

DEZ: You got to catch me in action first.

(Dez heads to the door.)

See ya'll at quittin' time. Shanita, I'll meet you out front to walk you to your car. Ain't safe out there after dark.

SHANITA: You hit on me and I'm gonna pepper spray your ass.

DEZ: Not till our first date, baby.

(Shanita grabs something nearby and throws it at Dez. Maybe a styrofoam cup. He disappears behind the door.)

SHANITA: I'ma go back too. Still got ten minutes, but I'm walkin' slow these days. Swollen feet ain't quick feet, you know? *(Shift)* Hey Faye, I'm bringing in a book of names tomorrow. You gonna help me pick somethin'?

FAYE: Thought you said you didn't wanna know the gender.

SHANITA: Somethin' unisex.

(Shanita leaves. Faye watches Reggie as he straightens things up. A moment of awkwardness.)

REGGIE: Was um . . . lookin' for you cuz I needed to talk . . . if you had a sec.

(Faye eyes Reggie intensely.)

FAYE *(Not a question)*: They shuttin' us down, ain't they.

REGGIE: How you—

FAYE: I know you, Reggie. Can read your face. Been lookin' stressed for a week and then some. *(Beat)* When you find out?

REGGIE: Last week. Harris pulled me into his office.

FAYE: Fuck.

(Pause.)

When they letting everybody know?

REGGIE: HR is sending out the notice as soon details are final.

FAYE: How soon this happenin'?

REGGIE: Within the year, Faye.

FAYE *(Sobering)*: FUCK.

(Another pause.)

I hit thirty years at the end of the year. In October. We gonna be around that long?

REGGIE: Ain't sure.

FAYE *(Almost to herself)*: Retirement package be real different for twenty-nine years versus thirty.

REGGIE: I know. I'm thinking on it. Was coming to talk to you. Get the scoop on folks. See what I might be able to figure out for everybody before the news hits. Cuz once it does . . .

FAYE: What you gonna do? What about Cheryl and the kids?

REGGIE: I've been trying to figure that out. I only got fifteen years on me.

FAYE: But you in a supervisory position. They gonna find you another job. Place you somewhere else.

REGGIE: Dalina just started high school. Got to save up for her college. And we just bought that house over in Sherwood. Couldn't hardly believe we could afford it. But we got it, Faye. It's ours.

FAYE: I know it.

REGGIE: I own something that can't nobody take from me. That mean somethin'.

FAYE: It does. Means a lot.

REGGIE: Now you can't say nothin' about this. I'll lose my job. You know that right?

FAYE: I know you don't expect me to sit on this. That's not what you was coming to ask me.

REGGIE: I was coming for your help. To work with you and fig- ure out what we can do to soften this blow. But you can't go taking this to the union yet. I need you to wait and let the company do this right.

FAYE: Do this right? Only right way is straight up. I'm still the rep. It's my job to protect these folks.

REGGIE: Faye, I'm confiding in you. I'm putting myself on the line for you cuz I'm on your side. But I need you on mine. I need your guidance. Help me figure this out without sounding the alarm.

FAYE: Reggie—

REGGIE: Please, Faye.

(Faye says nothing.)

I wouldn't be in this industry if it wasn't for you. My mama never stopped reminding me that, you know. You always been her most trusted soul sister. Recommended me to get a good job in the factory when wasn't nobody hiring a high school dropout. And now look. I'm wearing a tie to work and buying a house for my family. *(Beat)* I always appreciate that, Faye. You know that, right?

FAYE *(Softly)*: I know it. She'd be real proud of you.

REGGIE: I'm gonna work hard to get us outta here with somethin' we can exhale into. Just please . . . until I can figure this out . . .

FAYE: All right, Reggie. Fine. We'll do it your way.

(Reggie stares at Faye for a moment. He releases a smile.)

REGGIE: Thanks, Faye. You tough as bricks, you know that? Ain't nothin' can knock you down.

FAYE: See you in the mornin'.

REGGIE: All right then.

(Reggie heads to the door.)

And leave those cigarettes alone, Faye. If not for the plant rules, at least for your health. Jalen would kill me if he knew I let his mama smoke herself out of remission.

FAYE: My son ain't givin' two shits 'bout that. *(Shift)* Get outta here. I'll see you in the morning.

REGGIE: See you then.

(Reggie exits. Faye stands still looking after him for a moment. Then she reaches into her bosom, pulls out another cigarette. Lights it.
And puffs . . .)

SCENE TWO

In darkness, the humming of machinery creates a Midwestern hip-hop score, an extension of the factory-line soundtrack that opened the play.

Silhouetted workers are seen in action—their factory-line dance.
Suddenly, a chink in the machinery. The workers repeat move-
ments as if they are stuck between two motions, unable to complete
their tasks. Short-circuiting, caught in dysfunction.
Lights crossfade onto the breakroom.
It is early morning. Sunlight spills through the windows.
Clothes are laid out around the floor and on the dilapidated couch. A
locker is partially open. The heater is on.
Dez enters the breakroom wearing a coat and backpack. He
walks over to a boom box resting on a crate. Unplugs the heater
and plugs in the boom box. Puts on a CD. Slum Village's "Get Dis
Money" plays.
He notices the clothes lying about, the open locker. Registers it
questioningly.
He takes out his hard boots. Changes out of his nice gym shoes.
Puts his gym shoes in his locker. Takes off his backpack. Looks around.
Pulls a gun from his hip. Places it in his backpack and seals it well.
He pulls out his lunch and takes it over to the fridge. Opens the
fridge and sticks his head in, looking for something to drink. Shakes
the OJ cartons, smells the milk, etc.
Shanita enters, yawning. She walks right over to the boom box
and turns it off.
She goes to her locker and takes off her coat. She stores her
belongings, puts some new salad dressing in the fridge.

DEZ *(Rapidly):* Whoa whoa whoa what up doe? Why you turnin'
    off my music?
SHANITA: It's too early for this.
DEZ: Morning ritual. I'm sayin'. You messin' up my mojo. Slum
    Village is my muse. Make me feel like gettin' my hustle on.
SHANITA: I'm being selective about what I listen to while I'm
    pregnant. Only positive sounds for my baby to hear.
DEZ: What's more positive than makin' that paper?
SHANITA: Seriously, Dez. Mother-to-be. I get priority.

DEZ: Aiight, what you wanna hear? I got other stuff.

SHANITA: Silence. The sound of the refrigerator humming. The sound of the machines running. That's it.

DEZ: That ain't music.

SHANITA: To you, maybe not. To me, it is. Sound like harmony. Like life happening. Production. Good sound.

DEZ: I'm still pissed they busted me for playin' music on the floor. My mind goes numb listening to that stamping sound all day long. A dude could forget how to socialize with the outside world. Forget how to lay that pimp game down on a woman. Got nobody to practice with.

SHANITA: Don't think you 'bout to practice with me.

DEZ: Who else I'm s'posed to practice with? Faye? That's like hittin' on my Aunt Debra. You the finest woman up in this plant.

SHANITA: What am I—your default hottie? No thank you.

DEZ: You know you more than that to me.

SHANITA: Whatever.

(Beat.)

DEZ: Yo' baby daddy brought you here this mornin'?—

SHANITA: Do not ask me about my child's father. Not up for discussion, Dez.

DEZ: My bad—

SHANITA: You like pissin' me off early in the morning?

DEZ: You look cute when you pissed off. Got that pregnancy glow.

(She fumes at him. He backs off.)

Aiight. Too early for compliments I guess.

SHANITA: You don't know what a compliment is, I guess.

(Dez makes himself busy in the makeshift kitchen.)

DEZ: You want some coffee?

SHANITA: One cup. Milk—

DEZ: And two sugars. I know. I got you.

(Shanita folds the clothes.)

SHANITA: Who came in here earlier than us? That's Faye stuff?

DEZ: Yeah.

SHANITA: You heard them rumors down on 9-line yesterday?

DEZ: I heard 'em.

SHANITA: Think it's true?

DEZ: Bet' not be. I still got about six months left 'fore I have enough for my garage.

SHANITA: But what if they are?

DEZ: Can't stress over that. Rumors 'bout shuttin' down been circulating every year. Then it go away. That's just how it is. Can't worry 'bout it. Cuz if it don't happen, you done worried for nothin'. And if it do happen, you done worried twice. Better to wait to the last possible moment to start worryin', I say. Till then, just sit back and go with the flow.

SHANITA: Yo' philosophies be . . .

DEZ: Stupid?

SHANITA: Halfway comforting . . .

(Beat. Dez hands Shanita a cup of coffee. They sip in silence. The refrigerator hums. Shanita closes her eyes.)

DEZ: I wasn't sayin' nothin' about yo' baby's daddy. Just wanted to know—

SHANITA: Shhhhh . . . Listen to the music.

(Dez watches her . . . kinda smiles . . .
    Beat.
    Faye walks in, startled at the sight of them.)

FAYE: Oh—hey . . . ya'll ain't usually here this early.
DEZ: You in a lil' early yourself, ain't you?

(Faye avoids Dez's eyes. Goes to grab her clothes.)

FAYE: Forgive my mess . . .

(Faye puts the clothes away and shuts her locker.)

SHANITA: You made the coffee?
FAYE: Yeah.
SHANITA: Taste a lil' different.
DEZ: Better than this slop we usually drink.
FAYE: Brought some of my own beans in. Gourmet coffee beans or some shit. Christmas gift from my son. Ain't got no coffee maker, but he don't know that. So figured I might as well share 'fore they go to waste or whatever.
SHANITA: That's cool, Faye, thanks.
FAYE: Whatever. Better than wasting 'em. *(Shift)* Who workin' overtime tonight?
SHANITA: I'm gonna. Put in my request yesterday.
DEZ: Not me. I got a date.
SHANITA: A date?
DEZ: Yeah. Why—you jealous?
SHANITA *(A little)*: Pssshhhhh . . .
FAYE: What you gonna take her out in? Not that hooptie you got out there.
DEZ: Hooptie?
FAYE: So much rust on that car—look like it got a disease. Lesions everywhere.

DEZ: You talk shit now, but I'm 'bout to be working on her. She gonna look real pretty in a couple of months. Ain't gonna hardly be able to recognize her.

FAYE: Ya'll youngins don't know nothin' 'bout how to fix up no car. Treat 'em 'bout as dumb as you treat women. Put a bunch of pretty jewelry on her—gold rims—trick out her exterior, and on the inside, she ain't got nothin' to run on. No care. No substance. Just put all your attention on the shit that don't matter. That ain't how to make her purr like you really want.

DEZ: Like you know somethin'—

FAYE: I know how to get a girl in the back of my car faster than you. Tell you that much.

SHANITA: Faye be mackin' the ladies.

FAYE: I ain't said I be mackin' 'em. I just said I know how. If it's one thing I always known, it's cars and women. I keep all of it intact better than Dez keep his. Bet you that.

DEZ: I keep my cars and my women tight. Don't worry 'bout that.

FAYE: That ol' Betsy you drive ain't got nothin' to run on. Engine sound like it's gonna die on you any day now. Like a ol' dirty woman with a emphysema cough. Hear that girl hacking for her life every time you drive in the lot. Mile away.

DEZ: You gon' be that ol' dirty woman you keep smokin'—

FAYE: Hush that.

DEZ: Anyway, I'm fixin' to get a new engine. Got the hookup.

SHANITA: Where—at one of them auctions? Heard they for big ol' press machines. Cranes and lifts and whatever. Where you gettin' a new engine?

DEZ: My boy work over at the Briggs plant. Said he gonna hold one off to the side for me.

FAYE: That sound like some sideways and upside down shit to me. You better be careful dealin' with yo' boy. Police already arrested two fools last week for stealing plant materials.

Happenin' a whole bunch right now. Some of those ol' dusty ghost towns you talk about are getting ransacked. Poppy Johnson—the night watchman over at Kemp— got himself shot in the shoulder one night while he was patrolling the grounds. Didn't even get no disability.

SHANITA: Plants ain't safe no more.

FAYE: Nowhere safe no more. Everybody packin' somethin' these days. Can't go to the corner store without worryin' whether the person you blocked in is gonna come gunnin' at you cuz they got someplace to be in a hurry. Use to be able to offend somebody without losin' your life as the cost . . .

DEZ: How the hell else they s'pose to go around? Unarmed? You can't coast this city that way 'less you suicidal.

SHANITA: Why can't you? I do. I don't need my baby to come into this world armed and dangerous.

FAYE: Everybody handle tension differently. Some folks see shit fallin' apart and got to join in the destruction. Hands with no use find activity in useless shit. But some folks think on a different plane. Rather be part of the restoration. And some folks just . . .

SHANITA: What?

FAYE: Smoke a goddamn cigarette. *(Shift)* Where my pack?

(Dez holds up an empty pack.)

DEZ: You out.

FAYE: Hell, I got to go and get me some. Or you can get me a pack on your lunch break.

DEZ: I'll think about it. Don't know if I wanna be part of your destruction.

FAYE: Boy, I'll slap you.

SHANITA: Faye, you heard them rumors flying 'round the plant lately?

FAYE: What rumors?

SHANITA: Say we next on the choppin' block?

FAYE: Told you don't be listening to rumors. You inhale every rumor you clog up your lungs. Die of asphyxiation of other people's bullshit.

DEZ: I'm gonna get to the bottom of all that hearsay.

FAYE: How you figure that?

DEZ: Gonna ask Reggie straight out. He know somethin' and he ain't tellin' us? That's bitch-made to me.

FAYE: You back offa Reggie. Got himself a lot to deal with already. Counselin' all kinda folks losing they jobs. Ain't easy.

SHANITA: But he gotta tell us, right? I need to keep my benefits.

FAYE *(Changing the subject)*: Shanita, I almost forgot—I got somethin' for you.

(Faye goes to her locker. She pulls out a stack of paper and hands it to Shanita.)

SHANITA: What's this?

FAYE: List of names. Unisex.

SHANITA: For real?

FAYE: Printed 'em at the computer in Bea's old office. Go on look at 'em.

SHANITA *(Reading aloud)*: African baby names.

DEZ: Awww hell—African names? That kid ain't gonna be able to get no job.

SHANITA: Shut up, Dez!

FAYE: You a special kinda stupid.

SHANITA *(Reading)*: Akia.

FAYE: Yeah, I like that one. Means "firstborn."

DEZ: What kinda significance is that? That's like naming a kid "Born on Wednesday."

SHANITA *(Reading)*: That's Akua.

FAYE: Got significance, fool. Days of the week mean things to some people.

SHANITA: Wednesday mean something to me. Means a longer workday. Means being just like my daddy. Mean a lot.

DEZ *(Regretfully)*: I ain't sayin' it don't mean nothin'.

(Beat. Shanita checks her watch.)

SHANITA: It's almost nine o'clock. Gotta get on the floor.

(Shanita rises to her feet. Faye grabs a nearby deck of cards.)

FAYE: Who got time for a game of spades before the bell? Dez, lemme take your money right quick.

DEZ: Not me, nah. I already lost a bill yesterday. I'm off gambling today.

FAYE: Come back on break. Maybe you have a change of heart. Need me somewhere to play . . . keep my mind off shit.

DEZ: Off what?

FAYE: Just shit.

(Shanita heads to the door.)

SHANITA: I'll be back at break, Faye. I'll play you. *(Shift)* And don't let nobody take my salad dressing.

*(Shanita exits.
    Dez clears the table.)*

FAYE: I got that.

DEZ: Nah, I do. Let me.

(Dez throws the coffee cups away. Stops. Looks at Faye for a moment.)

FAYE *(Not a question)*: What.
DEZ: You . . . all right?
FAYE: I'm fine. What's your deal?
DEZ: The clothes—
FAYE: I'm fine. What's your deal?
DEZ: Nothing. I guess.

(Pause. Silence.)

I ain't gonna say nothin', but—
FAYE: Then don't.
DEZ: But the shit is concerning.
FAYE: Let it go, Dez.
DEZ: If Reggie find out—
FAYE: If Reggie find out what? Reggie ain't finding out nothin'. Reggie ain't finding out about my clothes lain around or me being here when ya'll arrived this morning. Reggie ain't finding out about me gambling on the premises. And Reggie ain't findin' out about that gun you keep in your locker. Right? Reggie ain't findin' nothin' out.
DEZ: How you—
FAYE: I know everything about this place, Dez. The walls talk to me. The dust on the floors write me messages. I'm in the vents. I'm in the bulletin boards. I'm in the chipped paint. Ain't nobody can slip through the cracks past me up in here. I can see through lockers. I know what you got in that bag you bring in here every day. But I don't expose it. Cuz everybody got they bag of shit. You got yours. And I got mine. Leave me to my own stink and don't go tryin' to air me out.
DEZ: What if we just worried about you?
FAYE: Worry 'bout that car need fixin'. Worry 'bout that darkness out there that make you afraid to coast without that metal. But don't worry 'bout me. I'm just fine.

(Beat.)

DEZ: All right.

(Dez grabs a pair of goggles and heads to the door.)

I'll come back with your poison at break.
FAYE: I'll come back here lookin' for it . . .

(Dez exits.
Faye stands alone for a moment.
She looks around the room, sighs and exits.)

SCENE THREE

Lights rise on Reggie in the breakroom. He is putting up signs on the
bulletin board.
The first sign reads: NO GAMBLING ON PREMISES. DEZ THIS MEANS
YOU.
Dez enters the breakroom. He sees Reggie, sees the sign. He rolls
his eyes and goes over to his locker.

DEZ *(Under his breath)*: Here we go.
REGGIE: Don't start with me, Dez.
DEZ: It's like a hundred less trees in the world cuz of all the
paper you use to cover this board. Can't you just spare us
all and say what you got to say?
REGGIE: I say it and you don't listen. But you better start listen-
ing real soon. Things are changing around here.
DEZ: Oh yeah? How so?
REGGIE: Plant was hit last night.
DEZ: Say word?
REGGIE: Took us for a good eighth of sheet metal off the 13-line.
DEZ: No kiddin'?

REGGIE: That's right. Upstairs is cracking down on all improper conduct on the floor. That means playing dominoes with Bony J. That means everything, Dez.

DEZ: What does me playin' bones have to do with the plant gettin' robbed?

REGGIE: They're losing patience. Zero-tolerance policy for any criminal activity on the premises.

DEZ: They got a zero-tolerance policy for the criminal activity happening upstairs? Or does that street only run one way.

REGGIE: Cool it with the back talk, Dez. I told you don't start with me today. I say cut out the gambling, that's what I mean. And whatever else you like to do in opposition to company protocol.

DEZ: I ain't got to move in opposition of nothin'. I understand the rules real clear, boss.

REGGIE: Good.

(*Beat. Reggie sighs. He continues to post signs on the board:* UNIT MEETING THURSDAY. KEEP THE BREAKROOM CLEAN. NO PERSONAL ITEMS LEFT IN THE BREAKROOM AFTER HOURS.)

DEZ: Speaking of protocol . . .

REGGIE: What of it?

DEZ: Folks startin' to talk on the shop floor.

REGGIE: Folks always talk on the shop floor. What of it?

DEZ: Sayin' this plant might be the next one to turn into a ghost town. Sound like HR is about to have a whole bunch of shit on they hands. Ain't that right?

REGGIE: I'm not speaking on hearsay.

DEZ: What you mean you not speakin' on it? Either it's happening or it's not.

REGGIE: What are you getting so concerned about HR for? You can barely focus on the line you're working on—why you worrying about HR?

DEZ: Cuz I wanna hear you say it. Tell us the plant is closing down and what we gotta do to make sure we get covered right.

REGGIE: You want me to tell you something that I can't.

DEZ: You can't, hunh?

REGGIE: What do you want from me, Dez? Didn't I just say I don't have nothin' to tell you? The company hasn't folded yet. You just focus on your job and keep your stat sheet clean, and stop worrying about things nobody can control right now.

DEZ: Can't control? Or don't wanna deal with?

REGGIE: You got something you wanna say to me directly? Or you gonna keep grabbing at stuff in the air without landing on nothing. Because I already told you what to do if you wanna make sure you're covered. Do your job. Lay off the disorderly conduct. And stay out of the shop room gossip. It doesn't suit you well.

DEZ: It doesn't suit me well?

REGGIE: No.

DEZ : What is it with you lately, man?

REGGIE: There's nothing with me.

DEZ: Act like you ain't come up in here the same way the rest of us did. The color of that collar don't change yo' origins. You forget that?

REGGIE (Getting heated): Don't question my collar, Dez.

DEZ: Ain't questioning the collar. Questioning the man wearin' it.

REGGIE: You question me again and I'll show you exactly what my origins are. I'm done being pushed this way and that, while you completely disrespect my position.

DEZ: Faye got you that position.

REGGIE: Who cares who got me the position?! I'm in it. And I'm your supervisor. And I'm telling you this as clear as I can think to say it . . . if I catch you doing one thing out of line anywhere on these premises, I will carry out the orders I've been given. And that's not just a write-up this time. It's not even suspension. It's the law. They're pressing charges to anyone stepping over the line. You understand that? That's charges, Dez. And you can push back at me and say whatever slick comment that comes out of your mouth, but it's not going to change a damn thing. You break the law, you're done.

(Faye enters the breakroom.)

FAYE: What's all this heat about in here? The radiator broken? Ya'll trying to create yo' own?

(Dez fumes. Reggie turns away and grabs his materials.)

Hey Reggie, you all right there? Need to talk for a minute?
REGGIE: Need to get back upstairs.
FAYE: You wanna come talk later?
REGGIE: Can't. Dalina got basketball practice. Got to take her to it. Cheryl's working a double tonight. Got to be home with the kids. Can't.

(Reggie leaves, disgruntled. Faye watches after him with concern. She turns to look at Dez.)

FAYE: You gon' get enough of sickin' at his heels.
DEZ: Lucky I ain't bite.
FAYE: Need to back off of him. Like to push people too far. He been a good supervisor to us. You know that.
DEZ: He holdin' somethin' back and I think you know it too.
FAYE: What's it matter whether or not he tells you what you wanna hear? Until word comes from HR, we ain't got much to stand on.

DEZ: You the rep. You supposed to be on our side. Fighting for us. What happened to all that union talk you got every other day? That only apply to everybody but Reggie?

FAYE: Oh I see, you in a fightin' mood today. Now you wanna throw punches with me? Hunh? You take yo' best shot.

DEZ: Ain't nobody tryin' to fight you.

FAYE: Naw. You feelin' froggy? Go'on and leap!

DEZ: Fine then. He ain't yo' son. That's what I got to say.

FAYE: Oh, now you just talkin' stupid.

DEZ: Am I? Then you tell me you don't got your blinders on when it come to him.

FAYE: I ain't got no blinders for nobody.

DEZ: Tell me why you ain't called no meetings down at the local or demand this company let us know our fate. Tell me why we ain't talkin' health coverage or severance deals? Ain't even gonna prep us for the blow that might be comin'?

FAYE: You talkin' premature. Got to let the man do his job first. Let him rise to the occasion. If somethin's goin' down, he can help fight for our jobs. Can't define what a man is until he got to take an action. You judge him befo' we even see what the action gonna be. And me—what I know 'bout that man . . . what I knew 'bout his mama and what he's made of . . . when it come to where his heart lie, he gonna rise to the occasion.

DEZ: And if he don't?

FAYE: If *if* was a fifth, we'd all be drunk.

DEZ: You trust him so much . . . why you ain't tell him you livin' here?

FAYE: And we are now done with this conversation.

DEZ: So you can get in my ass but I can't get in yours?

FAYE: You ain't got enough leverage to get in my ass. Besides, you talkin' 'bout somethin' you ain't got no proof about. You speculating and that's for lawyers and investigators, that ain't for you.

DEZ: Zero-tolerance policy. That's what Reggie say. For all disorderly conduct. How disorderly you think it is to be livin' at the job?

FAYE: I don't abide by no rules but necessity. I do what I do till I figure out another thing and do that. And that's all I got to say about it.

DEZ: Fine.

FAYE: Now sit down and let me take yo' money.

DEZ: I ain't supposed to be gamblin' no mo—

(Dez reluctantly sits. Faye pulls out a deck of cards, shuffles it.)

FAYE: Cut it.

(Dez cuts. Faye deals.)

This ain't a democracy. You in my personal breakroom and in the noble effort of thankin' me for not kickin' yo' ass out, you grant me the simple pleasures of playin' a game of cards so that I can graciously and repetitiously take yo' money. *(Shift)* Crazy eights. Twenty-five to start.

(She puts cash on the table. Dez matches her.)

DEZ *(Dropping his first card)*: Hearts.

FAYE: You know, you ain't the only one in tough shit. When I first come up in this plant, I was pregnant with my first and only. Kinda like Shanita. My son's father ran off and I was assed out. Had dropped outta school to be with him so I ain't have no family to fall back on. My mama didn't play them kinda games. —Your move.

(She throws a card on the table. Dez plays.)

She come from the real ol' school. Once you shame your mama and turn up with a fast tail, you got to be put out and ain't no lookin' back. I was scared shitless but somethin' in me knew I was gonna survive. Not cuz nothin' was promised to me or cuz I could see the light at the end of the tunnel or no shit like that. But somethin' in me knew what I was made of. I was gonna survive cuz I had to.

DEZ: On you.

(Faye's turn.)

FAYE: So I walked up, hiding my pregnant belly so I could get me a job, and I got it. Same day. Been workin' the line ever since. Survivin' ever since. —Take two.

DEZ: Awwwww . . .

(Dez takes two cards.)

FAYE: And it ain't been no easy work all the time. Even got the battle scars to prove that stamping doors ain't for sissies.

(Faye holds up her arm for Dez to see. A scar skates along her forearm.)

This beauty right here . . . from a press machine on 12-line. Years ago. Got backed up and tried to pull the sheet metal that was stuck in the gears. Press came right down by my hand, sparks burned the shit outta me. Coulda been a lot worse if I ain't move my hand quick. That's fast thinkin' like you ain't never seen. But I still got all my limbs. Everything intact. Twenty-nine years. —Knock.

DEZ: So that's the lesson? Faye's a survivor so shut the fuck up and leave her alone? —Spades.

(Faye's turn. She pulls cards.)

FAYE: You know, you really stupid. I'm tellin' you about being pregnant and alone. I'm telling you about having a son and bein' clueless. I'm telling you about not having the answers. Ain't never had 'em and probably never will. But whatever I'm doin', it's keepin' me here. And that's how I can be patient when the plane is headed toward a tree, cuz even if it crash . . . I don't think I'd die. I think I'd get scarred maybe. But I wouldn't die. Take the train next time. Keep movin'. —Hearts.

DEZ: Well I'm tellin' you somethin' right now, Faye.

FAYE: What you tellin' me?

DEZ: If the plane is crashing, I ain't gonna sit and watch it go into a tree. I'm goin' in that cockpit and I'm takin' the pilot's life jacket. I'm takin' the pilot's parachute. And I'm jumping from that motherfucker long before it goes up in flames. You can tell that to Reggie or whoever the hell needs to know. I'm gettin' what's mine . . .

(Faye glares at Dez. Faye pulls a card. Dez pulls and throws one. Faye pulls again. Her hand is getting full.)

FAYE: It's gonna come with a price. Just like that scar you got behind your ear.

(Dez stops playing for a moment. He touches his scar, strangely self-conscious. Then he releases, goes back to the cards.

Dez gains speed. He's down to only a few cards. Faye has a full hand.)

You can pretend you and me ain't affected by the same things, except we both got battle scars. But your way is impatient. May work for you in the short term. But in the long term, it kills.

DEZ: It's what I am, Faye.

FAYE: A hothead?

DEZ: A warrior. See?

(He drops his last card.)

Game.

FAYE: Fuck!

(Faye slams her hands down on the table.
    Dez scoops the cash.)

One more.

DEZ: Naw naw . . . can't. If Reggie catch me, he's gonna throw
    me to the wolves. That was my last game on the premises.

FAYE: He's just scaring you cuz you piss him off.

DEZ: Whatever. I ain't takin' that chance. Need me a good
    severance deal . . . *if* . . . shit goes down.

FAYE: If *if* was a splif, we'd all be high.

(Dez rises from the table, goes to his locker and grabs his gog-
gles, puts on his sweatshirt, etc.
    Shanita enters with tears in her eyes, visibly upset.)

Shanita, come let me take yo' money.

(Faye stops when she sees Shanita, who ignores both Faye and
Dez. Shanita goes to her locker.)

DEZ: What's the matter with you?

FAYE: You all right?

(Shanita doesn't answer. Her head in her locker, she bites back
a wail. Beat.
    She grabs her goggles, closes her locker.
    Then she moves past Faye and exits.
    Faye and Dez look after her with concern.)

DEZ: See that? Some people head right into that tree, crash, and don't survive. You gotta think about them, too . . .

(*Dez takes his goggles and exits.*
Faye, alone, shuffles cards. And shuffles cards. And shuffles cards.)

SCENE FOUR

Early morning in the breakroom. A new sign on the bulletin board reads: CRIME ALERT.
Shanita sips a cup of coffee. Silence.
Faye enters half dressed, putting on her work clothes.
Shanita says nothing. She reads a book of names.

FAYE: That coffee good today?
SHANITA: It's all right.
FAYE: I tried to make it like before. Don't think I mixed it the same.
SHANITA: It's all right.

(*Faye walks past the bulletin board. She sees the CRIME ALERT sign and shakes her head.*)

FAYE: You hear about the plant gettin' ripped off again?
SHANITA: Again?
FAYE: Say this morning on 9-line, more materials were missing. Don't even know how they got off with it.
SHANITA: Everybody on 3-line say they been installing more cameras on the floor. Heard they just hired a night watchman to patrol the grounds after dark.

(*A quick beat.*)

FAYE: That right? *(Pause)* Where he gonna be stationed?

SHANITA: Don't know. Just say they increasing security every-where.

(Faye registers this. Shift.)

FAYE: How that little honeybun you got cookin' in the oven? Started kicking yet?

SHANITA: Only sometimes. At night mostly.

FAYE: Started having cravings yet?

SHANITA: Not really. Tryin' not to eat a lot so I don't get fat. Gotta keep the weight off.

FAYE: Keep the weight off? If it's one time a woman supposed to feel like enjoying the full pleasures of eatin', it's when she's with child. Somebody done put that in yo' head? Got yo' mind on weight when it's s'pose to be on tendin' to your child's needs.

SHANITA: That's easy for you to say, Faye.

FAYE: How's it any easier for me than for you?

SHANITA: Woman with kids already got a uphill battle. It put a mark on you that keep everybody away.

FAYE: Like I say, how you figure it's easier for me?

SHANITA: Cuz you off men. That make it different, don't it?

FAYE: You think it's easier cuz I like women? Think heartbreak only come in opposites?

SHANITA: I ain't never known a woman to make me feel all the ways men make me feel. Crazy and so upset I can't breathe sometimes.

FAYE: Love ain't never had no kind of particulars, far as I'm con-cerned. Love just whatever it show up as. But love don't send you into the breakroom in tears every three days.

SHANITA: Don't talk about it, Faye.

FAYE: I ain't gonna talk about nothin'.

(Beat. Shanita changes the subject.)

SHANITA: Make you dream crazier though. Bein' pregnant.

FAYE: Oh yeah?

SHANITA: My Big Mama used to say dreams from a pregnant woman actually more like prophecies. You ever heard that?

FAYE: Sound like somethin' a Big Mama would say.

SHANITA: I don't know if it's any truth to it or whatever. But I been having these same dreams over and over. I'm standing on a concrete floor. Big empty space with nothin' in it. Dust covering everything. I call out the names of people. Ya'll mostly. But nobody answer. Then comes a strong gust of wind. When it stop, the dust is scrambled in a group of letters, that don't spell nothin'. Crazy, right?

FAYE: I'll say.

SHANITA: I think it could be a sign. From my baby maybe. Like whenever I can unscramble the message, everything's just gonna be clear.

FAYE: Everything like what?

SHANITA: I dunno. Life. *(Quick beat)* You think that's silly?

FAYE: Maybe so. But don't mean it ain't also possible.

(Quick shift.)

SHANITA: Where Dez?

FAYE: Think he must be runnin' late today.

SHANITA: Didn't walk me to my car yesterday. Guess he busy.

FAYE: If he don't punch in in the next five minutes, he gonna have a write-up on his hands.

SHANITA: Cassie Logan down on my line got written up yesterday for leavin' two minutes before her break cuz she had to pee. Try to tell me I can't break when my baby pressin' down on my bladder. I don't think so.

FAYE: They crackin' down like that, hunh?

SHANITA: Some folk say it's just a scare tactic. Downsizin' and trying to weed out the people who slackin'. I decided I ain't gonna listen to all that hearsay. Cuz people gonna end up sabotaging themselves and get fired . . . and that ain't gonna be me. Plus, you our union rep. Everybody know you ain't gonna take no company shit.

(Faye pauses, concerned.)

FAYE: You got a plan for yourself, regardless?

SHANITA: Got offered a job over at the Copy Center on Eight Mile. My cousin used to be the manager, but she movin' offices. Said I could come take over.

FAYE: That sounds good.

SHANITA: Not to me. What I'm gonna do at a copy center? Day in and day out, runnin' paper through these simple machines—for what? Don't got the same kind of pride this work got. Here, I feel like I'm building somethin' important. Love the way the line needs me. Like if I step away for even a second and don't ask somebody to mind my post, the whole operation has to stop. My touch . . . my special care . . . it matter. I'm building something that you can see come to life at the end. Got a motor in it and it's gonna take somebody somewhere. Gonna maybe drive some important businessman to work. Gonna get some single mama to her son's football practice. Gonna take a family on they first trip to Cedar Point. Gonna even maybe be somebody's first time. Who knows? But I like knowing I had a hand in it, you know? That's why I'm gonna turn her down.

FAYE: Your cousin?

SHANITA: Don't wanna work at no copy center. What's life at a copy center?

FAYE: Maybe you don't wanna do that yet. Always nice to have somethin' behind you in case you need to cover yo' ass.

SHANITA: Cover my ass for what? Do somethin' I don't believe in? I figure ya'll is right. Time to stop worryin' about something that may not happen. Workin' in this industry is what I do. Uncertainty is always there. But it's the work I'm made of. In me from my daddy. Wanted a son, but got me instead. Always been good with my hands, and this somethin' that makes him proud of me. Not bein' pregnant before I'm married. Not being over twenty-five and building a family by myself. But this? Being a highly skilled job setter . . . that's something I can stand on. Everybody can't say that. Everybody can't do what I do. I belong here. Ride it till the wheels fall off. Right?

(Pause. Faye rises from the table.)

FAYE: I need a smoke.

SHANITA: Need to quit, Faye. Ain't good for you.

FAYE: Where my pack?

(Shanita points to the counter. Faye grabs her pack.)

SHANITA: You better do it outside. Don't wanna get caught breakin' the rules right now.

FAYE: I'll be back in a few. See you out on the floor.

(Faye leaves.
    Shanita rises slowly. She goes over to the sink, washes her dish.
    Dez enters hastily, looking untidy.)

DEZ: Reggie been in here yet?

SHANITA: Not yet. You got like thirty seconds to punch in.

(Dez rushes to the clock and punches his card. Shanita turns to look at him.)

What happened to you?

DEZ: Nothin'.

SHANITA: Something.

DEZ: Got into a fight.

SHANITA: With who?

DEZ: Some fools on Gratiot. *(Pronounced "grash-it," like "mash-it")* Stopped at the gas station and them niggas tried to rob me.

SHANITA: You for real? This morning?

DEZ: Yeah.

SHANITA: What happened? You all right?

DEZ: Yeah I'm all right. Tried to jump me. We got into it for a sec but I got out of it.

SHANITA: How?

DEZ: I just did.

(Dez goes to make some coffee.)

SHANITA: What happened to you yesterday?

DEZ: Yesterday when?

SHANITA: After work. The parking lot? You wasn't there.

DEZ: Oh my bad. I had to run somewhere in a rush. Plus, I knew you was workin' late with Reggie. Figured he could walk you to yo' car if you needed somebody.

(Silence. Dez looks at Shanita. He cracks a smile.)

Why? You miss me?

SHANITA *(A little)*: Boy, please. I was just asking cuz you always make such a big deal of walkin' me, and then poof—you disappeared. Was just wonderin', that's all.

DEZ: Wondering for what?

SHANITA: Cuz you said you would. That's all. But obviously
you're the kinda person that say they gonna do somethin'
and then don't show up. Tell me everything I need to know.

DEZ: If I knew you cared, I'da shown up. To hell with my
meeting.

SHANITA: Meeting?

DEZ: With some of my business partners. For my garage.

SHANITA: Meeting? Not a date?

DEZ: Which one make you more jealous?

SHANITA : Tccchhhh . . . Neither.

DEZ: Neither?

(Pause. Shanita and Dez look at each other. A moment of possibility. Shanita considers it . . . then quickly decides to shut it down.)

SHANITA *(As if answering her own question)*: You too reckless.

(Shanita heads out of the breakroom.)

DEZ: I'll be there for you today. After work. Walk you to your
car. If you want me to.

SHANITA: I won't be waiting.

(Shanita exits.
Dez watches her go . . . his heart longing after . . .
Then he goes to his locker. Pulls a package wrapped in cloth from his locker. Peeks at the item and breathes a sigh of relief.
He finds a plastic bag nearby. He puts the wrapped item in the bag, puts the item back in locker. He closes and locks it and heads out onto the floor.
As a spotlight closes in on the locker, silhouetted workers are illuminated, struggling to complete stamping motions. More chinks in the rhythm. More dysfunction.)

SCENE FIVE

Morning in the breakroom. A bra hangs over the heater. The heater is on. Some panties lay across the heater.

The boom box is on. A song by Aretha Franklin plays.

Faye enters in pajamas, maybe a makeshift robe. She has a towel over her hair from recent washing. She goes through her morning ritual. She puts on deodorant.

She takes the towel off and begins to brush her hair into something presentable. Eats some toast.

She checks the panties on the heater. Feels that they are dry, slides them on. Pulls the bra off the heater.

FAYE *(To the heater)*: Better not burn my titties.

> *(She continues to get dressed, putting on socks, boots, lotion, etc.*
> *At the breakroom door, someone attempts to enter but can't get in. A knock.)*

REGGIE *(From off)*: Hello? Somebody in there?

> *(Faye turns off the music and quickly cleans up around her, hastily throwing things into her locker. She fastens her bra. Squirms a bit from the dampness. Throws on a sweatshirt.*
> *The beating at the door gets more rapid.)*

Whoever the hell is in there, you've got five seconds to open this door before I call the cops.

(Faye grabs a cigarette. Lights it, takes a few puffs.
The doorknob shakes and shakes. Loud banging. The door rattles.)

One.

(Faye takes another puff.)

Two.

(Faye puffs.)

Three, gotdamnit.

(Faye blows the smoke around the room. She fans it with her hands.)

Four, asshole.

(Faye puts out the cigarette. Grabs a room freshener and sprays.)

All right. Be stupid then.

(Faye opens the door, sees Reggie on his cell. He stares at her in disbelief for a moment and then hangs up.)

FAYE: My bad.
REGGIE: Faye? What are you—???

(Reggie enters the breakroom.)

You've been smoking?
FAYE: You can tell? Damn.
REGGIE: The room reeks, Faye!
FAYE: I'm sorry.
REGGIE: You've got to stop this. Why didn't you say anything?
FAYE: Ain't wanna hear your mouth. Was just trying to cover it up.
REGGIE: Well you did a terrible job. It smells awful in here. How long were you—do you know what I was thinking?

FAYE: That I was one of those rip-off artists?

REGGIE: Could've caused a big panic.

FAYE: And here you go—countin'.

REGGIE: I was trying to be fair.

FAYE: What were you gonna do if somebody opened this door ready to knock you silly? Count how many times they go upside your head?

REGGIE: You know I was about to call the cops on you?

FAYE: I figured I had till four and a half . . . four and three-quarters . . .

REGGIE *(Laughs faintly)*: That's not funny.

FAYE: Yes it is. I'm sorry. I just needed me an early smoke and it's too damn cold this morn' to do it outside. *(Shift)* They figured out who's been stealing that stuff anyway?

REGGIE: Not yet. Upstairs is cracking down on all of us.

FAYE: So what's that mean?

REGGIE: That means I'm going to be doing some investigating. I need you to report anything out of the ordinary to me. Everybody, for that matter. I want to make sure they know our unit is part of the solution and not the problem. Whole management team has a lot of pressure on us not to let this thing get any more out of control.

FAYE: Why's the pressure on you? How you supposed to stop it more than anybody else?

REGGIE: It's happening on one of our shifts. Somebody's got to be responsible.

(Pause. Reggie takes down old signs from the bulletin boards and posts new ones: "FRIDGE EMPTIED EVERY FRIDAY." "YOU SEE YOUR MAMA HERE? NO? THEN CLEAN UP AFTER YOURSELF!" "STOP AND SEARCH POLICY IN EFFECT."

Faye's eyes bore through Reggie.)

FAYE: You got a sign in there from HR?

REGGIE: Not yet, Faye.

FAYE: What about fighting to keep this place open? Shifting the production schedule to keep us working?

REGGIE: I brought that up. Harris says he'll give it some thought.

FAYE: Draggin' ya heels, ain't you?

REGGIE: . . .

. . .

. . .

There's a lot going on right now. This theft is throwing a monkey wrench and this production schedule is a tall task and—

FAYE (*Like a dagger*): Excuses.

(*Tense beat.*)

People need notice.

REGGIE: I'm pushing for that.

FAYE: Health care. Survival money.

REGGIE: You think I don't know that?

FAYE: This could sink some of us. Be the nail in our coffin. Folks got kids to provide for. Contracts demand we get a fair notice.

REGGIE: You bringing up contracts, Faye? You think I'm not doing my part?

FAYE: Tuition reimbursement. Retraining support. COBRA plans that don't kill us. You got a good relationship with Harris. Time to make it count.

REGGIE: You don't think I'm pulling his coat to all that? You think this is me?

FAYE: Ain't sayin' it's you.

REGGIE: Early panic, Faye. The company is afraid of it. Thinks it will impact production for the rest of the year.

FAYE: Is that what you think?

REGGIE: Doesn't matter what I think.

FAYE: It matters.

(Beat.)

REGGIE: Faye, I'm a good foreman.

FAYE: I know you are.

REGGIE: I'm not the enemy.

FAYE: I didn't say you were.

REGGIE: Then don't question me. Please. I'm doing everything I can.

(Reggie continues with his signs.)

FAYE: Shanita got a job offer.

REGGIE: She did? Where?

FAYE: Copy Center. Eight Mile. Can run it herself and probably earn a decent wage for her and her little one.

REGGIE *(To himself)*: Huh . . .

FAYE: She's gonna turn it down, Reggie.

REGGIE: She say that?

FAYE: Verbatim.

(Pause. Reggie contemplates.)

REGGIE: I can talk to Harris. See if we can get her placed somewhere else.

FAYE: Without seniority? She got a definite. You want her to wait on a maybe?

REGGIE: Her record is impeccable. I know we can get her resituated somewhere.

FAYE: Just like you?

REGGIE: That's right. Just like me. That's what I'm working on. That's the line I have to walk, Faye.

FAYE: You think about what walking that line is costing everybody else?

REGGIE: Of course I'm thinking about it! I don't like it. But what else can I do? I don't own this place, I just try to keep it running smoothly.

FAYE: I been holding off for you Reggie. Was a time when I'd grab these folk and take to the damn street. Shut this place down until they do right. To hell with company interests. You got the ear of your supervisor. That's a rare spot to be in. You tell Harris it's time to be transparent. Production'll just have to be what it'll be.

REGGIE: He's not going to listen to all of that, Faye!

FAYE: What is he going to listen to? You thought about that?

REGGIE: I'm thinking about that! I'm also thinking that I need my job just like everybody else. If this company folds, I could fold with it. I don't have a union to protect me. I just have my reputation. A rep that could get me placed some-where else. Ohio maybe. Out In Virgina would be nice. If I start rousing things up before it's time, I'm gonna be the one to lose out. My kids. My wife. I'm thinking about Shanita. I'm thinking about Dez. I'm thinking about you. Bony J. I'm thinking about Elder Johnson whose been working the line for forty-five years. The man's been in my house. Buys Christmas presents for my kids. And I'm thinking on what'll happen to him if he doesn't get the right package. I'm thinking about Dalina and Darnell . . . how much they love bringing friends over to the house now. How often they hang outside because they feel safe. How I could lose my job and make my family lose everything we've been— I'm walking the line, Faye. One foot in front of the other and trying not to fall and crash and break my spine. And who am I going to lift up when I'm broken? How can I help anyone else if I don't help myself? I'm thinking about it, Faye. I'm thinking about Shanita. I'm thinking about Dez. I'm thinking about you. I'm thinking and I'm thinking and I'm thinking—okay?!

FAYE: Okay.

(*Air.*)

Sound like your mama right now.

REGGIE: How's that?

FAYE: Just how she would say, "Shut up, Faye" or "Back off, Faye" without really sayin' nothin' at all.

REGGIE: I wouldn't tell you to shut up.

FAYE: No. You got too much sense to do that. But you tellin' me somethin' all right.

(*Beat.*)

REGGIE: Cheryl's been asking about you. Said to tell you she misses your peach cobbler.

FAYE: Yeah well . . . maybe I'll stop by one of these weekends and take over your kitchen.

REGGIE: Or we come to you. Whatever's easier.

FAYE: I come to you.

REGGIE: The kids'll be happy to see you.

FAYE: Sho.

REGGIE: I got to get on upstairs, Faye.

FAYE: Yeah.

(*Reggie heads to the door.*)

I know you thinkin', Reggie. But you come to a conclusion real soon, you hear me? Otherwise, I'm gonna come to one first. Cuz I can't let these folk fall with nothin' to stand on. Secret or no secret. Family or not. You understand that?

(*Reggie looks at Faye, almost incredulous.*)

REGGIE: What are you saying?
FAYE: Think fast.

(Reggie exits, concerned.)

SCENE SIX

Nighttime falls on the breakroom. It is empty.
Sounds at the door.

REGGIE *(From off)*: I need to get in there and there's not a damn thing you're going to do to stop me. You don't like to listen. You never like to follow any damn rules. Get out of my way, Dez. I swear to God you better get out of my way.

DEZ *(From off)*: What the hell you tryin' to go through my stuff for, hunh? I ain't see no warrant. You wanna go through my shit, you gotta get somethin' or else you gonna have to walk through me. I ain't movin' nowhere.

(Dez opens the door with Reggie at his heels.)

DEZ: I swear to God, you need a warrant.
REGGIE: I don't need a warrant while we're on work grounds. This isn't your personal house, Dez. That's what you don't understand.
DEZ: You don't know what I understand.
REGGIE: I'm going to ask you one more time, Dez. Open your bag, or else I'm getting the clippers and we're cutting this lock.
DEZ: What the hell am I? A criminal?
REGGIE: Better not be.

DEZ: Why you gotta act like such a bitch, man?!

REGGIE: Watch your gotdamn mouth, Dez!

(Faye and Shanita enter the breakroom hastily.)

FAYE: What's going on in here?

SHANITA: Can hear ya'll all the way down the hall.

DEZ: This nigga wanna test me—

REGGIE: I'm not yo' nigga—

DEZ: —cuz I didn't want him going through my bag.

REGGIE: Because you're being insubordinate.

FAYE: Why're you going through his bag?

REGGIE: Do you all even read any of the signs I post? Mandatory stop and search. Employees are asked to empty their bags when exiting the building—

DEZ: At random—

REGGIE: It happens to everyone.

DEZ: And today it only happened to happen to me.

REGGIE: It was a random search, Dez. We've been hit a lot lately. It's perfectly fair.

DEZ: Fair to who?

REGGIE: Fair to everyone! I put up a notice. It wasn't out of the blue. You act like it was out of the blue.

SHANITA: I got stopped yesterday. Just opened my bag and showed 'em it wasn't full of nothin' but prenatal pills. No big deal. They let me out and I went home.

DEZ: That ain't what this is about.

REGGIE: What is it about then Dez, hunh?

DEZ: You know what this is about, Faye.

FAYE: Faye? How'd I get into this?

DEZ: Cuz you always protecting this dude—

FAYE: Don't bring no Faye into this.

(The sound of radio static interrupts.)

VOICE THROUGH STATIC: Status report. All units in?

(Reggie grabs the radio on his hip.)

REGGIE *(Into the radio)*: Handling a dilemma. Status update in two minutes. *(Shift)* Dez, stop stalling. I've got to report back. Get past your foolish pride and open your bag. Or I'm going in the locker. It's that simple.

DEZ: I ain't opening shit.

SHANITA: Dez, just open the bag!

DEZ: Ain't right.

FAYE *(To Reggie)*: What you need to know about him? Tell me and I'll school you. Been watching him come and go every damn day.

REGGIE: It's simple protocol. I look in Dez's bag. He's cleared and goes home. It doesn't have to be this difficult. He's making it difficult.

DEZ: I ain't making shit difficult—

REGGIE: Unless he has something to hide.

DEZ: You accusing me of something?

REGGIE: I'm not accusing, I'm inquiring—

FAYE: Dez ain't stealin' nothin'. He's a fool but he ain't that stupid.

REGGIE: If I don't search him, the cops will. He can make this a lot easier.

DEZ: To hell with you and the cops.

REGGIE: Damnit Dez! I'm going to ask you one more time—

SHANITA: Dez, just do it!

DEZ: Do what?! Prove something? Won't matter! Once you got your mind made up about me you got your mind made up. What I'm supposed to do? Change it? Convince you I'm not the shit that you done convinced yourself I am? That's supposed to be my burden? My job? Hunh? Fuck that. Nigga always on me about something—

REGGIE: You break the rules!

DEZ: Always treating me like I'm up to no good. Like I ain't got a righteous bone in my body. Won't matter why I do what I do or what my intentions are. Won't matter what plans I got or what I'm trying to build. You got your mind made up that I'm shit and you just waiting for proof. So open the locker, then. Get your gotdamn proof. But don't ask me to volunteer for this bullshit. Just do what you gotta do.

SHANITA: Dez.

REGGIE: Fine then.

(Reggie picks up a pair of bolt cutters. He walks over to Dez's locker.

Faye looks at Dez with concern. Then she walks over to Reggie.)

FAYE: You don't gotta humiliate him like this now. Ya'll both just overheated. Step away, cool off and let me talk some reason into him.

REGGIE: I'm tired of being disrespected by him, Faye. I gave him a chance. He asked for this.

(Reggie reluctantly clips the lock. He opens the locker. He pulls out a pair of goggles, some boots, gym socks. Other personal items: deodorant, cologne, a brush, etc.

Dez stands defiant. Reggie finds nothing significant. He approaches Dez.)

The bag.

(Dez doesn't move.)

DEZ *(Sucking teeth in defiance)*: Tttttchhh . . .

REGGIE: The bag. Or we call the cops.

(*Dez stands defiant. Shanita and Faye look on with concern.*
Reggie reaches for Dez's backpack. Dez doesn't protest. He
doesn't resist. He remains stoic.
Reggie opens Dez's book bag. He pulls out the gun.
Shanita quietly gasps with concern.)

What—

(*Reggie sighs with disappointment. He pulls out a plastic bag.*
Peers inside. Sees the wrapped material.
He holds it out to Dez.)

Bullshit, hunh?

(*The radio on Reggie's hip goes off. The sound of static.*)

VOICE THROUGH STATIC: Unit nine, status update? . . . Unit nine,
status update?

(*Dez is silent. Reggie puts the material back into the book bag.*
Puts the gun back inside. Holds the bag.
All eyes on Reggie, waiting breathlessly for his reply.
Reggie looks at Dez. At everyone. He sets the book bag back
by Dez's foot, and exits.)

ACT TWO

Dez, Shanita and Faye in the breakroom. Five minutes have passed. Faye sits across from Dez. He is a wall. Shanita tries to fill the silent space.

SHANITA *(Nervous chatter)*: This whole city is under construction. That's what I discovered on my way into work today. Traffic on the 75 was crazy. They done took everything down to one lane. And people don't know how to merge. Cars backed up for miles cuz people don't know how to merge. Don't matter what freeway you take, it be the same selfish behavior on all of 'em. Everybody got somewhere to be and don't wanna let you in. Even when you honk at 'em. Even when you try to smile pretty and be polite with it. That shit used to work at one point. I could always squeeze into a lane with a smile. But not no more. Nobody wants to merge no more. We just gettin' squished into smaller lanes while they make these promises to fix the freeways and don't seem like they ever really get fixed. And at the end of the day, we just hate drivin' with each other cuz ain't enough space and assholes don't wanna let you in. And all I can think anymore is if we just merged, shit would flow so much better.

(Faye sets a cup of coffee in front of Dez.)

DEZ: No thanks.
FAYE: Drink.
DEZ: Not thirsty.
FAYE: Drink.

(Dez grimaces at Faye, then takes the coffee and sips. Shanita remains lost in thought.)

SHANITA: And I think I'm getting road rage. A big Mack truck ran me onto the shoulder of the freeway last week. I got so angry, I grabbed my chocolate Frosty from Wendy's and threw it at his window.
    But it just kinda sailed in the air and burst in the middle of the street. It was pretty anticlimactic. *(Beat)* Damn road rage. Damn construction. Maybe we just need a whole new city.
FAYE: You better take a yoga class and calm yo' ass down. Don't wanna throw your Frosty at the wrong car.
SHANITA: I need to quit Frosties anyway 'fore I get fatter than I already am.
FAYE: Don't start that talk again.
SHANITA: I been doing good except for those. And also brownies.

(She breaks a piece of brownie and slides it over to Dez. He sits stoic.)

DEZ: I'm good.

SHANITA: Eat it.

DEZ: Ain't hungry.

SHANITA: Don't matter.

> (*Dez looks at Shanita. She's not playing.*
> *Dez bites into the brownie unenthusiastically.*
> *They watch him eat. Silence.*)

What you think Reggie tellin' 'em?

FAYE: Ain't sure.

> (*Pause.*)

SHANITA: He don't seem like he would snitch. Think he would snitch?

FAYE: Reggie got a lot to deal with.

DEZ: Here she go.

FAYE: Don't start turnin' on me now. I done fed yo' ass some coffee.

DEZ: Ain't startin' nothin' with you.

SHANITA: Why you bringin' that gun up in here, Dez?

DEZ: Same reason you throwin' Frosties at Mack trucks.

SHANITA: Oh—so you pregnant and hormonal too?

DEZ: Shit gets personal on the street.

SHANITA: This ain't the street.

FAYE: You gon' tell us what that was Reggie found in yo' bag? Or you just want us all to pretend we ain't see that?

DEZ: What I got to answer to you for?

FAYE: Ain't said you had to answer to me.

DEZ: Tired of bein' questioned.

FAYE: Maybe if you gave some answers, folks wouldn't have so many damn questions about you.

DEZ: Maybe I don't need everybody in my business all the damn time. Ain't asked you for your help. And you ain't one to talk about answerin' folks. You the last person to point that finger.

FAYE: You ain't me Dez. When you gonna learn that?

DEZ: You slide around here under the radar and defend everything that dude do, and don't even got the decency to let us know the plant closing.

SHANITA: That's just a rumor.

DEZ: Ain't no rumor. That's a fact. And Faye know it too. Closing this year, ain't that right Faye?

FAYE: Dez, stop talking stupid. You gon' cause Shanita unnecessary stress.

SHANITA: Folks always talk about the plant closing. Always threats.

DEZ: 'Cept these ain't just threats. Management droppin' down every department. Keepin' on just enough people to get the job done. Anybody ain't crucial to the line gettin' cut. Ain't that right, Faye?

SHANITA: Faye, what's he talkin' bout?

(Pause. Faye glares at Dez.)

FAYE: This how you wanna do this? Really?

DEZ: I could ask you the same thing.

SHANITA: Rumors true?

(Faye looks at Shanita for a moment.)

FAYE: It ain't that I wasn't planning on sayin' nothin'. That ain't it. I was just handling things internally first.

SHANITA: We getting shut down, Faye?

FAYE: I ain't got no thorough report yet. Been working on getting as much info as I can.

DEZ: Info from Reggie, ain't that right? He told you somethin'. And 'fore we get dropped, you could be organizing with UAW to make sure we get took care of right, 'steada sittin' back protecting Reggie.

FAYE: Ain't nobody been sittin' back on nothin'. I been drawing out terms while Reggie works with management on—

DEZ: Work with management?! Since when is that how we negotiate?

SHANITA: Faye, what's gonna happen to us? We gonna lose everything?

FAYE: I ain't gonna let that happen to you.

DEZ: You done already proved where your loyalty be. Ain't with us.

SHANITA: I can't believe this. You wasn't gonna tell us, Faye?

FAYE: 'Course I was gonna tell you! You think I ain't been stressin' over this every night? Shit, I done had plenty of stresses and this plant closing is only one of 'em.

DEZ: We all got stresses but I think you got yo' blinders on for somebody ain't deservin'—

FAYE: What you know about deserving?!

DEZ: I know Reggie ain't on our side. I know he get set up right he be taken care of. Everybody just out to protect themselves—keep they own neck from gettin' broke. Don't matter how many other necks get snapped down below, as long as your family took care of.

FAYE: That's your problem. You only know how to see shit through small cracks and not the whole damn picture. You think he ain't got nothin' to lose? You think you the only one in limbo when this place shut down?

DEZ: Faye, what's the reason when it come to Reggie you can't see a spade for a spade? The rest of us see it and you still callin' hearts. That nigga ain't no heart. He's a spade.

FAYE: You blame Reggie for everything this plant do to keep you in line, but Reggie ain't make you bring that gun up in here. That was you. That wasn't nothin' but you.

SHANITA: Did you take them materials, Dez?

DEZ: What if I did, hunh? What difference will it make?

SHANITA: Makes a lotta difference. Makes you a thief.

FAYE: Thief and a liar.

DEZ: A liar? That's supposed to mean somethin' coming from you?

FAYE: I ain't took nothin' from nobody. That's a low I ain't never sunk to.

DEZ: Ya'll gotta be kiddin' gettin' moral on me right now. You think any of this is moral? Keep us workin' these presses till we pull a fuckin' shoulder blade, and then replace us in a heartbeat if we can't keep up the production. You think when this ship sinks the captain's going down? Ya'll got this blind faith in a crew that don't even eat lunch with you. Don't know your kid's first name.

FAYE: What's my son's name, Dez?

DEZ: That ain't the point.

FAYE: What's his name?

DEZ: You the one don't never talk about him.

SHANITA: What is your son's name?

FAYE: I rest my case.

DEZ: What case is you trying to make?

FAYE: Your whole philosophy is bullshit. You stealin' from the plant, don't try to make it nothin' righteous. Don't try to make it a cause. You want to be a thief? Be a thief. But don't try to hustle us into believing this is some sort of way to seek justice. You work. You sweat. You fight to have somethin' fair and right for yourself before you die. That's the industry. That's what we signed up for.

SHANITA: That ain't what I sign up for. A crapshoot. I signed up for a future.

FAYE: And you still gonna have one. You got a lotta potential to get placed somewhere else. Just keep doin' your best, and it's gonna mean somethin' for you. And Dez, if you ain't lose your cool, ain't no tellin' what you could build for yourself.

DEZ: Who say I'm not building? *(Beat)* I got this homie that used to work down at WDZH before they moved stations. They started layin' off cats one by one till it was just this small crew left to cover the basics. Five dudes doing the work of twenty. And my boy was one of the five. They stayed on till the last two days when the station was getting stripped. Had all these materials that were going to be tossed to scraps, sold at auctions and whatever. Meanwhile, the homie had all these dreams of being a DJ. Was gonna start his own station. Here he was, sitting in the middle of tons of resources. Mixers. Turntables. Full DJ starter kit. Two days before his last day of work, they fired him. Said he wasn't working up to performance. Bullshit. And the homie left with nothing. No severance. No bonus. No studio of his own. Nothing. That was like three years ago. Just saw him working security down at the casino. Ain't even talkin' DJ'ing no more. And I remember him saying—"If I'd've known I was getting fired, I'd've robbed them blind." I remember that real clear. *(Beat)* Don't assume we not building something. You don't even know.

FAYE: Did you take those materials, Dez?

(Dez and Faye glare at each other.
A moment.
The door opens and Reggie enters. Everyone is silent, waiting breathlessly for the decision.)

REGGIE: Time for everybody to leave.
FAYE: What's going on?
SHANITA: Dez in trouble?
REGGIE: You need to get on outta here. All three of you.

SHANITA: What about— *(Seeing Reggie's tone)* All right . . .
DEZ: Fine by me.

(Dez grabs his book bag. Reggie stands before him. They look at the bag.
   Reggie finally moves out of Dez's path. Shaking his head.)

REGGIE: You too, Faye. All of you need to go on home now.

(Dez stops at the door. Looks at Faye.)

FAYE: Okay. I'm right behind ya'll. Just gonna finish my pot of coffee. Ya'll go'on ahead.
REGGIE: Can't, Faye. Shift is over. I'm walking everybody out.
DEZ: I'll walk Faye out. Let her have her coffee.
REGGIE: You're in no position to give me orders. Get out of here, Dez. Shanita. Faye. Everybody, let's walk.

(Dez and Faye look at each other knowingly. Shanita heads to the door. Faye carefully gathers her clothing. Slowly. Calculatingly. She finally puts on her coat and heads to the door.
   Her eyes bore through Reggie. It's painful.
   Dez is last. He and Reggie look at each other. No words. Then finally:)

DEZ *(Shaking his head)*: Pssssshhhhhh . . .
REGGIE: . . .
   . . .
   . . .

(Reggie hits the light on the breakroom.)

SCENE TWO

Nighttime at the plant. The silhouetted workers on the line move slowly, rigidly. The sounds of the plant create a slow and chilling mechanical orchestra.

Moonlight peeks through the basement-like windows into the breakroom.

Lights up on Reggie, looking around the breakroom. In his hands, a piece of Faye's clothing.

Suddenly a noise of someone fidgeting with the door. Reggie turns to look at it.

The door opens and a hooded figure is revealed. The hood comes off and it's Faye. She stands to face Reggie.

They stare at each other silently—in disbelief.

REGGIE: Faye????

FAYE: . . .

    . . .

    Fuck.

(Uncomfortable silence.)

REGGIE: Faye. What are you— What the hell are you doing here?

FAYE: . . .

    . . .

    . . .

REGGIE: You . . . haven't been . . . steal—

FAYE: No.

(More silence.)

REGGIE: Then what is this? Why are you here?

FAYE: What do you want me to say?

REGGIE: Whatever the truth is.

FAYE: The truth? Okay. *(Pause)* It's cold as fuck out there tonight.

REGGIE: I don't understand.

FAYE: To sleep in my car, Reggie. It's too damn cold to sleep in my car. *(Beat)* The truth.

REGGIE: Why're you sleeping in your . . . something wrong at home?

FAYE: Let's just leave it alone.

REGGIE: I can't leave it alone.

FAYE: Better if you don't know.

REGGIE: I'll be the judge of that.

FAYE: Just let it go, I said.

REGGIE: Faye, why can't you go home?

FAYE: Cuz I ain't got one. Satisfied?

REGGIE: What . . . happened to your house?

FAYE: I lost it, Reggie. Bank took it from me. That's all there is to it.

(Long beat.)

REGGIE: . . .

　　. . .

　　. . .

　　Why wouldn't you say anything? Why wouldn't you tell me???

FAYE: I ain't tryin' to hear no lectures right now. Just came to get warm.

REGGIE: How long have you been sleeping here?

FAYE: Long enough to piss you off.

REGGIE: Faye, goddamnit!

FAYE: 'Bout a month! Maybe longer.

REGGIE: A month???

　　. . .

　　. . .

　　. . .

FAYE: Thought it'd be better if you didn't know.

REGGIE: That's all you have to say?

FAYE: What you want me to say?

REGGIE: Say how!!! Why???

FAYE: I don't know what to tell you Reggie. Ain't nothin' I can say that's gonna ease you none. I wasn't keepin' up the payments on the note. Goddamn property taxes killin' me. Roof was damn near cavin' in and I couldn't afford to fix it up. Cancer treatments kickin' my ass. What you want me to say? I ain't goin' through my whole list of finances with you. Shit got out of my hands. End of the damn story.

REGGIE: What about Jalen?

FAYE: You wanna know the last time I spoke to my son? Let's see . . . well he got married 'bout three years ago. Joined that new church on James Couzens. Had my first grandchild some months later and told me he had some concerns 'bout my lifestyle. Guessin' that pastor done convinced him a lesbian grandmamma wasn't the best influence or some shit.

REGGIE: Faye, I didn't kn—

FAYE: Fuck it. I see him on holidays. Ain't no tragedy. Just is what it is.

(Silence.)

What you doin' here so late? You come to snoop on us?

REGGIE: I come here to think. Look for answers.

FAYE: Answers to what.

REGGIE (Quick pause): They want me to fire Dez, Faye.

FAYE: No.

REGGIE: Yes.

FAYE: They determined him the thief—just like that? No hearin' or nothin'?

REGGIE: For his insubordination.

FAYE: What about the missing materials? The gun?

REGGIE: Didn't mention it. Tried to hold 'em off. Said I was delayed cuz of his insubordination. So they say, we've been needing to downsize. Why don't we release him.

FAYE: Dez a good worker.

REGGIE: I know it.

FAYE: Stubborn, but a good worker.

REGGIE: I know it, Faye.

FAYE: Don't do it, Reggie. Don't let 'em do it.

REGGIE: I'm trying—I just can't— *(Beat)* You know what Cheryl told me the other day when I come home?

FAYE: What's that.

REGGIE: I look like I'm disappearing from myself.

FAYE: You got a lotta stress.

REGGIE: I'm tired of hearin' that.

FAYE: You ain't in a easy position.

REGGIE: I'm sick of walking that line.

FAYE: What line?

REGGIE: Line that say I'm over here and you over there and even though we started with the same dirt on our shoes . . . I'm supposed to pretend like you ain't more than an employee ID number. Like I don't know what happens out there when you leave these plant grounds. Why every man feels the need to arm himself before he walks into the grocery store or drops his kids off at school. Like I don't know the fear that's come over all of us lately. Walk around with your manhood on the line cuz you never know who's gonna try to take it from you. Cuz you never know when you're gonna be the next one out there, desperate and needin' to feed your family by any means necessary. I know Dez well, Faye. I look him in the eye and he scares the shit outta me. Cuz that invisible line between us . . . it's thin as hell.

FAYE: We all walk that line. Any moment any one of us could
be the other. That's just the shit about life. One minute
you passin' the woman on the freeway holdin' up the "will
work for food" sign. Next minute, you sleepin' in your
car, damn near . . .

(A moment. Faye almost loses herself. Reggie sees this.)

REGGIE: Faye, what are we gonna do? You gotta tell me how
to help.
FAYE: See this the shit I ain't want.
REGGIE: What d'you mean?
FAYE: Bein' made helpless. Strippin' me to the last scrap. Lose
the house. The family. The job. Know what's left after that?
REGGIE: Faye—
FAYE: The soul. Then nothin'. I'm runnin' on soul now, Reggie. Only thing still got fuel in it. And you and this pity . . .
you gon' run me to empty.
REGGIE: This ain't about pride, Faye.
FAYE: I grew up on the East Side of Detroit, you know that?
Seen buildings burn to the ground on Devil's Night. People squattin' in houses with no running water. My mama
could barely afford to keep the gas on and we still found
ways to stay warm. I don't like nobody questionin' my
ability to rise up. I'm a born and raised East-Sider. If it's
one thing I know, it's how to rise the hell up.
REGGIE: How you gonna do that Faye??? With no help? We
supposed to be—I grew up at your house. My whole family—holidays. Barbecues. This don't just affect you, you
know that? You keepin' from this me—it ain't right and
it ain't fair!
FAYE: Don't tell me nothing about fair! It ain't fair, it ain't
fair— Life ain't fair! You think I don't know what I done?
You think I'm some victim? I gamble goddamnit. Blow

half my shit down at Greektown Casino. Now, you feel sorry for me? Started goin' down there twice a week. Then three times. You want me to tell you somethin' so it all make sense?

REGGIE: Yes I do—

FAYE: Your mama died.

REGGIE: . . .

FAYE: She was my heart and she gone and I couldn't move anymore without fuckin' somethin' up. I lose the people I give two shits about and I take it out on my pocketbook. Casino be the only place where nobody give a damn about you or your condition. They surround you with just enough strangers and noise that you feel halfway all right. And that was my choice. That's what I done. Now what about that? You still think that ain't fair? Or somewhere in your head, you figurin' I did this to myself?

REGGIE: I don't know what I think! *(Painfully)* Damnit Faye . . .

(Long beat. Then a shift. He tries a new tactic.)

We got a couch in the den. You come sleep there.

FAYE: Couch in here suit me just fine.

REGGIE: Faye, you can't . . . they'll find you. Tell me to let go of you next.

FAYE: I wish they would. Many years as I put in?

REGGIE: I don't know what's gonna come, Faye. You hear what I'm sayin'? I can't say it's gonna be good.

FAYE: I'm not asking you to make up happy endings. All I'm asking is that you tell 'em they can't write us off. We crucial to this production gettin' finished before they shut down. Tell 'em we need Dez. You got to fight for us, Reggie.

REGGIE: What about the materials?

FAYE: I don't think he stole nothin'.

REGGIE: You know that for a fact, Faye?

FAYE: I don't know nothin' for a fact. But I know Dez and he ain't no thief. You know it, too.

REGGIE: What the hell do I know? You living here right under my nose??? How in the hell did I not—like I'm some distant—

FAYE: Reggie.

REGGIE *(Urgently)*: Come home with me, Faye.

FAYE: . . .

   . . .

   Let me stay for the night.

REGGIE: We can get you situated somewhere.

FAYE: Just give me time to think.

REGGIE: They put up cameras.

FAYE: Not in here. Patrolman ain't gon' bother me none.

REGGIE: What if they have footage of you?

FAYE: I move off the radar.

REGGIE: Faye, don't do this to me. I can't leave you like this.

FAYE: Reggie, I need you to let me be.

REGGIE: Faye—

FAYE: Just leave! *(Pause)* Please. I need to do this. On my own.

REGGIE: . . .

   . . .

   I . . .

(Silence. They look at each other for a moment. Reggie is going to say more, but what's left to say?)

If my mother knew I left you like this . . .

(Reggie bites back his words. Walks out of the door. And disappears.)

SCENE THREE

Morning. The breakroom is empty. Shanita enters and digs in her bag. Pulls out a Tupperware dish and places it in the microwave.

Dez enters with his things and looks at Shanita. They are silent for a moment.

The microwave buzzes. Shanita's dish is ready. She goes to get it.

Dez goes to his locker and puts up his belongings. As he places things inside, his book bag falls to the ground.

Shanita looks at it curiously. She says nothing.

DEZ: I ain't that stupid. Don't worry. Nothin' in here today. Not with folk invading my privacy.

SHANITA: I ain't said nothin'.

DEZ: I noticed. Not even good morning. Not even nothin' mean or rude. A brother can't even get a eye roll.

SHANITA: Ain't got nothin' to say.

DEZ: Aiight then . . . Be that way.

(Pause. Shanita starts to eat her food. It is nothing skimpy or scarce like her usual. It's a full, hearty meal.

Dez pulls out a pathetic sandwich from his bag. Maybe the bread is stuck together. He sits down next to Shanita and picks at it pitifully. They eat silently.)

SHANITA: Just stupid.

DEZ: You talkin' 'bout me?

SHANITA: Thinkin' aloud.

DEZ: Whatever.

(More silence. Dez picks apart his sandwich. It is falling apart. Gone from looking sad to looking diseased. Shanita watches in disgust.)

SHANITA: Gonna make me lose my breakfast watchin' you eat
     that.
DEZ: It's a perfectly good sandwich.
SHANITA: It look like roadkill. Just stop. Here.

*(She grabs a nearby plate and puts some of her food on it. She
slides the plate over to Dez. He eats obediently.)*

DEZ: Damn, girl! You put your foot in this. I ain't know you
     could cook like this.
SHANITA: I do all right.
DEZ: What you put in these potatoes? Got extra flavor.
SHANITA: Curry.
DEZ: That's what's up.

(More silence. A beat.)

     Thank you.
SHANITA: Whatever.

(Pause.)

DEZ: Shanita . . . I—
SHANITA: Did you do it, Dez?
DEZ: I—
SHANITA: Did you steal them materials?

(Dez looks at Shanita in her eyes sincerely.)

DEZ: No.
SHANITA: You swear?
DEZ: I swear. I ain't stole nothin'.
SHANITA: Then what was that Reggie found in your bag?
DEZ: Some brass fittings. Been collectin' 'em for my new
     shop. My boy held some for me from the Briggs plant.

Had a auction. Went in there and got lots of stuff for my business. The fittings. Some weld caps. Even got me the hookup on a clean engine for my car. That's all to it. I got 'em legit. Plant auction.

SHANITA: You swear?

DEZ: I swear. That's it. Only reason I even been bringin' the stuff in is cuz I pick it up on my way into work. Ain't gonna leave it in the car so niggas can break in and steal the shit. These materials startin' to be like gold over here. Take out a little at a time, it add up eventually.

SHANITA: Why you ain't just tell Reggie?

DEZ: Reggie got in his head I'm shit.

SHANITA: But you coulda told him.

DEZ: So he can call me a liar? You know how exhausting that is? To waste your time explaining yourself to somebody who already got they mind made up about you? No matter what I say, he gonna be hearin' it with the screw face. Then after all that explainin', I done wore myself out and he still gonna believe what he gonna believe. I rather save myself the energy. Use it toward something I give a damn about.

SHANITA: He believe you. We all believe you if you just say so. You got it in your head that everybody your enemy, even when they ain't. You thinkin' we just waiting for you to prove us right. What we really doin' is holdin' our breath to God that we wrong. What we really doin' is wishin' on everything pure that our fears don't come true. Don't nobody wanna see you leave here defeated. Not none of us.

DEZ: Not you?

SHANITA: Not none of us.

(Beat.
    Silence. Dez looks at Shanita.)

That gun. What you got to say about that?

DEZ: I can't say nothin' 'bout that.

SHANITA: Don't make no sense. It's like you sabotaging yourself.

DEZ: I'm protecting myself.

SHANITA: From who?

DEZ: Everybody.

(Pause.)

SHANITA: I can't believe we getting shut down.

DEZ: We can all believe. Ain't the only ones. Been happenin' all over the city.

SHANITA: And still. Guess I just ain't wanna believe it could happen over here too. *(Beat)* What we gonna do?

DEZ: You gonna be fine.

SHANITA: You don't know that for no fact.

DEZ: I do.

SHANITA: How you know?

DEZ: Cuz you good with yo' hands. You got skillz.

SHANITA: Boy, stop tryin' to be slick.

DEZ: I ain't tryin' to be slick. I'm tellin' the truth. You one of the best out there—man or woman. Got like a talent in this or somethin'. You smart and you shine on the floor. That's not my opinion. That's a fact.

(Shanita looks at Dez. A moment of need. She grabs his face and kisses him spontaneously.

It gets deep and passionate for a quick moment. Then she abruptly pulls away.

Dez is stunned.

Pause. They look at each other. Shanita moves away.)

SHANITA: Shit. I'm sorry.

DEZ: Ummm . . .

SHANITA: I'm pregnant and my hormones are like shooting stars right now and I'm hungry and this is the first good meal I've had in like a month and I was tryin' not to get too fat and that was the nicest thing anybody's said to me in like a really fucking long time.

DEZ: Which . . . part . . . ?

SHANITA: It can't be duplicated. Don't try.

(Beat.)

I've been having these dreams lately. Crazy dreams.

DEZ: Like what?

SHANITA: Like this morning I dreamed I came into work like normal. Set my stuff up in the breakroom. Went on the floor and started work. And then I started gettin' these like awful contractions. And outta nowhere, I just start goin' into labor. Right on the shop floor.

DEZ: Aww shit. You better not. I ain't delivering no big-headed baby for you.

SHANITA: Shut up, Dez. My child will not be big-headed.

DEZ: I'm just sayin' though.

SHANITA: Anyway, I start pushin' and the baby wouldn't come out. And I'm pushin' like with all the might I got. And I'm sweatin'. And I'm overworked. And I can see the dirt on my boots. And I'm pushin' and screamin' and the sound of the machines is screamin' with me . . . And soon as somethin' was 'bout to give . . . I just stopped. Contractions stopped. Feelin' of labor stopped. And the baby stay there in my belly . . . all this potential . . . still waitin' to be delivered.

DEZ: When the time comes, that baby's gonna take over the world.

SHANITA: You think so?

DEZ: It's a fact.

SHANITA: What you gonna do, Dez?

DEZ: Try to stay on long as I can. Get my severance. Start my shop.

SHANITA: But what if they fire you?

DEZ: Then I just have to do somethin' else. That be the hustle.

SHANITA: You got quick answers for everything. You ever think anything all the way out?

(Dez is silent.
A moment of thought.)

DEZ: All the time.

(Beat.
Shanita moves close to Dez.)

SHANITA: How you get that scar behind your ear?

DEZ: You got a million questions today.

SHANITA: Just answer it.

DEZ: Car accident. When I was a teenager. Headin' to the Cass versus King football game with my boy Mike. Car rolled over on the shoulder of the 75. Flipped and landed right where I was sittin' on the passenger's side. Door near me got crushed and cut me along the back of my neck. Scar go down to the middle of my back. Folks had stopped along the side of the freeway and pulled me and my boy out. When the ambulance came, all I remember is folks sayin' how lucky we were to be alive. And I kept lookin' at that totaled car in disbelief. Wonderin' how I could survive somethin' so massive. And all them folks kept sayin'—if that car wasn't made good, we'd be dead. I remember that.

(Shanita moves close upon Dez. She touches his scar lightly.)

SHANITA: I feel like nothing is familiar anymore. Everything just feel like right now. Like there's nowhere before this and nowhere after. You feel that?

DEZ: Sort of.

SHANITA: You know I ain't never broke a rule on the job in my life?

DEZ: I can believe that.

SHANITA: I'm gon' break one now.

(*Shanita kisses Dez passionately. He receives it.*
They become increased in intensity. In need.
They are embraced in passion.
Clinging to one another for all they can.)

SCENE FOUR

On the line: the silhouetted workers move with precision, then pick up speed. The stamping motion increases in rigor. Suddenly the workers are overworking—too many miles per hour. The overload is too much to bear. They begin to turn the motion onto each other. Fighting on the line. Attacking one another and going for blood.

Lights cross-fade from the chaos to the breakroom.

It's evening. Faye sits on the shabby couch and begins to unwind in her space.

Suddenly Reggie bursts through the door looking distressed. He closes the door urgently behind him.

REGGIE: I—I've done it.

FAYE: Reggie what you doin' down here? Thought your shift been over.

REGGIE: Was in a—in a meeting.

FAYE: I thought everybody done went home 'cept the guards and the night shift. (*Sees Reggie's distress*) What's the matter with you?

REGGIE: I can't—fuck me. Fuck fuck me!

FAYE: Reggie . . .

REGGIE: Faye I—I came down just to say—cuz I don't really know where else to—

FAYE: Reggie, slow down, okay? You ain't . . . I can't follow you . . . Just slow down.

REGGIE: They pushed me, Faye.

FAYE: Who pushed you?

REGGIE: It just all went too far, you know?

FAYE: What you talkin' about?

REGGIE *(To himself)*: Goddamnit!

FAYE: What are you— *(Shift, with resolve)* They made you fire Dez.

REGGIE: No. I did it. I did what you said. I fought for him, Faye.

FAYE: Well that's good ain't it?

REGGIE: I told 'em he's too important. We need him on this crew. We need his skill to keep production moving on time. He's too valuable and we can't cut off our own hands to save our face. That's what I said.

FAYE: And what they say?

REGGIE: Said all right. Dez stays.

FAYE: Well good for you. That's a win.

REGGIE: Then Harris come talk to me private. Say . . . What about Faye Davison.

(Quick pause.)

FAYE: What about me?

REGGIE: Say we oughta . . .

FAYE *(Dangerously)*: What about me.

REGGIE: I don't even wanna—it was the way he said it that got in me wrong. It was the way.

FAYE: Said what.

REGGIE: Said to present you with the severance. Right now. Get you to retire.

FAYE: I just tell 'em no.

REGGIE: Say I oughta encourage it.

FAYE: Deal for twenty-nine years ain't the same as thirty.

REGGIE: I told 'im that.

FAYE: They can't make me retire. I know that much.

REGGIE: No but they can . . . they can make it real hard for you stay. They can do that real good. And I did what you told me to do, Faye. I was ready to fight. I say no deal. Faye been at this company too long. She one of the most skilled workers we got.

FAYE: Been puttin' in shocks. Sewin' interiors. Stamping doors. Been all up through this work.

REGGIE: I told 'im that.

FAYE: And what he say?

(Reggie's eyes shine with heartbreak.)

REGGIE: It was the way he said it that really made me—I just couldn't listen to him talkin' like that. Couldn't let him.

FAYE: What he say?

REGGIE: Spoke about you like you wasn't even—like you wasn't Faye. Like you had no name or no—history or no— "Dead weight," he say—just like that—like you wasn't even—I just couldn't let him. I felt it in my chest. Like dynamite burstin' inside of me.

FAYE: What you—what you meanin'?

REGGIE: I attacked him, Faye.

FAYE: You did what?

REGGIE: I fuckin'—I—I attacked him. I attacked my supervisor.

FAYE: No.

(Long pause. Breathlessness.)

REGGIE: I'm—I'm done.

FAYE: No. *(Beat)* WHY???—No. What'd you—how? How'd you attack him? You said somethin' to him?

REGGIE *(Beat)*: Didn't say nothin' I just . . . I went for him. Just for a second. Like a shock wave went through me. Lunged at him like I was gonna pound him into the fuckin' ground. Like I was gonna grab him by the collar and crush that shit in my hands. Looked at him in his eyes. Seein' through that emptiness. That lack of feeling. That—whatever you call it—that make you stop seein' yourself in somebody else. And I flexed on him like—"Nigga I wish you would say some shit like that again. I will fuckin' kill you." 'Cept I ain't say it with words.

(Beat) Then the shock wave left me. Real fast. And I ain't touch him at all. Just got swole on' him for a sec. But I came close enough. I would've. And he know it. And I know it too. I see him looking into my eyes like I'm the devil. Can smell his fear. Like if he even breathes louder than a sigh I might kill him dead. And I might've, Faye. I just might've.

(Beat) And I stand there, froze. Not knowin' if I really reached at him or if it was in my mind. But I see him lookin' at me—stiff. Like I scared the shit outta him. Like he was under attack. Like I'm that nigga. It's nothin' but silence between us for a sec. And then I just say, "NO DEAL." And I walk out.

FAYE: Reggie . . .

REGGIE: I'm done, Faye.

FAYE: You ain't done. You ain't even touch him. You just gotta fix it.

REGGIE: Can't fix it. Ain't no way possible. I saw his fear. It's the little shit like that. Just a little bit of unraveling. That's all they need to mark me dangerous. I'm done.

FAYE: You got to try to fix it.

REGGIE: I can't! I can't fix none of this!!!

FAYE: Apologize to him.

REGGIE: I did what you said. I fought. I did exactly what you said, Faye. You see that???

FAYE: I say fight! I ain't say sabotage yo'self!

REGGIE: You tell me how to do one without the other! You tell me how to fight and stand on some kinda ground in this industry without putting something massive on the line to do it! Ain't no way to fight without jumping on the goddamn grenade! Ain't no other way and you know it!

(Reggie bangs his fist against the bulletin board. A sign falls. He begins tearing the rest of them down violently.)

Goddamn lines. Goddamn rules. Goddamn everything!

(He falls against the wall and clings to sanity. Faye watches him painfully. Silence.
Long, long beat.)

FAYE: What if I took the deal?

REGGIE: What? I— No— What?

FAYE: What if you went back and told him Faye said she'll retire? Won't even cause no fuss.

REGGIE: No. You wouldn't get your— They'd cheat you. Rob you blind. And your health benefits wouldn't even— wouldn't fix it no way Faye. I did what I did. I made myself a threat.

FAYE: But if you apologized. Went to Harris. Told him you got Faye Davison to walk. It'd show a effort, wouldn't it? It'd show cooperation.

REGGIE: Faye I can't—

FAYE: Yo' mama was so proud of you when you got this job. I won't ever forget the look on her face. Her son wearin' a button-up to work. Saw a different life for you than the one she knew. Life with a future. *(Beat)* Me and her always joked that we wasn't never gonna be like none of these bums we seen on Woodward. Why be a bum in Detroit? Ain't make no sense, cold as it get. Soon as we get close to that last dime, we figure it make more sense to pay it on a bus ticket 'steada rent. Take us a trip down to Miami or Fort Lauderdale or somethin'. If we gon' be a bum, we'd say, might as well be a beach bum.

REGGIE: Faye . . .

FAYE: I could do that. Talk to Harris in the mornin' 'fore you even come in. By the time you get here? I already got my retirement deal and my one way ticket to somethin' else. Be like a ghost. A memory and nothin' more. And you stick around to fight another day.

(Reggie looks at Faye deliberately.)

REGGIE: I'm . . . *(Beat, tears in his throat)* I'm a man, Faye. I've done what I've done, and now I gotta go home. Gonna look my wife in the eye and tell her . . . cuz I've done what I've done. *(Beat)* Tonight's your last night in this space, you hear me? Tomorrow, I come in here, clear out my desk, grab my belongings, and take you home with me. *(Pause)* I'm taking you home.

(Faye and Reggie look at each other—a world of history and stories between them.
Faye reaches out to Reggie. For the first time, they touch. She holds his hand. Squeezes it.
Reggie holds on firmly.
Her grip the only thing keeping him from collapsing.)

SCENE FIVE

Lights up on the breakroom. It looks different. Hard to determine why, but some things are not in their usual places. There is no deck of cards on the table. Supplies may be missing from the shelves and the kitchenette. Perhaps stickers or pictures on a locker may be missing. Nothing completely obvious . . . but slightly emptier.

Dez enters and heads to his locker. He takes off his coat and begins to prepare for work. He looks around the room, noticing that it feels strangely different. He cannot put his finger on it.

Shanita enters. She heads over to her locker as well.

Dez and Shanita are strangely shy and awkward around each other.

DEZ: Morning.

SHANITA: Morning.

(They go through their routine. Shanita takes in the strangeness of the space, unsure of what's different. She heads over to the coffee maker.)

Nobody made coffee yet?

DEZ: Guess not.

SHANITA: Faye must not be in yet.

DEZ: Hm. Yeah . . . *(Dez looks around for Faye's things)* Must not . . .

SHANITA: I'll make some.

(Shanita goes to the shelf. A load of coffee sits in the basket. A note on it. She pulls out the note.)

Ohh . . . the good coffee! She got some more! *(Reading)* "Shanita and Dez—That good shit. Faye."—That's so sweet! I gotta make sure to thank her when she get in.

(Dez looks around curiously. Shanita eagerly puts the coffee in the maker. Finally it dawns on Dez:)

DEZ: The signs!
SHANITA: What's that?
DEZ: That's what's missing.

(Shanita looks at the board.)

SHANITA: Ohhhh—shit you right! I knew it was somethin'. Couldn't put my finger on it.
DEZ: That's gon' send Reggie through the roof.
SHANITA: Think it was whoever broke in?
DEZ: Maybe.
SHANITA: On my way in this morning that's all anybody was talkin' about. Say somebody jammed up the 16-line real good. Took some material off it too.
DEZ: 16-line? That's a mutha. Whoever did that ain't fuckin' around. They went straight for the biggest line up in here.
SHANITA: I know. Wonder what it'll mean. *(Pause)* Reggie tell you what they decided about your, um—?
DEZ: Guess I'm gonna find out when I see 'im.
SHANITA: Cool . . .

(The coffee maker runs. The refrigerator hums. Shanita sits and closes her eyes.)

DEZ: Ay, so I was thinkin' maybe later if you wanna—
SHANITA: Shhhh . . . don't mess up the music.
DEZ: You still on that?
SHANITA: Just listen with me.

(Dez sits next to Shanita. He watches her. She keeps her eyes closed.
   Dez looks at Shanita. She is glowing.)

I used to fall asleep to all kinds of electronic music. Sound of it come from the factory. Fills up the silence, like it ain't never gonna disappear on you or let you go.

DEZ: You worry 'bout that a lot don't you?

SHANITA: What's that?

DEZ: People lettin' you go.

(*Shanita looks at Dez and considers responding. She decides not to and instead closes her eyes again.*

Dez eyes her hands on the table. She continues to listen. Slowly he reaches his hand out and delicately touches hers.

Startled for a second, she opens her eyes and then closes them again quickly.

They breathe together and listen to the sounds.

The door to the breakroom opens. It's Reggie. Shanita snatches her hand away from Dez.

A look of urgent knowing on Reggie's face.)

REGGIE: Morning.

SHANITA: Morning, Reggie.

(*Reggie's eyes dart around the breakroom toward Faye's locker. Evidence of her presence is nowhere.*)

REGGIE: You all, um . . . there's a unit meeting today at three o'clock. You oughta both be there.

DEZ: Meeting for all staff?

REGGIE: That's right. For everybody who expects to stick around and learn the closing plan for the rest of the year. I'm gonna go through all of that.

SHANITA: You gonna talk us through post-closing too?

REGGIE: I am, Shanita. I'm going to make sure everything gets covered.

DEZ: So does that mean I should, um . . .

REGGIE: Means I'll see you at three o'clock, Dez. That's what it means.

(Reggie and Dez stare at each other. The silence between them speaks volumes.)

DEZ: Good then. I'll be there.

(Shanita breathes a sigh of relief.
   Beat.)

SHANITA: Faye ain't in yet. You seen her on the floor?

REGGIE: No, she um . . . looks like she won't be coming back to work. I've just been informed that she's . . . *(With difficulty)* retired early this morning.

DEZ: Retired???

SHANITA: Just like that??? Without saying goodbye???

REGGIE: I think she um . . . felt that was best . . .

DEZ: That's crazy . . .

SHANITA *(Softly)*: Damn . . .

(A moment. They settle into this new energy without Faye. It feels strange.
   Reggie regroups.)

REGGIE: Be prepared for new safety updates at today's meeting. There was another robbery last night. Some of the brass fittings on 16-line have been removed.

SHANITA: They still don't know who it was?

REGGIE: No . . . this job was a little different. Doesn't look like the same person. Production on 16-line is shut down for the day. The sheet metal's been jammed and the backup sheets are missing from the warehouse. We need your skills on that line, Dez. You're gonna be switched there for maintenance.

DEZ: Rippin' off the 16-line??? That's some pro shit right there. Gotta be an inside job.

(Something dawns on Dez immediately.)

Yoooo!

SHANITA *(Catching onto Dez's revelation)*: Ya'll don't think, um—

DEZ *(With amazement)*: Faye a OG!!!

(Beat.
Reggie, Dez and Shanita all look at each other knowingly.)

REGGIE: It's um . . . it's time for everybody to get on the floor. Over these next few weeks, management is going to be looking at me a lot closer. I can't let the same ol' same ol' keep sliding by. Shanita, doctor's appointments are going to have to fit into your lunch hour or you'll have to make them after work from now on.

SHANITA: All right.

REGGIE: And Dez, you punch in on time or you get deducted. You understand?

DEZ: I got it.

(Pause. They stand in the silence, unsure of what to do. Unsure of what they are without Faye.)

REGGIE: Good then.

(Reggie walks over to Faye's locker. Notices the pictures taped to her door are missing. He touches her locker for a moment.)

SHANITA: Can't believe she ain't comin' back.

REGGIE *(Resolved, not tragic)*: I know.

SHANITA: Did she do it?

REGGIE: Not all of 'em.

SHANITA: But this last job . . . was it her?

REGGIE: Does it matter?

DEZ: Only thing matter is if she good now. Somewhere mackin' the ladies and talkin' shit.

SHANITA: Can't imagine this place without her. *(Pause)* She was in my dream last night. I was layin' on the shop floor, covered in dust. Floor was dusty. Walls was dusty. Everything. And I was stuck there, trying to go into labor but couldn't. And then suddenly Faye appear. Not in person, but in spirit. The dust start to write me messages and somehow I know it's her voice. I don't know how, but I just did. She write *inhale*. So I inhale. She write *exhale*. So I exhale. Then just like that, I'm breathing . . . in and out, and I can feel my body goin' into labor. I can feel the contractions. It all started up again. And the machines is humming. And the presses are goin'. And I'm delivering the most brilliant light I ever saw. *(Beat)* Just when thought I wouldn't never go back into labor, Faye show up and help me give birth.

(Reggie opens Faye's locker. It is empty, except for one picture taped inside. Reggie pulls it out and looks at it. His heart swells. He flips it over and reads the back.
Pause.)

REGGIE: "Faye and Cathryn. Summer 1985. Love for life."

SHANITA: Who's Cathryn?

(Heartbreak and pride. It is his mother, but he is too full to speak. Reggie looks at Shanita but says nothing. Then, with determination:)

REGGIE: On the floor everybody. Got a full day today. Only way to get through it is to work together. Let's go.

(Shanita and Dez look around the room. They put their goggles on and head out of the breakroom.

Reggie stares at the room one more time. Moves into the space. Stands and closes his eyes. Inhales. Exhales.

Suddenly, the silhouetted workers come alive. They begin working the line. Smoothly. Collaboratively.

For the first time since the beginning of the play, the line has harmony.

Suddenly, Faye's spirit fills the breakroom, and Reggie can feel it. As if her name is being echoed across the lockers and the bulletin board and the floors. She becomes embedded into the soul of the plant.

Reggie inhales and exhales as Faye's spirit envelops him.

Lights fade on the breakroom as Reggie exits onto the floor, proudly.)

END OF PLAY

PHOTO BY JOSEPH MORAN

DOMINIQUE MORISSEAU is the author of *The Detroit Project* which includes the following plays: *Skeleton Crew* (Atlantic Theater Company), *Paradise Blue* (Signature Theatre) and *Detroit '67* (Public Theater, Classical Theatre of Harlem and National Black Theatre). Additional plays include: *Pipeline* (Lincoln Center Theatre), *Sunset Baby* (LAByrinth Theatre), *Blood at the Root* (National Black Theatre) and *Follow Me to Nellie's* (Premiere Stages). Dominique is an alumna of The Public Theater's Emerging Writer's Group, Women's Project Lab, and The Lark Playwrights Workshop, and has developed work at Sundance Lab, Williamstown Theatre Festival and Eugene O'Neill Playwrights Conference. Her work has been commissioned by Steppenwolf Theatre Company, Women's Project, South Coast Rep, People's Light and Theatre and Oregon Shakespeare Festival/Penumbra Theatre. She most recently served as Co-Producer on the Showtime series *Shameless*. Following its record-breaking run at Berkeley Repertory Theatre last summer, her new musical *Ain't Too Proud, The Life and Times of The Temptations* is set to open at The Kennedy Center (Washington, D.C.), The Ahmanson (Los Angeles) and The Princess of Whales Theater (Toronto) this season. Awards include: Spirit of Detroit Award, PoNY Fellowship, Sky Cooper New American Play Prize, TEER Spirit Trailblazer Award, Steinberg Playwright Award, Audelco Awards, NBFT August Wilson Playwriting Award, Edward M. Kennedy Prize for Drama, Obie Award, Ford Foundation Art of Change Fellowship and being named one of Variety's Women of Impact for 2017–2018.

Theatre Communications Group would like to offer our special thanks to the Vilcek Foundation for its generous support of the publication of The Detroit Project *by Dominique Morisseau*

THE VILCEK FOUNDATION raises awareness of immigrant contributions in America and fosters appreciation of the arts and sciences. Established in 2000 by Jan and Marica Vilcek, immigrants from the former Czechoslovakia, the Foundation's mission was inspired by the couple's respective careers in biomedical science and art history, as well as their appreciation for the opportunities offered to them as newcomers to the United States.

TCG books sponsored by the Vilcek Foundation include:

Five Plays by Sam Hunter
Mr. Burns and Other Plays by Anne Washburn
The Detroit Project by Dominique Morisseau

THEATRE COMMUNICATIONS GROUP (TCG), the national organization for the American theatre, promotes the idea of "A Better World for Theatre, and a Better World Because of Theatre." In addition to TCG's numerous services to the theatre field, TCG Books is the nation's largest independent publisher of dramatic literature, with 16 Pulitzer Prizes for Drama on its book list. The book program commits to the life-long career of its playwrights, keeping all of their plays in print. TCG Books' other authors include: Nilo Cruz, Quiara Alegría Hudes, David Henry Hwang, Tony Kushner, Donald Margulies, Sarah Ruhl, Stephen Sondheim, Anne Washburn, and August Wilson, among many others.

Support TCG's work in the theatre field by becoming a member or donor: www.tcg.org

tcg